The Making of a Moonie

For Peter with love and thanks

The Making of a Moonie

Choice or Brainwashing?

EILEEN BARKER

Basil Blackwell

© Eileen Barker 1984

First published 1984
Reprinted 1985

Basil Blackwell Publisher Ltd
108 Cowley Road, Oxford OX4 1JF, UK

Basil Blackwell Inc.
432 Park Avenue South, Suite 1505,
New York, NY 10016, USA

British Library Cataloguing in Publication Data

Barker, Eileen
  The making of a Moonie.
  1. Unification Church
  I. Title
  306'.6   BX 9750.S4

  ISBN 0-631-13246-5

Library of Congress Cataloging in Publication Data

Barker, Eileen.
  The making of a Moonie.

  Includes index.
  1. Unification Church.   I. Title.
  BX9750.S4B37   1984   289.9   84-12414
  ISBN 0-631-13246-5

Typeset by Katerprint Co. Ltd, Oxford.
Printed in Great Britain by Page Bros (Norwich) Ltd.

Contents

Acknowledgements

This book is not the result of one of those studies in which the academic, in scholarly pursuit, has been isolated in a library for years on end. In order to carry out the research, I have had to rely upon the help and co-operation of literally hundreds of busy people who have come to my assistance by talking to me, writing to me or sending me literature.

I am grateful for the financial support that I received from the Staff Research Fund of the London School of Economics. This allowed me to start work even while I was negotiating with the Unification Church for permission to do the study; it also enabled me to fill in odd gaps after the study was officially finished. To the Northern Studies Committee I owe the opportunity of researching (what I then believed to be) the absence of new religious movements in Scandinavia – it must be a rare occurrence, but one for which I was most grateful, to be granted money to examine a vacuum. The bulk of the funding for the research came, however, from the Social Science Research Council of Great Britain, a body which I would like to thank most sincerely not merely for the money but also for the invaluable help and understanding which its officers were always ready to give me.

Some of the photographs I took myself, but I should like to thank K. Eddy, who took most of them. I would also like to thank the Unification Church for permission to reproduce other photographs and the illustrations from *Outline of the Principle: Level 4* (New York, Holy Spirit Association for the Unification of World Christianity, 1980).

It is impossible for me to thank all the friends and strangers who have contributed to the research, but there are certain categories of people to whom I must express my gratitude. First, there are all those non-Moonies who filled in questionnaires, which were thirty-six pages long in the case of the main control group; secondly, I would like to thank the parents of Moonies, several of whom I now count among my friends, for the help they gave me in understanding the kinds of background from which their children had come. I would also like to thank a number of ex-Moonies, 'counsellors' and various organizations and people who have expressed concern about the new religions and the effects which they have on both society and their membership. Many of these people were generous with their time and in presenting me with information and a perspective which I could not have got from talking only to Moonies.

For assistance in some of the more tedious tasks, such as checking through lists and copying data from innumerable forms, I am indebted to a number of people, including Judith Barker, Rachel Barker, Bernadette O'Keefe, Sarah Mellor, Martin Shiels and Ruth Taylor. I simply could not have coped without the help of Gaie Davidson and William Kenny CP, who coded over 20,000 pages of questionnaires between them; the latter, as my chief research assistant, also helped me, with wisdom and with humour, in the layout of the main questionnaires and the creation of a codebook. Marge Blackwood, Cindy Celant, Josephine Johnstone, Isabel Metliss, Thelma O'Brien and Jean Ridyard all helped to ease the secretarial burdens with patience and with good-humoured efficiency; Penny Page cheerfully punched hundreds of datacards; and to Charles Sharp and Anne McGlone I offer profound thanks and deep admiration for their ability to tell the computer to do (almost) everything I wanted it to do.

There are several people whose research has overlapped with my own and with whom I have enjoyed exchanging both material and ideas – in particular, I would like to thank James Beckford, David Bromley, Karel Dobbelaere, Stilson Judah, Edward Levine, Warren Lewis, John Lofland, Casey McCann, Gordon Melton, Michael Mickler, James Richardson, Thomas Robbins, Anson Shupe, Rodney Stark, David Taylor and Roy Wallis. I would also like to thank a number of colleagues and the members of the LSE Sociology of Religion graduate seminar who have, over the years, commented on a series of tentative papers; such discussions have played an important role in helping me to formulate, analyse and clarify the raw data of my research. A number of friends, including Philippa Ingram, Jenny Mellor and Ann Trowles, have read drafts of the book; I (and, no doubt, the reader) would like to thank them for their help in expunging some less than felicitous sociological jargon which had crept into the text. I would also like to thank Elizabeth Bland for her painstaking copyediting. Intellectually, I owe a great debt to the scholarship and counsel of Donald MacRae. Bryan Wilson has been unfailingly generous in the advice, encouragement, inspiration and friendship that he has given me.

Of course, the most crucial factor for my research was the co-operation of the Moonies themselves. They allowed me to enter their lives, observe and question them minutely – sometimes on what most people would consider to be very private and personal matters. After years of trying to make me understand how they see the world, nearly all of them accepted, without bitterness or rancour, the fact that I could not share their beliefs. I know that what I have written will seem irrelevant and disappointing to many Moonies, but I do wish to express a very genuine gratitude to each and every one who has helped me to glimpse his or her world. There are, perhaps, a score of Unificationists who have been particularly important to me. I shall not embarrass them by listing their names – they themselves know who they are. I do, however, want to offer special thanks to two people, Michael Marshall and Jolanda Smalls, not for the information which they gave me but for the understanding.

Finally I must mention my own family. For years, the house has been cluttered with questionnaires and newspaper clippings; telephone calls have lasted for hours and have always seemed to occur just as we were sitting down for a meal. Strangers (Moonies, Moonies' parents, 'anti-cultists' or television crews) have arrived on the doorstep, frequently bringing with them proselytizing zeal, emotional distress or impossibly technical questions about the mains supply. My husband and children have (just like the families of Moonies, they complain) been abandoned for days, sometimes weeks – but I have always wanted to return to my home.

Eileen Barker
London School of Economics and Political Science

Introduction

Why should – *how could* – anyone become a Moonie? What possible explanation is there for the fact that men and women will sacrifice their family, their friends and their careers in order to sell tracts, flowers or candy on the streets for sixteen, eighteen or even twenty hours a day? How can well-educated adults be persuaded to abrogate the right to decide whom they will marry, whether they can live with their spouse and whether they can bring up their own children? How does a once poverty-stricken Korean, who speaks practically no English, manage to recruit thousands of Western followers who will accept his religious, political and social philosophy as the one and only Truth, who will be prepared to obey his every command and who will be eager to keep him in what would appear to be the lap of luxury while they themselves abjure the material comforts which they once enjoyed?

Mention the name 'Moonies' to anyone in the West today, and the chances are that you will receive an immediate reaction which falls somewhere between a delicate shudder and an indignant outburst of fury. The tenor of headlines around the world is consistently condemnatory: 'Parents fight "brainwashing" by bizarre sect'; 'Rev. Moon's plot to rule the world told'; 'Moonie cult faces probe by MP into "brainwashing"'; 'Tragedy of the broken families'; 'Mass suicide possible in Moon Church, 3 say'; 'Mother to fly out to brainwashed daughter'; 'Moonies have captured my Son'; 'Moonies: Maggie demands action'; '"Fanatical" Cult in Australia'; 'Le Dieu Moon nous arrache nos enfants'; 'Mil ochocientos parejas y el Reverendo Moon'; 'In Japan protestierten 500 Eltern gegen die Tätigkeit der Sekte'; 'Polícia investiga ação de seguidores de Moon'.[1]

In March 1982 eight Members of the European Parliament tabled a motion (at that time unsuccessfully)[2] for a resolution which began:

The European Parliament
 deeply concerned by the distress and family break-ups caused by
 Sun Myung Moon's Unification Church;

1. Welcomes the media's relentless exposure of the Moonies' activities;

2. Urges public authorities throughout the Community to ensure that the Moonies are not given special tax benefits, charity status, or other privileges;

3. Calls upon its Committee . . . to report on the activities of Sun Myung Moon's followers in the Unification Church and the danger to society that they represent.[3]

In 1978 a committee of the United States House of Representatives investigated alleged connections between the Moon organization and the Korean CIA and recommended further investigation.[4] In 1981 the Unification Church in Britain was ordered to pay an estimated £750,000 in costs to the *Daily Mail* when it lost a libel action against the paper over an article which, under the headline 'The Church that breaks up families', accused the movement of brainwashing.[5] The case, which lasted for six months, was the longest libel trial in British history. In 1982 Moon was convicted by a Federal Court jury of conspiracy to evade taxes and was sentenced to eighteen months' imprisonment. As this book went to press (July 1984), having lost his appeals, he began serving his sentence in a Connecticut jail.

In Massachusetts one can see bumperstickers bearing the legend 'Save the human race. Punch a Moonie in the face.' In August 1981 mobs, incensed by a television programme about the movement, stoned and burned a number of Unification centres in Brazil (a country with a tradition of religious tolerance), and police had to take about a hundred Moonies into protective custody. In 1976 a young Norwegian woman was badly injured as the result of a bomb attack on a Unification centre in Paris.

In a survey carried out towards the end of the 1970s, just over a thousand Americans born between 1940 and 1952 were given a list of 155 names and asked how they felt about each of them. Only 3 per cent of the respondents had not heard of the Reverend Moon. Only 1 per cent admitted to admiring him. The owner of no other name on the list elicited less admiration, and the only person whom a higher percentage of respondents did not admire was the ritual killer Charles Manson.[6] When I asked a group of just over a hundred people in Britain what they knew about Moonies or the Unification Church, nearly all of those who said that they knew anything at all responded with some kind of negative evaluation. They felt certain that the movement was a 'bad thing', but very few provided much in the way of factual information. There was a frequent use of words like 'scary', 'frightening', 'fake', 'impostor', 'rip-off', 'bizarre' and 'dangerous'. The main source of information was the media, though some did say that they had talked to a Moonie in the street, and a few said that they knew of someone who had become a Moonie.

The most commonly cited piece of information was that the movement used brainwashing or mind-control techniques. Exactly what these techniques were was not clear, although there were some suggestions that hypnosis or drugs were employed. The next most frequent report was that Moon was a multi-millionaire. One or two people explained that he was the anti-Christ. Some said that the movement was authoritarian, others that it took children away from their parents, that Moonies sold things in the streets, that they lied, that they were turned into zombies. Quite a few people advanced the theory that anyone who becomes a Moonie must be rather stupid, pathetic or inadequate in some way. Several said that once you get into the clutches of the Moonies you can never escape. Three or four people reported that Moonies kidnap their victims and lock them up. In some responses there was an obvious confusion with other new religious movements – with the chanting or the shaven heads of Krishna devotees, with the (erstwhile) teenage guru of the Divine Light Mission Premies or with the 'flirty fishing' (the use of sexual intercourse for recruitment) of the Children of God, or 'Family of Love', as that movement is now called. There were several references to the mass suicide of the followers of Jim Jones in Guyana.

What, then, *are* some basic facts about the Unification Church?

It is a religious movement, founded in Korea by the Reverend Sun Myung Moon in 1954 under the name of the Holy Spirit Association for the Unification of World Christianity. The theology, the *Divine Principle*, is a special interpretation of the Old and New Testaments with additional revelations which Moon claims to have received. It is a messianic, millenarian theology which enjoins believers to work under the guidance of the Messiah for the restoration of the Kingdom of Heaven on earth, and to follow their leaders with faithful obedience.

Missionaries first came to the West in 1959, but the movement had little success in America or Europe until the early 1970s, when Moon himself moved to the USA. Core members usually live in Church centres and work full-time for the movement, often selling literature, flowers or other goods for long hours in the street; there are, however, also 'Home-Church' members who, while sympathetic to Unification beliefs, live in their own homes and follow 'normal' occupations.[7] Strict celibacy is expected outside marriage and, indeed, for a period after marriage. Marriage partners are suggested by Moon, and mass weddings of hundreds, even thousands, of couples have been held. The movement is strongly anti-communist in its outlook. It owns valuable property and a large number of businesses (mainly in South Korea, Japan, America and Europe). It sponsors a variety of performing arts and international conferences for academics. It

(Above and opposite) Moonies selling literature in the street.

runs a seminary in New York State and the Little Angels school in South Korea.

As already indicated, the movement has provoked considerable antagonism from many quarters – particularly from the parents of members, the media and adherents of more orthodox religions. It has been condemned for using brainwashing techniques in order to gain and to keep its members who, it is said, are ruthlessly exploited in order to gain enormous sums of money for its leadership. It has been accused of illegally passing money and members across international frontiers. It is said to break up families and to cause physical and/or mental harm to its members.

Not surprisingly, the Moonies' vision of themselves and the Unification Church does not match (but is frequently a direct mirror image of) outsiders' conventional wisdom. From an outside perspective the Unification Church imposes bondage, exploitation and materialism; for the Moonie it offers freedom, opportunity and spirituality. For outsiders it is a movement of division, despair, deception and confusion; for the Moonie it is one of unification, hope, truth and enlightenment; while the outsider believes the Unification Church to be bad, wrong and evil, the Moonie believes it to be good, right and godly.

Of course, the world is rarely as simple as either of these pictures suggests. Rarely are social institutions unambiguously good or bad, social actions simply right or wrong, human actions the direct outcome of rationally thought out motives, or human beliefs systematic or consistent. We find ourselves doing things we never intended to do, and those things which we do have unintended or unforeseen consequences. Social interaction is a complicated, messy process which involves continuous renegotiation within an ever-shifting framework of expectations, rules and controls. Yet, despite all this, there is some order in the affairs of man. Most social phenomena can be understood more clearly if we care to look more closely. But clarification of human processes is rarely simplification.

This book is concerned primarily with an attempt to clarify an answer to the question with which it started: why should – *how could* – anyone become a Moonie? For many people it seems so incredible that anyone should *choose* to become a Moonie that the simplest resolution of the question is to deny that such a choice is ever made. The assumption is that Moonies are brainwashed, that they are subjected to mind-control or in some manner coerced; since no one, in his or her right senses would *want* to become a Moonie, becoming a Moonie must be the result of something that others do to the victim, rather than something that a convert himself decides *to do*; the victim is a passive responder, not an active agent.

The brainwashing thesis certainly has the advantage of simplicity. At first glance, it appears to account for the otherwise unaccountable. Since conversion is solely the responsibility of the brainwashers, it exonerates from blame the person involved, his or her parents and the rest of society. The only responsibility of non-members is to remove the hapless, helpless victim from the clutches of the Unification Church. The belief that Moonies have been brainwashed has been used to justify the use of 'deprogramming' – of holding a believer against his (professed) will until he can convince his captors that he is *de*-programmed and free from Unification beliefs. This practice, the illegal detention of a Moonie with the aid of physical force, has led some to argue that it is the deprogrammers rather than the Moonies who are using the methods of brainwashing.[8] It all depends, of course, on what is meant by brainwashing.

In its original and most narrowly defined sense, brainwashing refers to the techniques used by European and Chinese communists to produce enforced but real conversion of political belief and/or the sincere confession of crimes of which one is actually innocent.[9] These techniques include imprisonment and torture.[10] The Unification Church subjects its potential recruits to neither imprisonment nor torture. This is not to argue that no coercion of any kind is ever practised on (and, subsequently, by) Moonies, but to propose that, if it does occur, we need to know more about how the process works. Even the physical abuse that some deprogrammers have employed can hardly be said to be comparable with that used by the Russians during the 1930s, or by the Chinese on their own people during the 1940s, or on American prisoners during the Korean War.[11] What, we need to ask, is meant by 'enforced but real conversion' in the absence of physical force?

In its popular and most widely defined usage the term 'brainwashing' has been applied to almost any kind of influence, or attempt to influence others. A front-page headline in *The Times* on 14 May 1983 reads, 'Beware Tory brainwashers, says Foot'. We are all brainwashed by society, our parents, the media, advertising, the man who sells us insurance that we do not want to buy. But if this is all that is meant by brainwashing, we have explained away not simply the answer to our question but question itself. It is of little moment merely to assert that the brainwashing techniques practised by the Moonies are the same as those by which a television commercial 'converts' people to a new brand of toothpaste. It is the very fact that most of us find it difficult to understand why anyone would become a Moonie that makes us want to be able to distinguish between the process by which such a conversion occurs and other, presumably less important, influences.

While most people's antagonism towards the Unification Church can, rightly, present us with a challenging question, we cannot allow it to present us with the answer. We cannot assume that *because* the Unification Church is a bad/wrong/ill-conceived/incomprehensible movement, its membership can be recruited only by mind-control or deception. Such an assumption begs the crucially important question of whether any responsibility for the conversion can be traced to the individual himself, or to the wider society; it rules out of court any inquiry into the possible significance of the general social/political/economic *milieu* or the convert's more immediate social background (such as his family, his school and, perhaps, his Church). To assume that recruitment techniques are solely responsible for conversion is to ignore, and to leave unexplored, the difference between those who succumb and those who remain immune to Unification proselytizing.

There is, of course, no logical connection between what a convert believes and the process by which he came to believe it; nor is there any inevitable continuity between the reasons why someone joins a movement and the situation in which he finds himself once he has actually become a member. But if we want to understand more about how a movement 'works', and about the successes and failures it experiences in defining and achieving its goals, it is crucially important for us to have some knowledge of the 'raw material' with which it operates. When asking the question 'Why do Moonies *do* what they do?', part (though by no means all) of the answer is to be found through an understanding of how they came to be Moonies in the first place. Furthermore, such an understanding may also assist our knowledge of the limits to which Moonies can be pushed.

We are, however, anticipating a discussion for which there will be no space in this book. The analysis presented here is part of a larger study of the Unification Church, but it does, I believe, stand by itself as an attempt to deal directly with the question of recruitment into the movement. The contents of this book are confined almost exclusively to the Unification Church as it is presented to outsiders. Very little mention is made of the 'internal' aspects of the movements; there is little description of those parts of the ideology which are normally available to members only; there is only a limited discussion of what life is like once one actually becomes a member of the Unification Church, and not much more than a brief mention of the organizational hierarchy with its structured control of power and communication. These are, as I have just argued, matters which are largely (but not entirely) irrelevant to an understanding of why someone becomes a Moonie, partly because they are matters about which the potential Moonie is usually quite ignorant – which is certainly not to say that all the material which *is* included in this book is known to those who may become (or, indeed, who are) members of the Unification Church.

I start the book with a description of some of the ways in which I went about collecting and analysing the data upon which this and a further volume on the Unification Church are based. It is a personal account, written for those readers who are interested in learning something of the background to the study. In some ways this chapter might more sensibly have taken its place as an appendix, since it can be bypassed by those who are uninterested in such matters. I have, however, placed it at the beginning because some of the discussion supplements the argument presented in chapter 5, and an introductory account of the method adopted could be of help in understanding the perspective from which the research has been approached.

Chapters 2, 3 and 4 set the scene with descriptive accounts of what it is that the Unification Church offers to the potential recruit. First, I use an historical approach to present a picture of the movement as it has emerged during the last few decades. This is what the Moonies themselves would call a purely 'external' account, but there are two themes running through the chapter which are, I believe, interwoven with the history of the movement and which can help us to understand how it has reached its present position – particularly with respect to recruitment practices. The themes are, first, the crucial role played by Moon as the founder and leader of the movement, and, secondly, the crucial role played not by Moon but by his followers as, through a process of trial and error, they arrived at the institutionalization of certain practices and discovered which approaches to the public were the most successful. Chapter 3 describes those parts of Unification theology which are generally available to outsiders. (References to the *Divine Principle* will apply to the book and its teachings, while those to the Principle refer the more general Unification belief system.) Chapter 4 contains a description of the process of meeting Moonies and attending Unification 'workshops' – residential courses during which potential recruits, whom the Moonies refer to as their 'guests', are introduced to the beliefs and, to some extent, the practices of the movement.

Chapter 5 contains the theoretical argument of the book. In it I consider some of the contributions that have been made to the brainwashing debate in so far as these might apply to the practices of the Unification Church. I then propose a model by which it might be possible to circumvent some of the philosophical issues which have tended to drag the debate into mere polemical rhetoric. It is within the framework of this model that the subsequent data are presented and analysed.

Chapter 6 returns to the workshop but looks at it this time from the perspective of the guests' reactions to it, the members and the movement. In chapter 7 I consider the effects of deception, the controlled environment and the so-called 'love-bombing' (the showering of attention on their guests by the Moonies). In chapters 8 and 9 I look at the kinds of people who become Moonies and at their experience of society. Chapter 10 concludes by drawing together the various threads.

As a further, general point about reading the book, perhaps I ought to apologize to anyone who is upset by my use of the masculine pronoun when referring to Moonies. For purely stylistic reasons I could not bear the thought of continually writing s/he or him/her. Two-thirds of the Moonies in the West happen to be male; had the sex ratio been reversed, I would have used the feminine pronoun.

There are several ways in which the results of my research could have been presented. I have already written numerous articles on various aspects of the movement, some of them specifically for a sociological audience. In this book, however, I address a wider readership. My aim is to tell a story that is uncluttered by the language of sociological analysis,[12] but this does not mean that the underlying questions and perspectives are not those of sociology (which is, after all, little more than the systematic study of the manner in which human beings interact and the consequences of their interactions). Although I have tried to be as consistent as possible in the style of presentation, there are, inevitably, times at which I run the risk of being 'heavy reading' for some, while elaborating the obvious for others. This is partly because I have tried to combine a number of approaches in order to tackle a problem which I do not believe can be adequately understood by one approach alone. At one level I attempt to present a fairly straightforward, objectively factual account of the history and beliefs of the movement and of what 'goes on' at a Unification workshop; to complement this I have added a more subjective flavour, largely through the inclusion of a number of quotations from the people involved, in order to indicate the diverse ways in which a phenomenon can be viewed and to put some 'flesh' on the inevitably dry skeleton of statistical data. At the same time the statistical analyses are presented in order to balance, and thus to make it possible to assess the relative weight which ought to be accorded to, often conflicting data. The whole analysis has, moreover, been shaped and moulded by a 'model', 'paradigm' or perspective which I constructed in an attempt to confront and cope with some of the more confusing problems of philosophy, sociological theory and research methodology which have been raised by those who try to understand why certain people do things which other people find incomprehensible.

My hope is not just that readers of this book will find it easier to understand why people become Moonies, but also that I have presented my case with sufficient clarity and sufficient empirical detail to allow those who disagree with my conclusions to be able to produce data and arguments which will directly address the data and arguments that I have presented, rather than merely saying – as one 'expert witness' with whom I had publicly disagreed in the hope of initiating a debate, once said – 'Well, everyone is entitled to his own opinion.' Although no one who undertakes social research can ever hope to arrive at a definitive answer to the complicated questions posed by social phenomena, I hope that this book will offer more than mere opinion.

1   Access and Information-Gathering

It was not, in fact, I who initially sought out the Unification Church but they who, in a number of ways, sought out me. I first came across the movement in 1974 when I received an invitation from an organization calling itself the International Cultural Foundation (ICF). Would I present a paper at the Third International Conference on the Unity of the Sciences (ICUS) which was to be held at the Royal Lancaster Hotel in London? I had never heard of the sponsors, but I was told of the distinguished scientists who had attended the previous ICUS meetings in New York and Tokyo; I was also informed that a number of Nobel Laureates would be among those giving lectures at this coming conference. Flattered, and curious, as I was then conducting research into scientists' pronouncements on religious, moral and other ideological questions, I accepted. A colleague, who had also been invited, subsequently noticed that the name of the founder of the ICF was Sun Myung Moon. We both had a vague recollection of having read something not quite nice about him.

A visit to a newspaper-cuttings library revealed the information that Moon was a Korean millionaire who led a 'bizarre religious sect' and was thought by his disciples to be the Messiah; he had an entry in the *Guinness Book of Records* as a man who had married 791 couples at a mass wedding; the movement was an aggressively anti-communist organization; the previous summer some British students had gone to an 'International Leadership Seminar' in America: and "Immense pressure was put on us to join the movement" said one student who refuses to give his name for fear of the sect's attentions.' It was also reported in the *Sunday Times* on 16 June 1974 that a question was to be asked in the House of Commons as to whether the Attorney General would 'refer to the Director of Public Prosecutions with a view for prosecution for offences of deception under the Theft Act the body known as the Unification Church'. My family anxiously begged me to reconsider the invitation. But I was a sociologist of religion – nothing would have stopped me from going now.

Moon addressing the participants at the International Conference on the Unity of the Sciences, London, 1974.

The conference turned out to be disappointingly respectable. In fact, by academic standards, it was even rather a good conference. No one tried to brainwash us. We were allowed to say exactly what we wanted, and each word we had written was faithfully reproduced in the published proceedings.[1] There were, however, some awfully nice, young men and women who smilingly looked after us during the meetings. These, we whispered among ourselves, must be the brainwashed Moon people. It was hard to put one's finger on it, but there was definitely something 'different' about them. Perhaps they were a bit *too* nice.

My next contact with the movement came when I was invited to contribute to a series of three residential weekend 'Roundtables on Science and Religion' which were to be held at the Church's National Headquarters in Lancaster Gate, London. During the course of these visits we were taken to a farm in Wiltshire and had the opportunity to talk to several of the British members. I was unable to find out much about their beliefs or to form a very clear picture of the movement, but I did start to get to know a few of the individual members and to learn something of their backgrounds. Although they continued to be unusually pleasant and anxious to please, their unnatural niceness, which I had found slightly eerie at the

ICUS meeting, was not as noticeable when they relaxed on their own home ground.

At the same time, the media were becoming increasingly vocal and antagonistic in their reports of the movement. Some of the stories, such as rumours of child abuse, and allegations that the members held regular wild sex orgies,[2] I was fairly certain were untrue, but by now I was becoming fascinated by the Unification Church, and anxious to investigate some of the other reports. In those days, however, the movement was considerably more closed to outsiders than it is today, and it seemed unlikely that I would be able to obtain much more information – unless I were to pretend to become a member myself. This was out of the question for a number of reasons. First, I would have been unhappy about the deception on purely ethical grounds;[3] secondly, I had no desire to give up my job; and thirdly, even if I were to have joined, I would not have been able to go around asking questions on any sort of systematic basis without arousing suspicion. I dropped a few hints that I would be interested in doing a study, but I did not hold out much hope.

Then events took an unexpected turn. I was surprised one day to learn from my secretary that a Moonie about whom I had become rather interested (he had obtained a good history degree from Cambridge and I knew his father slightly) had been to visit me. My first reaction was that he might have been hoping to elicit my help in escaping from the clutches of the movement. I was afraid that he might get into trouble if I tried phoning, so I waited to see if he would make further contact. About a week later he found me in my office. He told me that he was worried about another sociologist of religion who, he had heard, was doing a study of the Unification Church from the 'outside', using information gleaned from people who were antagonistic towards the movement. He had also heard that the sociologist was intending to read a paper about withdrawal from the movement at an international conference of sociologists of religion the following year. I told him that I knew the sociologist (Dr James Beckford of Durham University) well, and that it was hardly surprising that he had to rely on negative reports, as it was well-nigh impossible to get any other kind of information. The Moonie then asked if I were going to the conference (I was), and whether I would be interested in writing a paper which drew on information from the inside? I explained that although I would be interested, I could not write a paper without first conducting a proper sociological study. I would need to have independent funding for my expenses, and I would require a complete list of the membership in Britain so that I could interview on a random sample basis (that is, each member would be allocated a number which would have an equal chance of being selected from a published table of random numbers), rather than seeing only those members whom the movement wanted me to interview.

It took several weeks to convince the British leadership that I could not do the study without the complete membership list. I tried to reassure them that as a sociologist I had no interest in, or intention of, divulging information about identifiable individuals. They were afraid, they said, that the media, or 'deprogrammers', would somehow get hold of the list and make trouble for the members. I suspected that the real reason was that they did not want to publicize the fact that the membership was much smaller than was usually assumed. In the meantime I applied to the Social Science Research Council, and my college, the London School of Economics, agreed to give me sufficient funding to start the project if the negotiations proceeded favourably.

It was at the end of 1976, more than two years after I had first made contact with the movement, that I finally got permission to do the study on my own terms,[4] with no conditions except for the promise, which I gave freely, that I would not publish personal details which could be related to identifiable individuals – except, of course, in the case of information which was already publicly available and/or related to the known leaders of the movement. The Moonie who had come to see me told me some time later that the reason why they had been prepared to let me do the study was not because they thought that I would necessarily support them – they did not, he admitted, really know how I regarded the movement – but because I had been prepared to listen to their side of the argument, and they could not believe that anyone who did that could write anything worse than what was already being published by people who had not come to find out for themselves. The final 'test' came on New Year's Eve, 1976, when one of the American leaders came to my house with two British Moonies. We discussed the research for about an hour and he then left, apparently satisfied. My children spent several exciting but ultimately unrewarded hours searching for the 'bugs' which they felt quite certain would have been planted in my study.

The Aims (and the Constraints) of the Research

The primary aim of my research was to find out what I could about Moonies – not about Moon, but about Moonies. As a sociologist I was less interested in how a leader 'ticks' or what his motives are than in how his leadership *works* – what his followers are prepared to believe and do for him as the (possibly no more than symbolic) focus of their attention.

In other words, it was not a central quest of my research to find out whether Sun Myung Moon is or believes himself to be the Messiah. I have been briefly introduced to him on a few occasions, I have heard him speak and I have read many of his speeches, but I have no special way of knowing what goes on in his mind. In my research the question 'how can a man, without the aid of guns or legislation, influence the lives of so many others throughout the world?' has been rephrased as 'under what circumstances will young, educated Westerners follow a man from Korea, accept a set of beliefs, adopt a style of life and perform actions which seem strange, wrong and unnatural to their parents, their friends and to most of the rest of society – and what are the consequences of such a phenomenon?'

The frightening thing about Jim Jones was not that he died, but that over 900 followers were prepared to die with him in Guyana; the strength of Hitler lay not in his ambitions, but in the fact that millions believed in him and obeyed him. It is not that I see the Unification Church as another People's Temple, nor, for different reasons, do I think that the Moonies constitute another Hitler Youth Movement,[5] but I am convinced that if we wish to further our understanding of how alternative movements actually 'work', we need to understand far more about what can make apparently unattractive, even repellent, beliefs and actions seem attractive to ordinary men and women. To say a leader must have charisma, or to 'explain' his following by reference to all-encompassing allegations of brainwashing or mind-control, is merely an obfuscating restatement of the problem.

To be more specific, some of the questions I asked during the course of my research were: why, and in what sorts of circumstances, will what kind of people become Moonies? Why, and in what sorts of circumstances, will what kind of people leave the movement? What is life like in the Unification Church? What kinds of communication system and power structure does the organization have? To what extent, and why, does the movement vary according to time and place? What is the range of the relationships which the Church and its members have with the rest of society? And in what kinds of ways can we best understand and explain the phenomenon of the Unification Church and public reaction to it?

An area in which I regretfully confess to a lack of expertise is that of the Eastern roots of the Unification Church. I have visited both Japan and South Korea, and I have some slight knowledge of Eastern religions, but this is not my 'field' and, speaking no Oriental language, I have been unable to comprehend with any depth or subtlety the specific perspective of Oriental Moonies. However, as most of the Western Moonies in whom I am interested have no more (usually considerably less) knowledge of the East than I, my ignorance need not interfere with my understanding of the functioning (as opposed to the origins) of the movement in the West, in so far as it is a movement mainly composed of, though not led by, Westerners.

Perspectives and Approaches

There are, as I have suggested in the introduction to this book, numerous perspectives from which people have looked at the Unification Church and its members.[6] On what might be termed the 'horizontal' level, there is a range of perspectives which encompasses, on the one hand, a picture of a scheming millionaire exploiting brainwashed robots who are unable to escape a life of abject poverty and misery, and, on the other hand, a picture of the man of God who has given love and liberty to his joyful followers as they realize their full potential in building the Kingdom of Heaven on earth. One of the questions that I had to ask was how one might reconcile these two pictures – or at least understand how such diverse views could be held of what is presumably one and the same reality. Another question dealt with what could be termed the 'vertical' perspectives. I wanted to analyse and, if possible, to integrate three different levels. First, there was the *personal* level, which was concerned with the individual Moonies; secondly, there was the *interpersonal* level, which was concerned with interactions between Moonies, and with relationships between them and those outside the movement; and, thirdly, there was the *impersonal* level, which was concerned with the more abstract phenomena in which sociologists are interested - things like structures and functions or unintended consequences, and systems which have properties that are not applicable to the individuals of which they are composed. At this impersonal level I also wanted to locate the movement as a whole within contemporary society and to compare it with other such movements both now and throughout history.[7]

It was obvious that no one method would be sufficient to obtain all the information that I would need for such a venture. In order to deal with the horizontal contradictions, I needed to speak to outsiders as well as insiders. To observe the vertical levels, I needed information about individual Moonies, their backgrounds, their hopes, values and general perspectives on life both inside and outside the movement. I also needed to observe them 'at work' as they interacted with other people in order to see how they were influenced by, and would themselves influence, others on a day-to-day basis. Finally, I needed to see how the movement as a whole was organized and how it influenced the day-to-day actions and interactions of its members.

I decided that three main approaches were needed: in-depth interviews, participant observation and questionnaires.

The Interviews

Thirty in-depth interviews were conducted at intervals throughout 1977. They usually took place in a quiet room at the centre in which the randomly selected Moonie happened to be living. The interviews were all taped, and the recordings were later transcribed. Most lasted between six and eight hours, the shortest was just under two hours, the longest a marathon of twelve hours. We would occasionally break for cups of coffee and sandwiches, but I tried to ensure that there were as few interruptions as possible. The interviews followed the general outline of a prepared schedule, but the actual order of topics was fairly flexible. We started comparatively formally, with straightforward questions about the interviewee's background, and then gradually relaxed until it seemed as though the interview was over. (Some of the most useful data I gathered came out in undirected conversation.) There was always a time when the Moonie would give his 'testimony', explaining, in a manner which had become polished with frequent telling, how he came to join the movement and how it had changed his life. We would spend quite a lot of time talking about his childhood, not so much for the value of the information itself – although it certainly had some – but because it helped to create an atmosphere in which the Moonie could feel that we were no longer strangers. Later we would move on to talk about life in the movement, and, finally, I would probe into the kind and the depth of understanding that the member had about what he was doing.

Participant Observation

Between interviews, and at odd periods throughout the next six years, I was also engaged in 'participant observation'. This entailed living in various centres with the members. I also attended a whole series of seminars or 'workshops' some of which were for potential members, but others were for academics or for parents, and there were yet others which were normally confined to the members themselves. I visited numerous Unification centres in North America. On the West Coast, early in the study, I nervously left instructions with a friend in San Francisco to rescue me if I did not return from a weekend at the notorious Camp K (see chapter 4).[8] Later I was to go, this time without a second thought, to the equally notorious farm at Boonville (sometimes spelled Booneville). On the East Coast I visited various centres in New York City and New York State. I stayed at the Unification Seminary in Barrytown, and I was taken on a tour of a 'Home-Church' area in Harlem. I got a supplementary grant to study new religious movements in all four Scandinavian countries, and

The author attending a lecture.

Conducting an interview.

whenever I happened to be in any other country I would make a point of trying to visit the local Unification centre.

   Although many of their interests and methods overlap, the social sciences are unlike the natural sciences in a number of ways. This is partly because they ask different kinds of questions. The chemist does not try to find out what molecules 'feel' when they are subjected to a particular process, but some degree of subjective understanding is necessary for the sociologist if he is to describe, let alone understand or explain, what his data are doing. The method employed in the attempt to gain some kind of empathetic understanding of what the world looks like from other people's point of view is frequently referred to as *Verstehen*.[9]

Although the two are frequently confused, empathy does not necessarily imply sympathy. *Verstehen* is a process of inquiry during which the researcher tries to put himself in other people's shoes or, to use another metaphor, to see the world through their glasses. He attempts to recognize the assumptions or 'filters' through which their world is seen, so that the actions and perceptions of the people he is studying begin to make sense. Obviously, this is an exercise which is much easier in some instances than in others. As a mother of teenage children, I found little difficulty in empathizing fairly quickly with most of the parents I met. It took a bit longer with some of my other subjects. The first time a young Californian Moonie rushed up and flung his arms around me with declarations of eternal love, I recoiled with truly British horror and only just managed to prevent myself from protesting that I did not think we had been introduced.

I found that the role I played as a participant observer went through three distinct stages during the course of the study. First there was a passive stage during which I did very little except to watch and listen (doing the washing-up in the kitchen was always a good place for this). Next there was an interactive stage during which I felt familiar enough with the Unification perspective to join in conversations without jarring; Moonies no longer felt that they had to 'translate' everything for me, and those Moonies who did not know me would sometimes take me to be a member. Finally there was the active stage. Having learned the social language in the first stage and how to use it in the second, I began in the third stage to explore its range and scope, its potentialities and its limitations. I argued and asked all the awkward questions that I had been afraid to voice too loudly at an earlier stage lest I were not allowed to continue my study. I could no longer be told that I did not understand because, in one sense at least, I patently *did* understand quite a lot – and I was using Unification arguments in my questioning. In this I angered some Moonies and saddened others, but there were those who not only tolerated my probing but actually discussed the problems that they and the movement were facing with an amazing frankness.

Of course, even in the interactive stage it was known that I was not a Moonie. I never pretended that I was, or that I was likely to become one. I admit that I was sometimes evasive, and I certainly did not always say everything that was on my mind, but I cannot remember any occasion on which I consciously lied to a Moonie. Being known to be a non-member had its disadvantages, but by talking to people who had left the movement I was able to check that I was not missing any of the internal information which was available to rank-and-file members. At the same time, being an outsider who was 'inside' had enormous advantages. I was allowed (even, on certain occasions, expected) to ask questions that no member would have presumed to ask either his leaders or his peers. Furthermore, several Moonies who felt that their problems were not understood by the leaders, and yet would not have dreamed of being disloyal to the movement by talking to their parents or other outsiders, could confide in me because of the very fact that I was both organizationally and emotionally uninvolved. It was not part of my duty to report which individuals were frustrated by the minor niggles of everyday life, or who was unhappily questioning some of the practices of the movement. I just listened. Fears and resentments could be expressed to someone who knew the context, yet would neither judge nor spill the beans. I found, furthermore, that I was the recipient of certain 'classified' information and, even without my asking for it, I was frequently presented with some of the less widely distributed Church literature.

My 'moles' fell into four broad categories. There were those who assumed that I knew everything anyway. Then there were those who wanted me to see everything so I would know that the 'secrets' were not as awful as I might imagine were I not to see them. There were others who, while generally loyal to the overall aims of the movement, wanted pressure to be put on the leaders by outsiders in connection with particular practices or policies about which they were worried. Finally, there were those who were generally disillusioned (and perhaps no longer members) and who wanted to expose what they considered to be the less attractive aspects of the movement without actually going to the media or the anti-cultists.

There were times when I found the study psychologically uncomfortable. One of the chief difficulties was something that might best be described as intellectual loneliness. I usually found my time with the movement interesting, and I grew genuinely fond of several individual Moonies, but at no time could I believe in the Unification version of reality. On the other hand, I could not accept the picture of the movement that outsiders kept telling me I ought to be finding. There was no one with whom I could share, or test, my own picture of reality. Then, just over half-way through the study, a BBC producer who was to make two films of my research for the Open University spent some time with me doing 'joint participant observation' in preparation for the filming. Each time we ended a visit I would thrust a tape recorder into her hands and beg her to pour out whatever occurred to her. The fact that her impressions largely coincided with my own did not, of course, prove that we were right and everyone else wrong, but it was enormously reassuring to learn that I was not totally idiosyncratic.

One question which researchers always have to ask themselves is how far they can trust their informants. I was continually being warned that, as Moonies practised 'heavenly deception' (telling permissible lies in order to further God's work in a satanic world), any information I obtained from a Moonie would be worthless.

I knew there was a problem, but I felt confident that, even if the Moonies did lie, to observe lying Moonies could produce more valuable data than would be got by confining oneself to the testimonies of ex-Moonies (see chapter 5). I did, however, need to discover which were the lies. This involved building up a very elaborate system of cross-checking between informants (particularly any discrepancies between information from those in the movement and those outside) and using several different approaches to a particular question – a procedure which was extremely time-consuming and which could not, by the very nature of the exercise, be hurried.

It seemed clear (and this has been consistently confirmed by members who subsequently left) that there was no general directive to deceive me. Having received permission from the 'top', I began my research in as low-key a manner as possible. Although I got to know several of the second-level leaders in Britain well, and would ask them for specific information (such as the whereabouts of someone who was on my inter-view list), I kept out of the way of the top-level leaders during the early stages of the study, and they, on the whole, left me to my own devices. It was not long before it ceased to be expected that I, as a visiting academic, should eat with the most important Moonies present, and when I was staying at a centre I soon found myself taking pot-luck with the 'sisters' as to whether I got a bed or had to spend the night in a sleeping bag on the floor. In so far as members were told anything about me – and I found to my surprise that often they were told nothing – they were usually asked to co-operate as (they were told) I was a friend of the Family. It was obvious from interviews, questionnaire responses and casual conversations that there were plenty of Moonies who were only too keen to talk not just about how wonderful the movement was but also, as I have already said, about the problems it and/or they were facing. I was the recipient of floods of complaints about local and national leaders. Some Moonies did un-doubtedly lie to me, but it did not take me long to find out who was not to be trusted. The most blatant falsehoods tended to come from a few in fairly exalted positions of leadership, and, interestingly enough, from one or two of the newer, more fanatical recruits. A far greater problem than outright lies was the probability that the Moonies were suppressing certain information. To get round this barrier I had to collect and piece together odd snippets of information bit by bit. This I did partly by letting it drop that I knew certain things in order to inspire the confidence of confirmation and perhaps further, associated information; alternatively, I might suppress the fact that I was aware of something, and in this way I was able to check how 'open' my informant was being.

To some Moonies, especially those with whom I did not wish to have too much contact during the early stages of the research, I appeared to be a rather dull but harmless presence, to whom one did not have to pay much attention; for others I was a chatty companion with whom one could discuss day-to-day existence. Some treated me as a maternal confidante; others decided to mother and look after me. A few of the members were anxious to treat me as an academic and to have long philosophical, political or theological discussions, mostly, although not exclusively, concerning their beliefs and practices. One or two Moonies treated me with the utmost suspicion and made it quite clear they did not wish to have anything to do with me. It was the very variety of these different relationships (which 'happened' rather than being carefully planned) that provided me with the opportunity to accumulate and check, slowly but surely, a multi-dimensional picture of the movement.

As I got to know and be known by the members, I started dropping in at various centres unannounced. This provided me with a further means of checking on such things as normal living conditions (the sort of food that was being eaten), the general state of the members (how many had streaming colds) and who was living where.

One set of information of which I was particularly anxious to check the accuracy was the basic lists of members and the details which were documented about them (such as age, date of joining, nationality, who had introduced them to the movement and what 'mission' they were on). At the start of the study I had been given the list of British membership without the disclosure of the full names.[10] I was soon finding that I could complete the names and some time later, when I had already collected a considerable amount of information about the members and when those in charge of the British 'office' were confident that I could be trusted not to publish any details concerning individual members, I was given access to files of present and past members' application forms. I was also, over the period of the study, able to collect a series of complete membership lists which allowed me to calculate the previously unknown but crucially significant rates of defection from the movement.

I found no instance of 'fudging' in the lists or the various forms and documents that I obtained from the British headquarters (except in the case of the date of birth of one woman, and I presume that it was not me, but her fellow members, whom she was hoping to mislead). From a variety of sources I checked and double-checked the figures I was given for people joining, leaving, going abroad, attending workshops and so on. Again, while I sometimes uncovered inefficiency, I never came across deception in such matters in Britain. Most of the European centres that I visited towards the end of the study were prepared to give me the membership information that I asked for, and, although I had little means of checking their figures, I have no reason to believe that they were anything but accurate. In the USA, the story was different. I could get numbers for certain centres, even for some states, but I never had access to official national figures, and some of the estimates I received differed enormously, although not as much as did those for Japan and South Korea. I knew some of the American leaders exaggerated their figures, sometimes by tenfold or more, and I found some of their other information unreliable. But, as I have already said, by the end of the study I had a fairly clear idea which sources I could trust and which I could not.

Finally, mention ought to be made of the fact that the people I was studying could be influenced by my presence *because* I was studying them.[11] The observer of the natural world is not (unless he is doing experiments in which Heisenberg's Uncertainty Principle is of moment) nearly as likely as the observer of the social world to influence the data he is studying. It is impossible to know just how much my research 'disturbed' what was happening. There were several occasions on which I mediated between a Moonie and his parents, and I frequently tried to persuade the movement's leaders to see that the members kept in touch with their relations. These interventions, and the giving of information to parents, the media, members of the 'anti-cult movement', and religious and various other officials, I undertook with an awareness that what I was doing could affect the situation. There were also numerous occasions on which my influence was unintended. A couple of extreme examples will make the point.

The first incident occurred while I was on a twenty-one-day course at which the participants were expected to deliver a lecture. The subject I was allocated was 'The Purpose of the Coming of the Messiah'. I did not exactly enjoy this aspect of my research, but participant observation does involve participation, so I gave the talk, carefully punctuating its delivery with phrases such as 'The *Divine Principle* teaches that . . .' or 'According to the *Principle* . . .'. When I had finished, a member of the audience declared that she had been extremely worried about that particular part of the doctrine, but she now understood it, and she fully accepted that the Reverend Moon was indeed the Messiah. I was horrified. 'But I don't believe it,' I insisted. 'I don't think it's true.' 'Perhaps not,' interrupted the Moonie in charge, 'but God has used Eileen to show Rosemary the truth.'

I had, from the start, excluded 'witnessing' (or 'spreading the truth') from the activities in which I was prepared to participate. I immediately vowed to refuse to give lectures in any further workshops I might attend. I have, however, given numerous talks at universities, colleges, schools church halls and at various conferences on the subject of new religious movements in general and the Unification Church in particular. On such occasions my audience has usually consisted of people who knew little about the Unification Church – except that it was 'a bad thing'. Every once in a while, however, a Moonie (usually a CARP member)[12] has stood up and made himself known (sometimes to my embarrassment and some-times to the astonishment of his fellow students who had thought until that moment that he was an 'ordinary' student). The information about the second example of my influence on those whom I was studying came to me through a friend, one of whose students was an ex-Moonie who told him that she had heard me giving a lecture on the movement and had consequently realized for the first time that it was possible for her to take what she called 'a middle-way position'. She had reached a stage of not accepting everything that was taught or expected of her in the Unification Church, but at the same time she had felt that she could not deny the good things which she had experienced in the movement in the way that she assumed would be necessary (because of the attitudes of Moonies on the one hand and that of 'outsiders' on the other) if she were to leave. But when she had heard me give, from an outsider's perspective, what she considered to be a fairly accurate account of the movement, she had concluded that she did not have to make an absolute 'yes or no' choice but was able to leave, rather than feeling forced to stay because of her ambiva-lent feelings.

Of course, most of the effects of research were unlikely to be as dramatic as tipping someone into joining or leaving the movement, but it would be hard to believe that my presence in the centres did not make some difference, especially in the early years of my research when the rank-and-file Moonies very rarely talked to anyone who was not a member except for the specific purposes of fund-raising or finding new recruits. When I began the interviewing I was uncertain about the consequences of my asking difficult and searching questions which anyone, not just Moonies, would have found hard to answer. My interviewees told me that they had, in fact, enjoyed the experience, although it had often been pretty exhausting. They said that it had made them think about things they had not really thought about before; but when I pointed out inconsistencies in their arguments they were unlikely to crumble and express doubts about their faith – instead they tended to say that I had presented them with a challenge to look more deeply at the beliefs and so discover the answer, which they felt certain could be found were they only to study or think about it. I also found that I became a source of certain kinds of information for the Moonies, and, as I have already stated, I found that several Moonies would contact me for the odd chat. In this position I played the role of the 'stranger',[13] which was, as I have already indicated, extremely useful for my research, but in so far as there was unlikely to be a 'substitute stranger' for many of those who confided in me, I must, once again, acknowledge that I could have made a difference to the situation I was studying – indeed, in some instances, I hope I did.

The Questionnaires

If the researcher wishes to test the generalizations upon which any scientific explanation has to rest, then he must, to some extent, obtain data which can be subjected to qualitative and/or comparative analyses. For various reasons, some of which are fairly obvious, the subject matter of the social sciences is considerably less amenable to research than that of the natural sciences. But this does not mean that we cannot improve our knowledge of social patterns, trends and tendencies and gain a more reliable understanding of regularities between variables – of 'what goes with what'. By looking at groups as a whole we can begin to see patterns of relationships, and it becomes easier to detect which occurrences are incidental, even if sensational, and which are 'normal'.

By the beginning of 1978 I had formulated some of the hypotheses which I wished to test on a more systematic basis. I also hoped that I was sufficiently well acquainted with the beliefs and practices of the movement to be able to compile a questionnaire that would be couched in terms which would 'show off' enough internal background knowledge to give members the confidence to answer fully and openly questions which they would not normally discuss with outsiders.

After trying out some initial drafts on my long-suffering students, I distributed twenty copies to one large Unification Church centre, asking the members to point out any ambiguities and to make any suggestions for improvements or additional questions. This pilot study yielded several very helpful ideas that were incorporated into a final forty-one page questionnaire which was given to all the British members and to those foreign members in Britain whose English was of a sufficiently high standard. The questionnaire was also distributed to all the Moonies studying at the Unification Seminary in New York State and, on a somewhat haphazard basis, to a small number of other American members. Some of the questionnaires I handed out personally while going round centres. The rest I sent to individuals through the post. I allocated each Moonie a number, and this alone identified the returning questionnaires. I am (and intend to remain) the only person who has access to the key which connects each number to a name. Attached to each questionnaire was a stamped envelope with my university address.

The response rate was exceptionally high. I sent letters to those British members who had not replied and then, to those from whom I had still not heard, I sent a single-page questionnaire asking for basic background information in order to check whether those who had responded were different from those who had not (with respect to such factors as sex or length of membership). In the event I was unable to detect any significant difference. By the end of the year (1978), and after one further reminder, I had received some sort of reply from all but eleven of the full-time English-speaking Moonies who were still in the movement in Britain, and I had been able to collect quite a lot of information about the majority of these eleven. Only three of the non-respondents admitted to objecting in principle to filling in the questionnaire. The others claimed either that they had had no time to do so or that they had lost their original questionnaires.

The questions were of two kinds: those that were 'pre-coded' and those that were 'open'. For the pre-coded questions the respondent would ring the most applicable of a series of possible answers; the open questions could be answered by the respondent in any way he chose. Many of these answers were very detailed and continued on to the back of the page. Two research assistants coded the response so that the information could be fed into a computer.[14]

I have no intention of turning this section into a methodological text, propounding statistical theory or techniques, but as some of the statements in this book question a number of assertions made by Moonies, by the media, by the anti-cultists and, indeed, by some academics, I would like to mention briefly the quantitative methods and principles which I consider crucial to my challenging of their conclusions – and the vindication of my own.

It is understandable that people confuse visibility with quantity. In the course of a radio programme I once announced that there were about five hundred Moonies in Britain. An active opponent of the Church telephoned the BBC to say that there were at least twice that number. I was fairly certain that there were 517, but I asked him on what he based his figures. 'Well, people keep complaining, and anyway you can see them everywhere – walk down any big shopping centre and you'll see what I mean.' My figure could have been wrong. It came from the most up-to-date Moonie list, but, as I have already indicated, I checked these lists frequently and carefully through unannounced visits to centres and reports from parents and apostates and, indeed, against names supplied by the anti-cult movement itself. On this comparatively simple point I had no hesitation in believing that the basis for my assertion was infinitely superior to his, and that if I were wrong, I certainly was not as wrong as he had been (and he did, indeed, use my figures in some of his subsequent pronouncements).

Another, more complicated way in which visibility and quantity become confused is when a true story is told over and over again in connection with a particular movement and it becomes assumed that this is *typical* of the movement in question (that the rate of such occurrences within the movement is high), and that it is *atypical* of the wider population (that the rate of such occurrences in 'normal' society is much lower or even non-existent). The next stage in the argument is usually that the (assumed) high rate of occurrence is taken to 'prove' that it is the movement which is responsible for (is the primary cause of) the occurrence. Such assumptions may or may not be true, but it is only through systematic investigation, including the careful use of control groups, that we can ever hope to find out.

A related problem which a researcher often has to face is that he cannot always get information about *all* the people he is studying. He is, consequently, forced to work with a sub-group or sample. If he wants to generalize from the sample, he has to try to gauge how accurately it reflects the whole group: if, for instance, 21 per cent of his sample comes from a Roman Catholic background, how probable is it that 21 per cent of the whole group comes from a Roman Catholic background? If we have a randomly selected sample for which each member of the whole group has had an equal chance of being selected, and if the sample is of sufficient size, then we can accurately calculate the probability that our sample will faithfully reflect characteristics of the whole group. But if the sample is not randomly selected, we must ask whether there was a factor which was responsible for the selection that could bias the sample's representativeness with respect to the information about which we wish to generalize. Most people would agree that the evidence of divorcees is not necessarily the most reliable basis from which to study the institution of marriage, yet one sample that has frequently been used for generalizations about the Moonies consists of those who have been deprogrammed and, in the process, *taught* many of the things that they now say about the movement (see chapter 5). When assessing the extent to which one can generalize from their statements, one has to take into account, both this and the fact that they were the sort of people who *could* be deprogrammed (while others, going through a similar process, have returned to the movement.

In my research I used a variety of groups for comparative purposes, but there were two non-Moonie groups which were particularly important. General population statistics told me, for instance, the extent to which

**Workshop
Application**

2-DAY WORKSHOP : £ 5.00
7 DAY WORKSHOP : £16.00
21-DAY WORKSHOP : £25.00

Workshop Application

NAME _____ SEX _____

ADDRESS _____

OCCUPATION _____ TEL _____

DATE OF BIRTH _____ RELIGIOUS BACKGROUND _____

CONTACTED BY _____ CENTRE _____

TALENTS AND SKILLS _____

NATIONALITY _____

I would like to attend the _____ day workshop at _____

on _____ in order to understand better the principles of your Unification movement.

DATE _____ SIGNATURE _____

NOTE: We cannot be responsible for accidents or stolen property.

*One of the application forms (for a British workshop) which provided some of the basic
data for the study.*

Moonies differed from their fellow countrymen in terms of such variables as sex, age and social and religious background. As the necessary information about certain other variables in which I was interested was not available, and as these variables were liable to be affected by sex, age and background, I gave a questionnaire, similar to that which I had given to the Moonies, to a group of people who were 'matched' with the Moonies with respect to sex, age and background.

I did not have the resources (time or money) to select my control group as systematically as perfection would have demanded, but for the purposes of the study the method was adequate. I compiled a thirty-six page version of the forty-one page questionnaire that I had given the Moonies. It differed only in that it contained some questions asking what the respondent knew about the Unification Church, and, obviously, it did not contain questions directly related to life in the movement. I then found about two dozen people who had access to the sorts of social context from which Moonies might be recruited. These contacts included teachers at universities and colleges around the country, a Roman Catholic priest, a Presbyterian minister and members of various youth groups and other organizations associated with people in about their early twenties. The only instruction I gave the contacts was not to pass on the questionnaire to anyone under eighteen years of age. I distributed just under 200 such questionnaires and received 110 codable responses.

In addition, from 1,017 application forms for workshop attendance in the London area during 1979 I was able to gather a considerable amount of information about a group of people of whom most did not become Moonies but who did represent the constituency from which Moonies were recruited.[15] I sent a six-page questionnaire to the applicants who had supplied legible addresses. This produced 130 codable responses, and these reflected the already known characteristics of the 1979 London workshop attenders with a gratifying closeness. Then, as most of the respondents had not joined, the same six-page questionnaire was sent to British Moonies who had become members during 1979 or 1980 in order to secure a number of 'joiners' which would be sufficiently large to enable me to make meaningful comparisons.[16] Details of the numbers of the respondents to all the questionnaires are given in table 1.

Other Sources of Information

During the course of the research I had contact with just under a hundred sets of parents. Some I had met at Unification Church centres, others I met at anti-cult meetings, but most of them had contacted me because they had heard, one way or another, that I was doing the study and were desperately in need of information. As with the Moonies, several of these

Table 1   Sources of quantitative data

Source of information		Respondents
Full-time Moonies		
Main UC: 41-page questionnaire (1978)		380
Follow-up: 1-page questionnaire (1978)		45
		425
Major breakdown		
British members of British movement	224	
Non-British members of British movement		
(not falling into another category)	11	
European other than British	77	
Asian	13	
American seminarians	67	
Non-American seminarians	8	
Non-seminarian Americans	16	
New Zealanders/Australians	9	
	425	
Control Group		
36-page questionnaire (1979)		110
Workshop Group		
6-page questionnaire sent to all 2-day attenders in London		
area (1979)		130
Additional questionnaires sent to all who joined in 1979 or 1980		87
		217
Major breakdown		
Non-joiners	104	
Leavers (joined and left within few weeks)	25	
Home-Church joiners	11	
CARP joiners	13	
Full-time joiners	64	
	217	
		Persons
Data from application forms for 2-day workshop during 1979		
(London area)		1,017
Data from application forms for 21-day workshop during 1979		
(London area)		604
Data from available membership forms for Home-Church members		140
Data from application forms of apostates		
Data from 8 (up-dated) UC membership lists between 1976 and 1983		
4-page questionnaires administered by Stilson Judah to San		
Francisco Bay Area Moonies in 1976		50

parents felt a need to talk to someone who knew what was going on, yet was not a member of the movement. Most of the parents had experienced difficulty in communicating with the members, including, perhaps, their own child who could not or would not understand why they could not or would not understand why he had to sacrifice his career, his family and his friends in order to 'fund-raise' on the streets for eighteen hours a day. ('Fund-raising' is the term used for the collection of money, usually by asking for donations in exchange for literature or by selling flowers, plants, candy or other merchandise in the streets or by knocking on people's doors.) 'They just won't listen to what I want to tell them. They keep changing the subject to talk about something unimportant – like the price of butter, or what my cousin's new dress is like,' complained a frustrated Moonie after a visit to her parents. An equally frustrated parent complained, after his son had been home for a rare weekend, 'Every time I try to have a serious conversation with him, he just starts jabbering like an idiot about our fallen nature and what happened in the Garden of Eden.'

At the same time, parents have frequently found that the outside world does not offer much in the way of support and understanding. Friends may talk about how their own children have just completed degrees at Cambridge and then look at them with embarrassment; uncles may tell the parents to take hold of the situation and get George out of it at once; women may look pityingly at mothers and say how lucky they are that *they* have always had a close relationship with their children; other kind friends may send cuttings of the more sensational reports in the press with 'Just in case you didn't see this' or, more cruelly, 'Is *this* the thing Henrietta escaped to?' scribbled accusingly in the margin. It was through getting to know such parents that I had an opportunity of seeing how different interpretations of what was happening could lead to some of the tragic rifts which sprang up between them and their children – and, of course, the parents provided me with a great deal of factual information which I could compare with the information which the Moonies were giving me.

A further, invaluable source of information (but again one that I found I could not always trust) was the 'anti-cult movement'.[17] I received the literature and met a considerable number of representatives of several of these groups. Talks with deprogrammers included a twelve-hour interview with an extremely obliging and utterly charming gentleman in an office decorated with firearms and cultist spoils. On another occasion I sat in on a 'counselling session' for a young man who had just left another new religion, the Way International.

I had innumerable exchanges – some friendly and mutually helpful, others less so – with the media in their various forms. I discussed the Unification Church with a number of interested government officials in Britain and Germany and with representatives of many different religious organizations. For the sake of comparison I also visited and interviewed members of a dozen or so of the other new religious movements.

Perhaps the most valuable sources for checking information, however, were the twenty or so people with whom I kept in touch after they had left the movement. There were many other former members with whom I talked, but those whom I had known both as Moonies and as ex-Moonies were the ones from whom I could learn the most.

My Diary and Learning the Moonie Perspective

Whenever I was engaged in participant observation, after each of the hundreds of informal interviews I held, and during every telephone call connected with the research, I made copious notes as soon as I could, both on factual information and on my personal reactions to what was happening. Often these notes were spoken into a small portable tape-recorder which went everywhere with me. At the start of the study I was terrified lest the tapes or the notes would be found, and I went to great lengths to hide bits of paper or to whisper my observations into the recorder so furtively that my secretary could not transcribe the tape because it sounded, she complained, like heavy breathing down the telephone. With time I found these 007 tactics totally unnecessary. Apart from one occasion (when I was spending a weekend at the Californian Camp K and my notebook disappeared for a couple of hours), I have no reason to believe that anyone ever showed the slightest interest in the observations I was making. There was, indeed, one time when, feeling particularly exhausted, I suggested to an even more exhausted Moonie that we should 'escape' for a short holiday. She agreed, summarily informed her 'central figure' that she would return to New York in two or three days, and off we went. (We learned later there was some speculation as to whether I was deprogramming her or she was brainwashing me, but in fact we did little more than relax and enjoy ourselves.) Then one evening we started a discussion on a subject that had been both fascinating and puzzling me for some time. Before long, however, the effects of a day in the sun, the sea and a night club we had rather daringly visited caught up with me, and I fell asleep. Still having quite a bit to say, my companion found the tape-recorder which I had left lying by my bed, switched it on, and was able to present me with one of my most rewarding 'interviews' when I awoke in the morning.

The 'diary', which filled half a dozen large files by the end of the research, was obviously useful for recording factual data. It also served to remind me about what I had taken to be strange or exotic at the start of the study but had begun to stop noticing as I discovered how it fitted into the internal logic of the movement or turned out to be based on rumours that I had long since discounted. An early entry which caused me some surprise when I came to read it a few years later, for example, was that the keys for a particular centre (in which I had heard Moonies had been kept locked up) were kept hanging in a place accessible to all and that the front door could easily be opened from the inside. One rather exotic entry noted the rate at which Tampax and sanitary towels were being replaced. (This was because I had read that females always ceased menstruating on becoming Moonies.)[18]

The record of my reactions was especially helpful in reminding me what would need to be communicated to outsiders if they were to understand more about the Moonie perspective. The problem of communication has been brought home to me forcibly on several occasions. One of these was when my husband and I met two Moonies whom I knew fairly well. (This was during the second, 'interactive', stage of my participant observation.) We had had a pleasant coffee with the Moonies, and had then parted company. 'They weren't bad, were they?' I asked my husband, who generally refused to go anywhere near a Moonie because, he said, they gave him the creeps. 'No, they seemed rather nice,' he admitted, 'but you – you were so different!'

What had happened was that, on the one hand, the Moonies had been behaving 'naturally', without doing the 'translation' that they usually do for outsiders (which involves the 'being awfully nice') that my husband disliked so much, and, on the other hand, I had 'changed gear' so that I was communicating by means of a set of concepts and assumptions that were unlike those I adopted in everyday life. It was not, as an anti-cultist who heard me tell this story suggested, that my involvement with the Moonies was so strong that my family noticed that I had started using Unification Church terminology and that I was thinking like a Moonie in my 'ordinary' life.[19] My husband had been surprised because he had *not* seen me behave like a Moonie before.

The surprise for me was that the difference in style was so marked. My husband had seen me behave in one way with elderly relatives, another way with our children, another way with our close friends and in yet another way with my students. I was unaware that the 'suitable' (and largely unconscious) change in behaviour with the Moonies differed from any of these other 'suitable' (and largely unconscious) changes in behaviour. The point is that my husband, like those to whom I was going to have to communicate my findings, was so unfamiliar with the Moonie perspective that it seemed to him totally unnatural that anyone, especially someone known intimately over many years, should behave in such a manner. It is my diary that has helped me to recreate a bridge between the two 'realities' as I have looked back on my own journey of 'translation'.

I know, of course, that no one can ever provide an entirely satisfactory translation from one view of reality to another. This is partly because each perspective will have so many different facets, but it is also because there will always be those who are so suspicious or frightened of unfamiliar views that they will not allow themselves to 'hear' a translation. One distraught mother, for example, was quite convinced that her son had suffered irreparable brain damage as a result of his becoming a Moonie. There was, she said, no other possible way of explaining why he would believe such utter nonsense. After about an hour's conversation I thought I had calmed her down, on this point at least, by convincing her that one did not necessarily have to be brain-damaged in order to believe in the contents of the *Divine Principle* (see chapter 3). Suddenly, there was a renewed outburst of hysteria. You're making it all sound so sane and understandable' she cried, 'You must believe it – you must be a Moonie.' And we were right back where we had started. She, like several of the Moonies with whom I have discussed Unification theology, seemed to think that one cannot understand something without believing it to be good or true. Yet, perhaps paradoxically, it is often these very people who seem to believe that one can know with certainty that something is false or bad without understanding it.

Facts, Values and Science

I believe that it is perfectly possible to learn to see things from other people's point of view without necessarily agreeing that they are right. At the same time it seems to be self-evidently true that, whatever judgements we make, they will be 'better' judgements to the extent that they are based on an accurate understanding of whatever it is we are judging. There are, however, those who think that it is immoral for the sociologist to sit on the fence. Both Moonies and their adversaries have complained bitterly about certain of my articles in which I have not come down on one side or the other. One crusading anti-cultist, incensed by a paper I had written, phoned up the editor of the journal in question and complained that doubtless this was all the result of academic research, but it was so balanced and objective that he demanded the right to redress the balance.[20] When I challenged a clergyman, who had told some parents that I was unreliable, to tell me what it was that I had got wrong, he replied, 'Oh, you get the facts right, but it's no good if you don't come out strongly and clearly against them – people will be lulled into thinking everything's all right.' A Moonie complaint, on the other hand, is more likely to be that my writing is 'accurate enough as far as it goes but, sad to say, uninspired'. Why, they tend to ask, when I have been given the opportunity to observe the living truth, do I not want to proclaim it from the rooftops with shouts of ecstatic joy?

I suspect that there are enough campaigners on both sides. Those who want stirring polemic, asserting that the Moonies are evil and ought to be stamped out, can go to an anti-cult centre, those who want stirring polemic asserting that the Unification Church is the only righteous hope for the world can go to a Moonie centre. It is not that I am against campaigning in principle (I have already admitted that I frequently jeopardized my role as an 'uninvolved researcher' by actively mediating between the movement and the parents of several of its members), but I do believe that passing value judgements should be an enterprise that is separate from social science. Of course, the separation between fact and value is an ideal standard that is easier to state than to achieve – and one certainly hopes that one's research has practical *relevance*[21] - but, while engaged in the exercise of describing and explaining phenomena, it is my belief that social scientists are useful only in so far as they communicate information which corresponds to the object of their study rather than colouring, distorting, confusing or over-simplifying an already messy and complicated reality with the addition of their personal beliefs and values. The 'purer' the information, the more helpful it will be in enabling us all (as citizens) to implement our values.[22]

If social scientists have no special expertise in moral judgements, can they claim any epistemological expertise? Can they, that is, have special, superior, ways of *knowing* about social phenomena? Of course, they have no mystical powers of divination, and most of the sociologists' research is little more than hard sweat. They do, however, have the advantages of access to a body of accumulated theory and background knowledge concerning their area of study, a familiarity with certain techniques and an awareness of certain pitfalls. Like all scientists, they have to recognize, that their expertise is confined to empirical reality – that is, to reality which is observable through the five senses. Statements such as 'The successes of the Unification Church proves that God is on our side' or 'the set-backs the Unification Church faces prove that God is on our side because Satan is working so hard against us' cannot be assessed by the social scientist, since there is no way in which they could be refuted.[23] (Of course, the fact that people make use of such arguments is part of the sociologist's *data*.)

This leads me to another way in which my research has irritated both some Moonies and some evangelical Christians who are convinced that Moon is really the anti-Christ. How, I have been asked, could I hope to explain why someone converts to the Unification Church when the real explanation is that God (or Satan) has guided or called the Moonie to the movement? It is, of course, impossible for someone to judge the truth or falsity of claims concerning the direct intervention of God (or Satan) in another person's life. By definition, a supernatural act is beyond the ken of any kind of science. But while I have insisted that I have had to remain agnostic about whether or not God (or any supernatural being) really had intervened, in defence of my research I have argued that it is usually possible to observe that if God (or Satan) *were* intervening, He would appear to be making considerable use of secondary causes or intervening variables to implement His intervention.

In other words, one does not hear of people suddenly becoming Moonies without their going through some kind of social channel. Even the most unexpected revelation – that, say, the Messiah, in the person of Sun Myung Moon, is upon the earth – does not occur (or, at least, is not interpreted as such) without some preliminary introduction to the idea through a less direct route. Mundane factors, such as a previously developed susceptibility to something like the Unification Church, a precipitating 'push' from society or an alluring 'pull' from proselytizing Moonies, would seem to be an inevitable part of the process involved in the making of a Moonie – and these are factors which are accessible to empirical investigation.[24]

2 The Unification Church: An Historical Background

Origins of the Movement in Korea

There is as yet no official history of the Unification Church, and it is difficult to verify some of the stories that are told about the early life of the movement or its founder, the Reverend Sun Myung Moon. It does, however, seem clear that Moon was born, the fifth of eight children, to a rural family in Cheong-ju, Pyeong-an Buk-do, northern Korea, on 6 January 1920 (this date being calculated from the lunar calendar which is used in Korea).[1] It is reported that Moon was initially named Yong Myung Moon, but twenty-five years later he changed his name to Sun Myung Moon.[2] His family converted to a Presbyterian version of Christianity when Moon was 10 years old, and as a young man he taught in Sunday school.[3]

Although he appears not to have publicized the event at the time, Moon was later to report that on Easter Day 1936 Jesus appeared to him and revealed that God had chosen him for the mission of establishing His Kingdom of Heaven on earth.[4] Moon 'then wandered through the invisible (spirit) world. . . seeking to solve all the fundamental questions about life and the universe. . . . In search of the truth, he walked a path of suffering and fought a bloody battle against the forces of Satan.'[5] We are told that over the next nine years Moon received revelations through prayer, meditation, the study of religious scriptures and spiritual communications with such key religious leaders as Jesus, Moses and Buddha and, directly, with God Himself.[6] These revelations were written down by his followers in Korea, the first text appearing in 1957.[7] A subsequent text, translated and published in English as *Divine Principle*,[8] has been used as the official doctrine of the Unification Church. Further explications of the Principle have been and still are being written,[9] and it has been announced that further revelations will be released, although these will depend upon progress made in the task of establishing the Kingdom of Heaven on earth.[10]

On a more mundane level we learn that Moon received a traditional

Chinese education in his village, then began Western-style elementary school in his teens.[11] In 1938 he went to High School in Seoul, and in 1941 he enrolled as an electrical engineering student at Waseda University, Japan.[12] He returned to Korea in 1943 and found work as an electrician in a construction company, but the following year, because of underground political activities (in support of Korean independence from Japan) in which he had been engaged while a student, he was arrested by the Japanese police and tortured for four months.[13] After Korea's liberation from Japan at the end of World War II, Moon began full-scale religious activities, and on 6 June 1946 he is said to have received a revelation that he should go to Pyeong-yang in northern Korea. This he did immediately. For the next six years his then wife, who at that time had a two-month-old baby, did not know what had happened to him.[14]

In Pyeong-yang Moon established the independent Kwang-ya Church and started to gather a following of people who accepted his new revelations, but, we are told, 'the atheistic Communist Party despised him.'[15] In August, following rumours that he was teaching heretical doctrines and that he was a spy for the President of South Korea,[16] the communist police arrested him and put him in jail.

> He was tortured, severely beaten and deprived of both food and sleep. . . . Finally he was so severely beaten that he began to vomit great amounts of blood, and the jailers thought he was dead. They threw him outdoors on the pile of bodies awaiting burial beside the police station.
>
> There his followers found him and took him home. They expected him to die and began funeral preparations, but with the devoted care of his followers and the assistance of Chinese herbal medicine he recovered and began to preach his message even more powerfully than before.[17]

His renewed efforts brought him some more followers – and further complaints. He was arrested again in February 1948.[18]

One of his first disciples, Won Pil Kim, writes that at Moon's trial the communists wanted to show that Moon was crazy because he believed in God, while they taught that God is man-made:[19]

> The communists also tried to prove that Father [Moon] deceived people in order to deprive them of their joy and precious valuables. It is very easy for them to accuse a religious leader because a church always operates on contributions from the members. Today in America churches operate on the same principle.[20]

Mr Kim also reports that women who were joining the movement were instructed by God to live like virgins until their marriage was blessed

Moon at High School.

The shack made with rocks, earth and cardboard boxes which was Moon's Church in Pusan, South Korea in the early 1950s.

by Moon. Their husbands were suspicious about Moon's role in this and they banded together, calling him a heretic who disturbed their family life. This provided ammunition for other Christian ministers to use against Moon:

Moon giving a Sunday sermon at the Chungpadong Church in Seoul, 1960.

Father was totally innocent. You know what he teaches, and how he emphasizes purity. That's the way it was from the very beginning. Furthermore, Father never asked those wives to give up their family life. God directly intervened, and thus the misunderstanding was born.[21]

Moon was sentenced to five years' imprisonment in Hung-nam labour camp where he is reported to have impressed not only his fellow prisoners but also the communist guards with his physical and spiritual endurance of the appalling conditions within the camp.[22]

On 25 June 1950 the Korean War broke out, and Moon was released by the United Nations forces in October, after just over two and a half years of imprisonment.[23] With Won Pil Kim and another disciple, who had a broken leg, he fled on foot from the communists to the south and, after a series of adventures,[24] reached a refugee camp in Pusan at the beginning of 1951. There he lived in a hut made out of mud and US Army ration boxes[25] and continued with his teaching (known as the Principle). Then, having moved to Seoul, the capital of South Korea, Moon established a Church called the Holy Spirit Association for the Unification of World Christianity (HSA–UWC) on 1 May 1954.[26] Later that year the movement was given a considerable fillip when the authorities at Ewha Women's University sent one of their professors to investigate the Principle. Instead of condemning it, however, she was converted, became a member and was followed into the movement by several other professors and students.[27]

But the following year Moon was imprisoned again. The Unificationists say that this was on a trumped-up charge of draft evasion,[28] but it has also been reported that he was charged with 'injuring public morals',[29] or, according to another account, that 'his indictment was initially draft dodging but was later changed to adultery and promiscuity.'[30] Similar rumours (which persist to this day in Korea)[31] alleged that he was engaging in ritual sexual practices. The movement's explanation is that these rumours originated because there was a curfew, and as people could not return home after the long services, they had to stay at the Church centre all night, thus giving rise to unfounded speculation on the part of hostile officials of other Christian churches. The Unification Church, however, persists in its assertion that Moon was never arrested on sexual charges, but that the 1955 arrest was for 'violation of Military Draft Law' for which he was found not guilty[32] after three months' imprisonment. A few days after Moon's release the Church moved to a location at Chungpadong, which became the site of its world headquarters.[33]

Many stories are told about the suffering and persecution that Moon underwent during these early days.[34] Not all of these match each other in detail, but there seems to be little doubt that Moon did endure considerable hardship during his twenties and early thirties. He was, however, even during his time in prison, clearly able to convince some people that he was a very special man of God who had a very special message for the world, and slowly but surely there grew around him a band of faithful followers.

The establishment of a new religious movement was by no means a rare event in post-war Korea. In a land torn by political, social and religious divisions, a movement offering Unification would have obvious attractions. Several scholars have tried to explain the rise of the movements in general, or the Unification Church in particular, in terms of both Korea's recent history and her cultural heritage.[35] Such theories cannot, however, explain the attractions that the movement was to have for young people in Japan – (where Koreans have, traditionally, been regarded as an inferior race);[36] even less can they explain the growth of the movement in America or Europe.

There is, none the less, an important point concerning the subsequent development and organization of the movement in the West which can be made at this stage. The Unification Church is fundamentally dependent upon Sun Myung Moon for its existence. It did not originate as the result of a schism, or because a group of people decided that they wanted to return to some pristine version of the Truth.[37] Nor was it merely the result of a reinterpretation of Holy Scripture. The theology is not new in its particulars – scholars have pointed to roots or precursors in a variety of traditions,[38] claiming that it is syncretistic or that it is drawn from a conglomeration of heresies – but in its *structure*, in its entirety, it is an original whole. And the source, the only source of the picture as a whole, is Moon himself. It is he, his followers believe, whom God has chosen to reveal the Truth (and he it is whom nearly all of them believe to be the Messiah). If there is any disagreement or misunderstanding about God's divine Principle, then it is to Moon that the movement's membership must ultimately turn. So long as he is alive, no one within the movement can claim a better understanding of God's will. The fact that there are some members who believe that he makes mistakes, a few who use other sources to check his revelations and a few, a very few, who are uncertain whether he is in fact the one chosen to fill the office of the Messiah does not detract from his unique position. The explicit *raison d'être* of the Unification Church is to restore God's Kingdom of Heaven on earth. Sun Myung Moon is the man who has the hotline to God. Thus it is that both power and communication structures will naturally focus on one in his position, and, other things being equal, his followers will be accorded respect and authority to the degree that he permits them to be close to him

– or close to those who are close to him. The origins of the movement suggest, in other words, a hierarchical organization of authority, with Moon at its apex. And, moreover, the followers believe that it is an authority which has divine sanction.

The Unification Church Goes West

Although this book is concerned mainly with the recruiting practices of the Unification Church since the mid-1970s, some background knowledge of the movement's early days in the West is necessary to set the scene for the later period. There exist two reliable studies describing the early days of the Unification Church in America. The first, the result of first-hand research done for a doctoral thesis in sociology by John Lofland, deals with the period up to 1964 and is published, with the use of pseudonyms, under the title *Doomsday Cult*.[39] As this excellent study is readily available, there is little point in my going over ground Lofland has already so well covered. The second study is less available, being an as yet unpublished MA thesis by Michael Mickler,[40] who is himself a member of the movement. Mickler's thesis provides an informative and painstakingly documented history of the movement in the San Francisco Bay Area until 1974 (the year in which I first met the movement).

Early in 1959, Dr Young Oon Kim (commonly known as Miss Kim) enrolled as a student at the University of Oregon in Eugene and began the task of introducing the *Divine Principle* to the citizens of the United States of America.[41] Miss Kim had been professor of New Testament and Comparative Religions at the Methodist-affiliated Ewha University in Seoul until she, with some other teachers and students, was expelled in 1955 for refusing to leave the Unification Church.[42] She was no stranger to the West, as she had held a scholarship to do post-graduate studies at the University of Toronto for three years and had subsequently spent six months in Europe.[43] From her early teens she had had a series of mystical experiences including visions of Emmanuel Swedenborg, about whom she wrote her thesis while in Canada.[44] Since 1954 and her own conversion to the movement at the age of 39,[45] she had been resolved to take the Principle to the West, and, in 1956, she had made the first of several translations of the *Divine Principle* into English.[46]

For some time after her arrival, her endeavours met with little success, but in 1960 she had gained the interest of a small group which included Doris Walder who became one of the first converts in the West. In September 1959 David S.C. Kim (who had gone to Britain as a United Nations scholar in 1954,[47] was one of the charter members of the HSA–

UWC and is now President of the Unification Church Theological Seminary) also arrived in America. (David Kim is not related to Miss Kim; Kim is a very common name in Korea.) Two years later another early member of the Korean Church, Colonel Bo Hi Pak (who was later to be Moon's chief public interpreter and the chief Unification witness at the investigation of Korean–American Relations hearings), became assistant military attaché at the Republic of Korea Embassy in Washington.[48] Then, in 1965 Sang Ik Choi, a Korean who had spent most of his

Moon with Dr Young Oon Kim (Miss Kim) in 1959 before she was sent as the first missionary to the USA.

formative years in Japan, arrived in America. Under the name of Nishika-wa he had smuggled himself into Japan to become the first successful Unification Church missionary there.[49] A fifth Korean missionary who was to have an important influence in the development of the movement in the West, was (Onni) Yun Soo Lim. She was one of two people who had 'won' the right to come to America through being the most effective evangelizers in Japan. After a few months in Washington, she moved to the Bay Area in December 1965 to work with Choi.[50] She was married by Moon to Dr Mose Durst in 1974, and together they were to run the 'Oakland Family', the most successful recruiting centre in the West, until May 1980 when Durst became the president of the Unification Church in America.

Among the early members who joined in the United States were a number of immigrants who were still nationals of countries in Europe. In 1963 some of these were sent back across the Atlantic.[51] They could scarcely be said to have met with immediate success, however. By the end of 1964, of the seven members in Germany, six had joined in the USA.[52] It was, however, Germans who established centres in Austria, Spain and France during the following year.[53] In April 1965 Doris Walder went to Italy to become the first missionary there, although she spoke no Italian.[54] At the same time, Moon gave Miss Kim 'the assignment of teaching the Principle to the English people', but she was back in America before the end of the year.[55] Although there was some other missionary work in England during the 1960s, this had not been very successful, but there were five members when Doris Walder arrived from Italy in 1968.[56] In 1969 she was married, by Moon, to one of her British converts, Dennis Orme, and the couple were to run the 'British Family' for the next decade.

In practically every country in which it has evangelized, the Unification Church has had a very slow start. One or two missionaries by themselves have seldom, during their first year or so, managed to persuade many, if any, to join. In some non-Christian countries, lone missionaries have spent far, far longer with practically no results whatsoever. As in many other enterprises, this is partly a story of success breeding success, or, rather, of lack of success perpetuating failure. Few people are likely to join a movement when they cannot *see* it as a movement but are just hearing, without the reassuring backing of a social context of believers, a strange new philosophy from an individual (who is frequently a foreigner).

It is also true that it takes some time to acquire effective proselytizing skills. In the movement's early days in America, there was a great deal of experimentation, and considerable amounts of time and energy were expended on fruitless enterprises.[57] Lofland, who studied the various strategies and tactics employed in the early recruitment practices, de-scribes how members of Miss Kim's group vacillated over a number of issues: whether initial contacts should be made on a face-to-face level, or through impersonal means such as newspapers and radio; whether the members should disclose their theological, apocalyptic message immediately, or wait until they had secured the potential convert's interest on some other pretext; whether to contact people in a religious or a secular place (in a church or at a street corner) – and if the former, whether 'deviant' places, such as spiritualist meetings, were more promising than the main-line churches. There was also some indecision about whether to seek out important, influential people or a rank-and-file membership of followers, and whether to concentrate on the old (over forty) or the young?[58]

These were dilemmas that were faced not only by Miss Kim's group. There are numerous reports that Moon gave little, if any, specific instruction to his early missionaries on matters of organizational or proselytizing procedures[59] – each was left to his or her own devices. This meant that a process of trial and error was going on not just *within* each group, but also *between* the groups, and this in itself could well have contributed to the (relative) success of the movement in the early 1970s, when it was to draw on the experiences learned through a number of trial experiments. A sort of 'natural selection' came into operation. Not all the movement's eggs had been put into one basket.

As the membership was small, the character of the leaders had a significant influence on the 'style' of each group. The early missionaries from Korea had diverse personalities with pronounced individual perspectives which led to widely differing methods and results, despite the fact that they all professed an intense loyalty to the one cause and to Moon's leadership.[60] Miss Kim, as the intellectual theologian with a deep concern with spiritual and spiritualist happenings, is a very different character from David Kim who had been an official in the Korean government,[61] who refers to himself as a fighter[62] – and who now inspires his seminary students with fear, respect and devotion. Both differ greatly from the military Colonel Pak who, in turn, had a completely different approach from the 'politician', San Ik Choi.[63]

Even today it is possible to detect the (sometimes indirect) influence that the different personalities and 'Unification styles' have on a much younger membership through a selection of the kind of people who would *respond* to one approach rather than another. There are Moonies in Britain who, attracted by the theological focus of the movement presented in the tradition of Miss Kim through Doris (Walder) Orme and the members whom she brought into the movement, probably would not have been attracted by the ebullient enthusiasm to be found in California during the Dursts' regime, which was itself in the Choi tradition. Conversely, members of the 'Oakland Family' have frequently reported finding the

'British Family' cold and uninviting. On the other hand, seminarians, the elite of the Western Moonies, who have been exposed to a wide range of influences under the presidency of David Kim, tend to raise a critical eyebrow in both directions, no matter where they themselves may have joined.

These different 'styles' were, furthermore, fostered during the 1960s by the fact that a series of attempts to forge a national movement had been generally unsuccessful, and the different groups remained relatively autonomous, with a considerable amount of rivalry between them.[64] (Indeed, in June 1967, the group under San Ik Choi, which was known as the 'Japanese Family', asserted its autonomy by incorporating as the International Unification Church – a separate incorporation from Miss Kim's HSA–UWC.)[65]

Miss Kim had moved to the Bay Area in 1960 with her first converts. By mid-1963 her group had acquired twenty-one converts. These were 'primarily white, Protestant . . . some had college training, most were Americans from lower-middle-class and small-town backgrounds, and the rest were immigrants.[66] Most of the early converts were in their late twenties or early thirties; one, exceptionally, was seventeen. At that time there were about thirty-five members of the movement in the whole of the West (the United States and Germany). A year later there was an estimated minimum of 120 converts.[67] Lofland's assessment of these new recruits was that there

> had been a significant upgrading in the level of social and verbal competence. . . . Outsiders could no longer so easily dismiss [members] as sickly incompetents huddling together in an obscure religion. The cult was acquiring converts who could give it a respectable front . . .This is only to say that many new converts did not wear their physical and mental sores so openly. They all seemed to be troubled people as pre-[converts]. The very respectable and competent new recruits were simply better bandaged and made up for public display.[68]

After her brief visit to Europe in 1965, Miss Kim went to Washington to join Colonel Pak, and the movement in the Bay Area took on a very different profile from the one Lofland describes in *Doomsday Cult*. This was partly in response to the changing environment. The Bay Area was in the vanguard of the changes that were affecting Western youth during the second half of the decade. There were, for example, the student protests at the University of California at Berkeley, and there were the hippy communes in the Haight-Ashbury district of San Francisco.[69] But the changes

within the movement in California were also due to the different personalities and experiences of Miss Kim and Mr Choi. Mickler contrasts these
two periods in some detail:

> If the middle sixties were years of transition for the Unification
> Church in the Bay Area, the late sixties were years of transformation.
> This transformation was reflected, most fundamentally, in a radical-
> ly different membership profile and approach. Whereas members
> had previously been older, often married and 'established', the
> accent in the late sixties was on youth. Members who joined during
> this period were, for the most part, in their early twenties, unmar-
> ried and unattached. At the same time, whereas previously the
> Church had been concerned with proclaiming its message, the accent
> in the late sixties was on action. 'Salvation', as one piece of church
> literature put it, 'is not to speak about [the] heavenly kingdom, but
> to actualize it.' . . . the thrust of the church in the late sixties was
> less theological than educational and finally utopian. . . . Rather
> than through spiritualists or prophecy, hope and excitement were
> generated through a consummate effort to set up the 'International
> Ideal City'.[70]

The Influence of the Japanese Experience

The lessons learned by the Japanese branch of the Unification Church
were to be crucially important to the subsequent development of the
movement in the West. The first three missionaries to Japan had failed
totally.[71] When San Ik Choi smuggled himself there in 1958, he was
imprisoned for some months and, like his predecessors, was to have no
success for well over a year before he eventually managed to convert the
first Japanese member (a 'very active woman').[72] The real breakthrough
came in late 1962, when the conversion took place of a group of young
leaders of Rissho Kosei Kai, a Buddhist sect of the Nichiren tradition,
established in Japan in 1978.[73] From then on, the Unification Church, like
hundreds of other new religious movements in Japan,[74] seemed to go from
strength to strength. Then in 1965 Choi, having been deported from
Japan,[75] moved to California, bringing with him many of the practices that
had been developed in Japan.

One feature of the Japanese movement that was to become a hallmark of
the Church in the Bay Area and, as a result of its success, was later to give
rise to the widespread accusations of mind-control and brainwashing
techniques, was the development of a systematic training programme. In

contrast to the rather haphazard and informal methods employed by the movement in Lofland's day,[76] the Japanese had achieved a significantly higher level of sophistication in their 'training sessions', for both potential recruits and the members themselves. Regular staff were employed in the teaching, and the sessions followed a clearly organized pattern. Mickler quotes a 1966 'Report from Japan':

> The schedule is characterized by intensive group activity. Trainees meet regularly in groups of eight to ten to eat, to pray and to discuss questions and difficulties; they are under the direction of a leader at all times. After the trainees bed down, the leaders gather for evalua-tion and planning. They watch the trainees carefully for qualities of leadership, for participation, and for any problems that might arise.[77]

Because of the bitterness that has existed between Korea and Japan, the Unification movement in Japan tended to focus on the teachings them-selves, rather than on their origin.[78] This was a practice which persisted throughout most of the 1970s in the Bay Area, where converts often did not hear Moon's name mentioned until they had been with the group for several days or even weeks (see chapters 4 and 7). The negative publicity which the movement started receiving in the 1970s certainly made the evangelizers less likely to proclaim themselves Moonies until they had established a firm relationship with a potential recruit, but the fact re-mains that members of the 'Oakland Family' have, generally speaking, been far less forthcoming about the connection with their Korean Messiah than most other members in the West.

Employment in Japan usually implies a lifetime's commitment to a firm which provides considerably more in the way of a 'family' concern for welfare and leisure time facilities than one finds with firms in the West. This, coupled with the fact that students held a prestigious and influential position in post-war Japan, led the members to concentrate their prosely-tizing activities on the student body.[79] It was at Waseda University in Japan that the National Student Movement, later to be renamed the Collegiate Association for the Research of Principles (CARP), was found-ed in 1964.[79] CARP was not organized in the United States until 1973, but it is now one of the main recruiting bodies of the Unification Church in the West.

Mickler reports that while Miss Kim may have generated hope for her hearers through spiritual prophecies, Mr Choi generated hope through utopian ideals.[80] Japan was in the midst of unprecedented economic expansion. New religious movements, caught up with the reconstruction fervour, focused on this-worldly rather than other-worldly expectations.

Choi, too, envisaged a concretized ideal for the Kingdom of Heaven on earth: 'He filled us with a lot of hopes. An apple became as large as a water-melon. On going to the neighbourhood, we can go there by escalator. . . .'[81]

Such was the vision that was exported to California and incorporated in what was to become known as the Re-Education Center. It was, moreover, a vision which translated a strictly theological reading of the *Divine Principle* into the far more humanistic philosophy that would be taught to Californian recruits throughout the following decade (see chapter 3). Thus it was that Unification theology was interpreted to meet the interests first of the Japanese and then of the secular, idealistic young seekers of the Bay Area: 'If Miss Kim responded to metaphysical truths reminiscent of Swedenborg and a personal healing [in Unification theology], Mr Choi responded to ethical truths and the possibility of social reconstruction.'[82] Instead of teaching a fairly direct translation of the original Korean theology, Choi was to teach an adaptation called *Principles of Education*, published as a series of booklets in 1969.[83]

Another practice which Choi had initiated in Japan was that of communal living[84] – something which had not, and still does not, occur in the Korean branch of the movement. This provided the group with the strength and coherence of a community of like-minded believers, and protected it from the erosive scepticism of outside contact. Although Miss Kim's group had referred to itself as a 'family', Mickler argues: 'The lack of a strongly communal lifestyle and sharp disparities of age made more for peer relationships than the more defined lines of authority characteristic of a family.'[85] He quotes a member's description of the community under Choi – a description which, with its emphasis on distinctions and strong parental control, could have been written about many communities, not only those of the Unification Church, throughout the following decade:

The structure of our family stands with Papasan [Mr Choi] and Mamasan [Mrs Choi] as the heads of our family. Papa is involved with the educational-movement part of our family. He is continually thinking what is the best way to publicize our Principle . . .; how he can best teach the brothers in our family to speak and lecture well; how he can influence prominent people . . . Mamasan works from the other end, internally rather than externally. She involves herself with family members' problems in their family relationships, in the understanding of themselves and then the overcoming of their own weak or negative points such as impatience, arrogance, and insensitivity. Papasan works with the collective family . . . Mama works with each individual brother or sister. Papa is a great extrovert, always thinking big things . . . Mama is an introvert, thinking about her development of character . . . so they are like the yin-yang symbol, complete opposites, but extremely complementary.[86]

With the advent of communal living, the Japanese had also started working together, first by collecting junk from door to door, and later in small Church-run businesses.[87] The organization of the Church in Japan was, furthermore, far more structured than it was in America, at least until the early 1970s when Moon settled in New York. The Japanese Church had a strong headquarters which was organized into several different departments and controlled a system of districts which were in turn divided into prefectural churches of which there were thirty-six by 1966.[88]

Under Choi's leadership the Californian movement started to grow – slowly at first, but by the end of 1967, the original community of eight (which consisted of a handpicked, elite corps of missionaries including 'Onni' Yun Soo Lim, who had worked with the Japanese movement) had doubled itself with eight new American members. It was to continue doubling its membership each year until 1971.[89] By 1970 the group was operating on a budget of a quarter of a million dollars.[90]

It was in 1970 that Choi announced the next stage of the community's development:

> From now on, we will increase our project to actualize the international ideal city based on our land in Calistoga . . . we will look for even more and better land . . . Later, we will expand, make our own city, our own bank and currency, our own everything. We will experiment. If we can establish the ideal city-system, we can win the whole world.[91]

The political principle was to be one of 'divine democracy'. There was to be free enterprise with social welfare; freedom was to be 'allowed only under the truth which is constructive and instructive for all'.[92] Three phases of construction work were planned for the following three years, and work was enthusiastically started on 600 acres of land in Boonville, Mendocino County, California. After about six months, however, the building and improvements came to a halt and the Boonville site became not the 'International Ideal City' but a place for festivals and training sessions.[93]

During the early 1970s Mr Choi's group continued to grow. It no longer conceived of itself as a local movement. The Re-Education Center became the International Re-Education Foundation (IRF).[94] It developed a number of small businesses, and it sponsored a series of banquets to which local dignitaries were invited.[95] An International Pioneer Academy was set up at the imposing headquarters in Page Street, San Francisco.[96] Then, in

1971, the Federal Government's Alternative Service Program approved the Foundation as 'an acceptable alternate service to the draft for conscientious objectors'.[97] Within the community the 'house organization' proliferated into twelve discrete departments with individual heads.[98] Choi's group was no longer a family, it had become an organization.[99]

By this time, as well as Mr Choi's International Re-Education Foundation there was Miss Kim's Unified Family and David Kim's United Faith Inc.[100] Each group had its own newsletter, its own membership, and its own interpretation of the Principle,[101] Miss Kim stressing the spiritual or metaphysical, Mr Choi the utopian and Mr Kim the ecumenical (he was particularly keen on the unification of all religions within the Principle.)[102]

Miss Kim's Unified Family (which became the Unification Church in 1971) was based in Washington but had centres in various other cities, the most successful one being in Berkeley, California. Originally consisting of a single bedroom apartment that had housed a member of Miss Kim's original Bay Area group, this centre had three houses and forty members by the end of 1970. A Princeton graduate whom Miss Kim had converted and sent from Washington, wrote of the Unified Family in Berkeley: 'We just put in hours of witnessing, hours of teaching, a lot of fasting and it was very exciting.'[103] In Washington too, there was a concentration on 'witnessing' (trying to gain converts): 'Witno-captains' took the members in a 'Witno-bus' on 'Witno-ventures' to campuses, laundromats, the National Zoo and airports.[104]

Until the late 1960s the movement in America had not shown an active interest in politics, but anti-communist activities had played a significant role in the movements in Korea and Japan for some time,[105] and it was partly in order to forge a link with the Church there that Miss Kim's group founded the Freedom Leadership Foundation (FLF) in the summer of 1969.[106] The stated primary objective of the FLF was 'to develop the standards of leadership necessary to advance the cause of freedom in the struggle against communism'.[107] One of the first FLF activities was to organize a three-day fast for freedom in Vietnam. This produced a telegram of gratitude from Richard Nixon.[108] Not all the members were (or are) happy about all of the anti-communist activities in which the group became involved.[109] Later the FLF was to come under the scrutiny of the 'Fraser Committee'.[110] One of the chief witnesses testifying against the Unification Church (falsely, according to the Moonies)[111] was Allen Tate Wood, who had been in charge of the FLF for a short time in the early 1970s. In his book *Moonstruck* he writes:

Life in the center was communal, in everything but sex and money
. . . The Washington center was busy, businesslike, and the work went along two fronts, religious and political. . . .

Here began my political education. The hard fact was that Reverend Moon was an utter hawk, totally for the Vietnam war and for America's armed intervention.[112]

Moon in the West

Moon himself (if we can somewhat artificially separate him from his teachings) exerted relatively little direct influence over his movement in the West before 1972. Throughout the early days the members had continually been hoping that he would visit them, and eventually, after disappointed expectations in 1959 1961 and 1964, he made his first world tour in 1965. During this he spoke at a number of meetings, answering questions from members and guests at centres throughout the United States. The transcriptions of these sessions were to form the first in a series of documents which were circulated internally under the title 'The Master Speaks'. Moon also did a phenomenal amount of sightseeing; he had a sitting with the psychic Arthur Ford;[113] and while in Washington he sought out various political figures in order to introduce them to the movement and ask for their support. The most famous of these figures was the former President, Dwight D. Eisenhower.[114] The accomplishment that the members were to consider one of the most significant of this world tour was, however, the establishment of 120 Holy Grounds,[115] fifty-five of them in the USA.[116]

Moon's next world tour was in 1969. The highlight of this visit was the first multiple wedding ceremony, or 'Blessing', to be held outside Korea. Thirteen couples were blessed in Washington, and two weeks later eight more couples were blessed in Germany. This last group included some of the husband-and-wife teams that were to provide European national leaders during the 1970s. A further twenty-two couples were blessed in Japan the following month.[117] A third world tour began in late 1971. At the end of this tour Moon returned to America, the country which has remained his base ever since. Although during earlier visits he had obviously instigated certain changes and provided a focus for enthusiasm for the members, it is clear that his settling in the United States ushered in a completely new era for the Unification Church.

The third world tour was to mark the beginning of three years of all-out evangelism by the movement in America and a new phase in Moon's ministry. He had not spoken publicly in the West before,[118] but for the next few years he was to be seen and heard by hundreds of thousands of people in cities throughout Europe and North America, and the publicity he was to receive was to turn Moon into a household name.[119] The organization needed for these tours was one of the chief instruments in

The Holy Ground rock at Belvedere, Tarrytown, New York.

Moon and followers climbing the In Wang mountain to establish a Holy Ground, 1965.

uniting the various groups to form a national movement, but behind this
there was also the fact that Moon himself had very definitely arrived to
take charge. It is reported that when asked how two of the groups would
relate in the future, Moon expressed 'hurricane-like fury at Satan and the
division of the American family: "They are one" he thundered. "There is
no Miss Kim's group and Mr Kim's group and Mr Choi's group. They are
all Mr Moon's group. Missionaries will be recalled to Korea. Members
will be interchanged, and all members will go through my training, even
your president Farley Jones."'[102]

The whole structure and organization of the movement was changed.
Members from all three groups were transferred to different 'missions' in
different locations. Special training programmes were set up, and there
were lectures on 'the Principle as it is taught in Korea'.[121] Specially
selected and trained members were sent to prepare the way for Moon's
revival meetings in seven major cities throughout the States, starting at the
Lincoln Center, New York, in February 1972.[122] 'Pioneers' would spend
eight to twelve hours in the streets trying to sell tickets; local members in
the different cities arranged dates, rented halls, printed posters and adver-
tised the event in every conceivable way. In the final city, Berkeley, there
was, for the first time, a full house.[123]

In his public speeches, Moon's approach has not been very different
from that of other crusaders.[124] He has stressed the Christian side of

Unification beliefs, and he has urged America to turn again to God.[125] The advent of the Messiah is announced, but audiences are not given much information on this subject other than the warning that if they fail to recognize him, Christianity will have no hope.[126] The style of Moon's oratory is expansive. His followers will sit with shining faces, hanging on his every word. Not all his hearers share their enthusiasm, however. Some feel upset by the shouting, saying that it reminds them of Hitler, others find the whole thing slightly embarrassing, or amusing, or just plain boring. One problem is that whenever Moon speaks in public it is almost always in Korean, and he seldom uses a text. His hard-pressed interpreter has written: 'Because he speaks entirely in the spirit of God, as it manifests through him, the content of his messages often varies from one city to another . . . My heart was truly aching because I was really the only one who knew how much was lost in translation.'[27]

Expansion and Opposition

One of the innovations which emerged during the early 1970s, and which contributed towards uniting local groups into a national movement, was the emergence of small teams of people who travelled around the country in buses. Liaising with 'state representatives' and local centres, these teams were initially developed in 1972 for evangelizing purposes. They were referred to as the One World Crusade (OWC), and were joined, in early 1973, by members from Europe and Japan to form the International One World Crusade (IOWC).[128]

But all this needed money. Each of the tours cost hundreds of thousands of dollars, and the Eight-City Tour (which included a massive rally at Madison Square Garden on 18 September 1974) was reported to have a budget allocation of $1 million.[129] It was not long before the hard-selling evangelism was matched by equally aggressive fund-raising campaigns. Door-to-door sales had been tried (unsuccessfully) as early as 1961,[130] but until 1972 the movement in the West had relied mainly on either small Church businesses or the members' tithing of their income from outside employment. The breakthrough came, almost by accident, when members in Maryland realized just how successfully they could garner 'donations'.[131] They produced thousands of candles which were sold to other centres. In the summer of 1972 the members found themselves under pressure to raise $294,000 as a downpayment for a 22-acre, $850,000 estate, 'Belvedere', in Tarrytown, New York State.[132] 'Candle factories' were set up in various centres and 'express candle vans' took the still warm candles to other centres. Two mobile teams, each with about fifteen members, sold candles full-time, one on the East Coast and one on

Moon addressing an audience in Atlanta, 1974. On the right is his interpreter, Colonel Pak.

Poster announcing Moon's sermon on Capitol Hill to senators, congressmen and aides.

Poster announcing the Day of Hope Festival in Korea, 1975. At the bottom are pictures (left) of the New Hope Singers International and (right) of the Korean Folk Ballet.

the West.[133] These were the first of the Mobile Fund-raising Teams (MFTs) which were to become not just the source of a huge income for the movement – by July 1973 individuals were averaging sales of nearly $1,000 a week[134] – but also part of the life of practically every new recruit for the next ten years.

Belvedere having been purchased, the Church proceeded to acquire the nearby East Garden (which was to become the home of Moon and his family) for $625,000.[135] In 1974 it paid $1,500,000 for 250 acres of land and a seminary which had belonged to the Christian Brothers in Barrytown, New York.[136] In September 1975 the Unification Theological Seminary was inaugurated there with an interdenominational faculty and its first class of fifty-six students.[137] The movement's income in 1974 was estimated to be $8 million, almost all of which, according to the then president of the movement in America, Neil Salonen, came from street

The Unification Theological Seminary, Barrytown, New York.

sales of peanuts, candles, flowers and dry-flower arrangements.[138] The MFTs had split, during 1974, into National Headquarters MFT for general Church expenses and Father's MFT for special projects.[139] But Mickler estimates that money sent from Japan (where there were 120 flower-selling teams, working seven days a week) was probably even more important for the tours and the property purchases than the American MFTs.[140] And Moon himself has declared, 'I have brought millions of dollars from Korea and elsewhere to buy so many buildings.'[141]

In Korea the Church had a growing number of businesses. The Tong Il Industrial Company made machine parts. (Earlier Moon had wanted the movement to export its airguns to the West, but had been persuaded that such activities in a religious group would not go down well with the American population). The Il Hwa Pharmaceutical Company made and exported (mainly to the Japanese movement) nearly $1 million worth of ginseng tea during the year following its government authorization in February 1972. Also in 1972, two factories producing paints and coating materials started operations near Inchon, South Korea.[142]

The Unification Church was concerned not merely with the numbers of people who were to learn of its existence but also with attracting the attention of people with important or influential positions in society. The Korean Cultural and Freedom Foundation (KCFF), founded by Colonel Pak in 1964 to foster Korean–American relations, promoted, among other cultural organizations, the Little Angels. By 1974 this Korean ballet company had completed seven world tours and given over a thousand performances, including one at the White House and another at the London Palladium in the presence of the Queen.[143] During the various tours local dignitaries were invited to banquets. Members employed in public relations work would stress the Christian and ethical values of the Church;[144] members who, through the FLF, made contacts with the political world stressed the anti-communist stance of the movement and arranged for a series of meetings between Moon and various US Senators and Congressmen.[145] Since 1972 academics have been invited to the annual International Conference on the Unity of the Sciences.[146] From late 1973 professors and students were also contacted, through a series of programmes and meetings on campuses throughout the USA, by CARP. A further development was the organization of International Leadership Seminars (ILS) which brought hundreds of students from European and Japanese universities to America in order to introduce them to Unification beliefs.[147] It was as a result of English students' attendance at the ILS that Reverend Moon and the Unification Church first hit the headlines in the British papers – and the reports were far from reassuring (see chapter 1).

Initially, the publicity which accompanied the increasing visibility of Moon and the Unification Church was comparatively benign.[148] The

The three-day fast for the Watergate crisis on the Capitol steps, July 1974.

public image which the Church presented was of idealistic young Christians who wanted to raise the moral standards of the nation and help to win the fight against communism. The movement's relative success at achieving this image is illustrated in a book produced in 1974 called *As Others See*

Us,[149] in which were printed about a hundred letters from public officials, clergy and private individuals expressing (albeit usually rather bland) support for Moon and his movement. One of the letters was from Richard Nixon.[150]

The very fact that such a book was produced could, however, have been a sign that the Unification Church was beginning to come under fairly severe attack on several counts from a number of sources. Visibility was turning into notoriety; the Unification Church was achieving not only fame but also infamy. The movement had been the recipient of sporadic protests on previous occasions, but in January 1974 the Christian Student Coalition in Berkeley, an association which included a motley assortment of Christian groups, organized a formal disavowal of 'any spiritual kinship with the Unification Church and its founder, Sun Myung Moon'.[151] From then on, an increasing number of Christian organisations and individuals, particularly those of a right-wing, fundamentalist or evangelical persuasion, were at pains to declare that Moon and his beliefs were not Christian but, according to a few, Satanic.

Antagonism was exacerbated by the Unification Church's overt support for Nixon's continuing Presidency during the Watergate affair from late 1973. Throughout the United States, Moon's 'Answer to Watergate' statement appeared in full-page advertisements asserting, 'America must live the will of God, and God's command at this crossroads in American History is Forgive, Love and Unite.'[152] A forty-day 'National Prayer and Fast for the Watergate Crisis' was begun in December. More than a thousand members demonstrated in Washington, DC on the occasion of the annual Christmas Tree Lighting and were personally thanked by Nixon. Moon was invited to the Presidential Prayer Breakfast on 31 January 1974, and the following day he had a twenty-minute audience with Nixon, when he reportedly told the President to stand up for his convictions.[153] In July, when the scandal was at its crisis, 610 members held a three-day fast and vigil on the steps of the Capitol and received national coverage in the media,[154] most of it unsympathetic to either Nixon or the Unification Church. Fundamentalist Christians were joined by left-wing militants in demonstrations against the movement. There were several unpleasant incidents: bricks were thrown through the windows of the campaign headquarters in Washington, DC; van tyres were slashed, telephone lines were cut, and a series of hoaxes were perpetrated – an unordered termite exterminator arrived, for example, to fumigate the centre in Philadelphia.[155]

The movement was also beginning to have trouble with the authorities. Visas for members of the IOWC ran out, and by September 1974 there were 583 foreign members who were subject to deportation proceedings.[156] But the most persistent resistance came from the parents of some of the members themselves. Worried families began to get together to form small self-help groups. The term 'anti-cult movement' came into being to describe the growing number of groups and individuals who were opposed not only to the Unification Church, but also to the other new religions which were attracting public attention.[157] Members of the anti-cult movement disseminated critical information through newsletters and the media, lobbied government and other officials and employed or advocated a variety of ways to restrict the practices of the new religions and/or to persuade individual members to sever their association with a cult. The methods of persuasion have ranged from informal counselling, during which devotees have been free to come and go as they please, to illegal kidnappings and 'deprogrammings'. At its most extreme, the process of deprogramming has involved pushing the 'victim' into the back of a van and driving him to a motel. There he has been woken whenever he has tried to sleep, subjected to both verbal and physical abuse, and told that he will be kept under lock and key and constant surveillance until he has 'come to his senses' and renounced whatever beliefs the deprogrammer has been hired to eradicate.[158] By no means all deprogrammings have involved aggressive techniques, but fear of the practice has increased the suspicion felt by members of the new religions towards outsiders.[159] Exactly (or even roughly) how many deprogrammings have been carried out it is practically impossible to find out, but it has been reported that 400 members of the Unification Church had been subjected to deprogramming by mid-1979. It has also been claimed that just over half of them subsequently returned to the movement.[160]

Although Mr Choi's and Miss Kim's groups had become considerably more successful towards the end of the 1960s, they had not matched the growth in numbers or the organizational sophistication of the movement in Japan and Korea. It is difficult to obtain accurate figures. One early member reports that there were probably about fifty members in America when she first met the movement in 1967.[161] Despite the fact that far higher numbers have been reported, it seems unlikely that by 1969, after ten years of missionary work, the number of converts in the whole of the West exceeded 250.[16]

It is probable that there were fewer than a total of 300 American converts in 1970,[163] still about 300 in 1971,[164] and about 400 by 1972.[165] One erstwhile high official, who has now left the movement, tells me that he has a list of 500 names, which constituted the entire American membership in 1973. From the time that Moon moved to America, the movement is reported to have expanded rapidly.[166] In December 1974 Neil Salonen, then American president of the movement, told members that the membership was nearly 3,000.[167] Although both the movement and its opponents sometimes put the figure as high as 30,000, Lofland reports that in their planning documents around this period (1974) the leaders never spoke of more than 2,000 members, plus about 600 foreign members who were in America on missionary training visas.[168] In 1978 Salonen is reported as having claimed an American membership of 35,000, of whom 7,000 were full-time.[169] A year later the figure was reported to be 37,000, of whom, again, 7,000 were full-time.[170] It is, however, possible that the number of full-time members has never been more than 4,000.[171] In the summer of 1981 one of my more trustworthy informants told me that he had seen a list which contained the names of 1,800 members for the United States. There were, of course, far more members gathered together in New York for the 'Blessing' in 1982, but many of these had come from 'more than seventy countries'.[172] It has frequently been claimed that the worldwide membership runs into several million. I cannot be certain of my 'guestimate', but I would be surprised if the total number of full-time members has (by the early 1980s) exceeded 50,000.[173] I would also be surprised if the total number of affiliated members has reached 250,000.

High numbers of voluntary defections are often ignored by both Moonies and their detractors, both sides preferring to point to recruiting successes. The ex-member with the list of 500 members told me that 300 of these had left by the summer of 1980. From another, usually very reliable, source I heard that about 30,000 people had both joined *and* left the Unification Church in America during the 1970s. I shall return to this subject later, but it should be observed here that a high turnover rate seems to have characterized the movement throughout most of its time in the West.[174]

During the second half of the 1970s both the Unification Church and the anti-cult movement expanded their activities. I shall be referring to different aspects of these later developments in another book, but perhaps a brief survey of some of the major events would provide a useful overview with which to conclude this introductory account of the history of the Unification Church in the West.

In 1970 the Church had qualified for *The Guinness Book of Records* when Moon had 'blessed' 791 couples in a mass wedding ceremony. This record was well and truly broken on 8 February 1975, when the Church made international headlines with the Blessing in Seoul of 1,800 couples from twenty different nations – a record that was to be surpassed on 1 July 1982, when 2,075 couples were blessed in Madison Square Garden, New York[175] and, once again, on 15 October 1982, when 5,800 couples were blessed in Seoul.[176]

In May 1976 the Church bought the New Yorker hotel in Manhattan for a reported $5 million. The following year Tiffany's was sold to the movement for $2.4 million. The movement went into the fishing industry and has provoked a considerable amount of hostility in Gloucester, Mas-

'Matching' ceremony at the Little Angels School in Seoul, 1982, when Moon (assisted by David Kim) selects marriage partners. The 'brothers' are sitting on one side of the hall and the 'sisters' on the other.

Blessing of 5,837 couples in Seoul, October 1982. Moon and his wife are in white robes, sprinkling Holy Water over the couples as they file past.

sachusetts, and elsewhere for purportedly threatening the livelihood of the local community; it also developed a ship building and a machinery business.[177]

The year 1975 saw the expansion of missionary activities throughout the rest of the world. Teams of American, Japanese and European missionaries were dispatched to spread the message. Moon continued with his speaking tours. On 7 June 1975, at a 'World Rally for Korean Freedom' held in Seoul, he addressed a gathering of (reportedly) over 1 million people.[178] In 1976, the year of America's bicentennial celebrations, a special 'God Bless America' committee was formed by the Unification Church. Two enormous rallies were planned. The first took place on 1 June at Yankee Stadium, New York,[179] the second on 18 September at the Washington Monument. Despite the time of year, it poured with rain on the day of the Yankee Stadium rally. Whether the event was acclaimed a success or failure depended quite markedly on the perceiver. According to a Church spokesman:

> Over 45,000 people braved rain, wind and cold to express support of the Festival, and most improbably, to hear the address of the Festival's Founder, the Reverend Sun Myung Moon. Those who came were not disappointed. Reverend Moon's message, majestic in its depth and scope was that of a prophet.[180]

Time Magazine told another story:

> . . . the stadium seating 54,000 was only about half full. Many who did come left long before the end of Moon's hour-long harangue, punched out in rough, gutteral Korean and translated into English paragraph by paragraph. Outside the stadium, fifty groups of Moon's foes paraded and picketed with signs like A PROPHET FOR PROFIT and NO SLAVE LABOR ALLOWED.[181]

The Washington Monument rally involved a massive 'forty days' preparation' campaign, in which hundreds of Moonies from all over the world canvassed invitations by knocking on virtually every door in Washington, DC, and arranging for busloads of people to be brought into the city from the surrounding states. This time there was an estimated audience of 300,000. Moon declared that his public speaking appearances were over after the Washington Monument rally. He has, however, made several public speeches since then, and in December 1983 he began a ten-city speaking tour through South Korea's provincial capitals, addressing an estimated audience of 250,000.[182] Most recently there has been an increased emphasis on witnessing in America, and members from Europe and Japan have joined fifty IOWC mobile teams who are touring around the USA, organizing lectures, trying to recruit new members and, of course, fund-raising. CARP teams also continue to be active on numerous campuses.

The Church's interest in communication has not, however, been confined to the spoken word. It (or, to be more precise, organizations such as the News World Communications Inc. which were founded by Moon) have invested millions of dollars in a variety of publications. In January 1975 the movement launched its first daily paper, *Sekai Nippo*, in Japan. A couple of years later another daily, the *News World* (later to be renamed the *New York Tribune*),[183] appeared on the streets of New York. This was joined by a Spanish-language daily, *Noticias del Mundo*,[184] for the New York Hispanic community. In 1982 the *Washington Times* started publication,[185] and the following year saw the introduction of the *Middle East Times*[186] News World Communications also owns a news service, Free Press International, which publishes a bi-weekly newsletter. Another venture, which lost the movement a large fortune, was the production of a film about the landing at Inchon during the Korean War, which starred Laurence Olivier as General MacArthur.[187]

The ICUS conferences have continued to draw scientists and other academics from around the world to meetings each Thanksgiving weekend. They have been joined by 'God conferences', to which theologians of a number of different religions are invited in order to discuss various doctrines, including the *Divine Principle*; the 'Media Conferences', which are attended by a bevy of somewhat bemused journalists from around the world; and numerous smaller-scale meetings of groups such as lawyers, ministers, counsellors, evangelicals and academics. These (and other) gatherings have resulted in the publication of collections of papers by the movement's publishing houses. Other Unification-sponsored movements include the Professors' World Peace Academy, which has attracted a large number of academics in the East and is starting to grow in Europe and North America, and the Confederation of the Associations for the Unification of the Societies of the Americas (CAUSA), which is particularly concerned with combating communism in Latin America.

It should not, however, be thought that the movement has concentrated only, or even primarily, on influencing or gaining the support of those in positions of authority throughout the world. Towards the end of the 1970s Moon instituted what became known as the Home-Church movement. Each Moonie was meant (in theory at least) to be responsible for a 'parish' of 360 families whom he would visit and try to assist in some way. Old ladies were to be helped with shopping or decorating; lonely mothers would be helped with baby-sitting or heart-to-heart chats. And if the people in a Home-Church area were impressed with the caring service they received and, as a consequence, thought better of the Unification church, perhaps a grass-root movement of support would slowly grow to combat the antagonisms which the Unification Church has continued to engender.

The year 1978 saw the Fraser Committee meetings and the publication of its report which requested a further investigation of the movement.[188]

This, and the tragedy of the mass suicide by the followers of Jim Jones in November, produced a flurry of renewed activity from the media and the anti-cult movement. There were continual battles with deprogrammers and legislators over conservatorship orders as parents sought legal custody of their adult children in order to try to persuade them to relinquish their beliefs in the Unification Church and other new religious movements. In March 1977 Judge S. Lee Vavuris, awarding the parents custody of five Unification Church members for thirty days, made the following declaration: '[The parents] are in charge of their children. And these are adults, but as I said before, a child is a child even though the parent may be ninety and the child is sixty. They are still mother and child, father and child. The parents are still in charge, and they are to work for the benefit of their children.'[189] The decision was later to be overturned on appeal, but by then four of the five had been successfully deprogrammed, and the foundation had been laid for a succession of further attempts to obtain legal control of members of new religious movements – attempts which were to worry not only the new movements but also some of the older, traditional Churches and, in particular, the American Civil Liberties Union.

The legal position of the Unification Church – and possibly also that of other religious bodies – entered into an even more public debate when Moon was convicted of charges connected with tax evasion, fined $25,000 (plus costs) and sentenced to eighteen months' imprisonment. Moon's defence was that, although the money was banked in his name, he was holding it in trust for the Church and it had thus been assumed that the interest on the capital was not liable for taxation. A considerable number of other organizations filed amicus curiae briefs, testifying that their practices and interests would also be in jeopardy if the conviction was upheld and, as the time for Moon actually to go to prison approached, a rally was held in Washington at which several hundred clergy from a wide spectrum of religious denominations protested against the Court's decision on the grounds that the case was, fundamentally, one of religious persecution.

Although the Unification Church would seem to have lost its legal battle, Moon's imprisonment is interpreted by the Moonies as a supreme act of sacrifice and as a crucial event through which the movement is unifying the churches of America and, perhaps, the rest of the world in the fight against not only religious bigotry, but also atheistic communism, in the name of freedom and a God centred society.

3 Unification Beliefs

It is sometimes suggested that the Unification Church is not really a religion. This is nonsense. By any criterion the Unification Church is quite clearly a religion.[1] It is, of course, much else besides, but few members stay in the movement without accepting the broad outlines of its theology, a theology which is arguably the most comprehensive of any of those offered by the new religious movements that have arisen during the latter half of the present century. The *Divine Principle* has its own cosmology, theodicy, eschatology, soteriology, Christology and its own interpretation of history.

Its theology is, I believe, one of the Unification Church's most crucial resources. Not all Moonies accept all the doctrines; some Moonies have a sophisticated understanding of their theology, others have but a superficial grasp of its basic tenets. But there is a sense in which every Moonie 'lives' the *Divine Principle*. If one is to understand the Moonies, it is necessary to understand at least as much of the theology as the least theologically-minded of their number, for it contains an endogenous logic which is drawn upon in every aspect of daily life within the Church. The theology provides a *Weltanschauung*, a world-view, a perspective on life, which unites those who believe, and divides them from those who do not share their faith. It provides a context, a direction and a meaning; it provides a language, a means of communication and of interpretation; and it provides a reason for performing unpleasant tasks and a justification for the demands of unquestioning obedience.

So far as our interests for this book are concerned, Unification theology plays two important roles (one direct, the other indirect) in the recruitment of new members. First, it is the theology which, in one form or another, is the central focus of the workshops. The majority of the activities are organized around lectures on or discussions about the *Divine Principle*. Secondly, the members present themselves as having become the sort of people they are *because* of their living according to the Principle. It is knowledge of this new revelation which, the Moonies tell their guests, gives them the hope, happiness and purpose that makes them 'different'. If only, it is suggested, the guest can understand the Principle, he too will be able to be part of this happy, loving community; he too will be able to hope for a better life for himself, his family and, indeed, the whole world.

The theology is also a source of much of the antagonism engendered by the movement. It is, perhaps, to be expected that those who strongly hold to other faiths could consider it a heresy or a blasphemy. Because it claims to be a Christian religion, it questions and threatens existing boundaries of permissible interpretation of the Testaments. And because it provides a new, *internal* world-view and channel of communication, it confuses and disrupts previous patterns of mutual understanding between Moonies and their families and friends, causing the latter to fear for the sanity or health of the Moonie.

Validatory Claims

It has already been explained that Sun Myung Moon claims to have had communications from God, Jesus and other spiritual persons, and that these communications are the special source of the revelations contained in the *Divine Principle*. Moon also denies that the Principle was just handed to him on a plate. He claims that he had to study and pray hard in order to 'work it out' for himself. His spiritual contacts gave him clues and provided access to a source of knowledge against which he could check (and be checked) to make sure that he was getting it right. The formulation of the theology, like that of the organization, has, it seems, been developed on a trial and error basis.

> Suppose you want to know about the tree of the knowledge of good and evil. . . . Up to a certain level, spirits can tell you what it is. But for the highest truth, spirits cannot help you. They will not tell you because they don't know. And God will not tell you outright. Therefore you have to search, to find out by yourself. So, from this 90° position [of a clear, unbiased conscience], you may ask God, 'Is this tree of the knowledge of good and evil a real tree?' You immediately know that is not right. It is something else. You continuously inquire and eventually find out what it is . . . when you become one with God, you can know the answers. . . . In that way, I [Moon] discovered the crime of Satan.[2]

But even when Moon arrived at the right answer, it is said, God tested him by twice denying that he was right. When Moon persisted for a third time, God knew that he really did understand and was steadfast.[3]

When teaching the *Divine Principle* to potential recruits, the lecturer, in order to justify the truth of the theology, does not rely on the argument that the revelations were made to Moon. Other proofs are offered. These differ in emphasis from place to place. In Europe and most of America a primary claim to validation rests on Holy Scripture. There is usually at least one, sometimes a dozen or more, references to the Bible on each page of the *Divine Principle*.[4]

Another kind of 'proof' comes not from Moon but, it is claimed, directly to others from the spirit world. An association with spiritualists and psychics has been a prominent feature of Moon's life, and from earliest times many of his followers have been people who are 'spiritually open' and who report having experienced communications with the 'beyond'.[5] For the considerable number of people who accept the validity of such experiences[6] numerous stories are told of independent revelations testifying to the truth of Moon's message.

One of the most widely quoted of the disclosures from the spirit world is published in a book called *Unknown but Known* by one of America's best-known psychics, Arthur Ford. While still in America during the early 1960s, Doris Walder had met Sir Anthony Brooke, an old Etonian who had been a 'white Rajah' of Sarawak and had led an English metaphysical group, the Universal Foundation.[7] Brooke became enthusiastic about Moon and visited him in Korea. In 1964 he had a sitting with Ford and was told by a medium called Fletcher that: 'The divine purpose for which Mr Moon is brought to your consciousness is simply stated in this way: "It is necessary (he is the voice of inspiration, guidance) to restore to mankind an understanding of his full nature and his relationship to God."'[8] Brooke then arranged for Moon himself, while in America on his first world tour, to have a sitting with Ford. Fletcher transmitted a message from the spirit world to the effect that 'The Holy Spirit, the Spirit of Truth, can speak through Moon more clearly – more completely – than he is able to speak through any one individual today'.[9]

But it is by no means only professional psychics who report having received a sign that the *Divine Principle* or Moon is of God. Guests at workshops are frequently told that they themselves must pray for guidance if they have any doubts about whether or not to accept Unification teachings. Many say that, having prayed, they have indeed received some clear manifestation that the teachings are true. This is a particularly convincing kind of validation for those with such experiences, not least because it seems so direct and non-social. It can, however, be observed that while individuals relate dreams or experiences which they have had, these are frequently *interpreted* by, or in the social context of, people who already accept the Unification perspective (see chapters 3 and 5). When the information from the spirit world has seemed on occasion to result in

someone's receiving an incorrect communication, this has been interpreted either as the result of satanic forces or, less drastically, as misinformation, which comes through because those in the lower regions of the
spirit world are themselves ignorant.[10]

Unification theology also appeals to science for proof of its truth –
indeed, it claims to bridge the gap between science and religion. The
Divine Principle presents a kind of 'natural theology', especially in its
opening chapter, by arguing that we can understand the nature of God by
studying His creation.[11] God's Principle, His purpose and His desires are
also, it is said, revealed in and throughout history – especially Jewish
history up to the time of Jesus and Christian history since that time. In
California particularly, but also in other Unification centres, considerable
emphasis is also placed on each individual's own personal experience of
the natural and social world. A socratic method of questioning is employed
to elicit from the potential recruits 'obvious' answers which point towards
the truth of the teachings.

But there is one further proof of its truth which the *Divine Principle* is
accorded: the claim that it 'works'. Unification theology is a pragmatic
theology in that its followers believe that it is empirically manifested – one
sees that it must be true because of the visible effects of believing in it and
following it. To some extent such proofs can be confirmatory whatever
their form. If the movement is succeeding, this shows that God is on its
side because it is doing what He wants; if it finds itself facing strong
antagonism and opposition, this shows that Satan is worried because the
movement is doing what God wants. There have, of course, been many
religions throughout history that have used such arguments to support
their own position. However, any 'practical theology' which affirms a
connection between divine truths and what is happening in this world also
runs the risk that people will find apparently disconfirmatory evidence.
While there is no doubt that many Moonies do have their beliefs strengthened by their interpretation of whatever is going on around them, the
pragmatic theology has proved to be a double-edged sword for the movement: many of its members have left either because they have ceased to
believe that the Principle 'works', or because they no longer welcome the
ways in which it works.

The Divine Principle

It is always difficult for the non-believer to produce a satisfactory account
of what it is that others take to be important, fundamental truths. It
should also be acknowledged that the *Divine Principle* cannot be summarized without doing gross injustice to the complexity of its dogma. Many

of the more obvious 'but surely. . .?' thoughts that will be evoked by a brief account would be answered were the theology to be studied in its entirety. It would, in other words, be unfair to judge the *Divine Principle* theologically on the account that follows.[12] Here, and elsewhere in this book, descriptions of Unification beliefs are intended primarily to help to illuminate a social phenomenon.

The Unification Church sees itself as not just another religion but one which has come to unite all Christians and, indeed, all faiths. Just as the New Testament offered a new way of seeing the Old Testament, so, the members believe, the *Divine Principle* represents a further interpretation of the Bible and other Holy Scriptures. Many Unification beliefs are familiar and acceptable to orthodox Christians and, to a lesser degree, to Jews and Muslims. The main points of divergence lie in the interpretation of the Fall, the meaning of history, the conception of the Trinity, the Christology and the messianic millenarianism of Unification theology. It is on these points that I shall mainly concentrate. (The page references in the text refer to a version of the *Divine Principle* that is popularly known as 'Level 4'.)[13]

An important feature of the *Divine Principle* is its emphasis on 'process'. It is a theology which concentrates on relationships between structures rather than on the structures themselves – it is a theology of 'doing' and 'becoming' rather than of 'being'. The *Divine Principle* presents God as a personal God who created the world according to a few basic, universal principles. All creation is composed of positive and negative (male and female) elements or units which, when they come together in a relationship of 'give-and-take' action, make a more organized whole which can itself then have a give-and-take relationship with a further unit. The distinction between male and female is not one of sharp opposition, but is similar to the complementarity of the Taoist yin and yang (p. 11).

Nature is a reflection of God, so God has masculine and feminine aspects to His/Her nature (p. 12), and S/He experiences emotions in the same way that human beings experience emotions. The most essential of God's characteristics, however, is 'Heart'. Heart is the impulse to love and to be united in love with the object of its love (p. 13). 'If there is no object, God cannot satisfy His impulse to express care and love, which springs limitlessly from within Himself. God made the Creation to be the object which He could love' (p. 22).

All living things have to pass through three stages of growth, during which time God can relate to them only indirectly through His Principle (universal law). But while passing through these stages, man, unlike other living things, has to be willing to develop his capacity to love. He is not just a puppet, mobilized by the influence of the Principle, he has a responsibility to obey God's commandments and cannot reach perfection and a 'direct' relationship with God unless he does so of his own free will (p. 29). In fulfilling God's will, man's responsibility can be seen as '5 per cent' and God's as '95 per cent', but, in order to accomplish his 5 per cent, man has to put in 100 per cent effort (p. 89).

When God first created Adam and Eve, His plan, according to the *Divine Principle*, was that they should pass through the necessary stages of growth, and that they would then be ready to be joined together in matrimony. They would become True Parents, and their children and their children's children would populate the world. As husband and wife they would have a horizontal give-and-take relationship with each other; they would have vertical relationships 'upward' with God and 'downward' with their children.[15] This would establish what Unification theology calls the Ideal Four Position Foundation, the basic foundation upon which God can operate (p. 21). This God-centred Four Position Foundation is achieved as man fulfils what are known as the Three Blessings: God's First Blessing is man's ability to perfect his character, the Second Blessing is his ability to have an Ideal Family, and the Third Blessing that God gave man is the right of dominance over the whole of Creation (p. 24–5).

> The world where the Three Blessings are realized is the ideal world in which God and man, and man and the cosmos, are in complete harmony. Such a world is the Kingdom of Heaven on earth. . . . Such a world would have no conflict or crime . . . when his physical self died after such a life on earth, [man's] spirit self would leave his physical self and pass into the spirit world. There he would live eternally in the Kingdom of Heaven. (pp. 25–6)

Unfortunately, as we all know, this was not to be. Moon's special revelation was that the Archangel Lucifer, whom God had entrusted to look after Adam and Eve as they grew to maturity, became jealous of God's love for Adam and developed an emotional relationship with Eve which culminated in an illicit (spiritual) sexual relationship (p. 46). Eve then persuaded Adam to have a (physical) sexual relationship with her. As a result of this premature union, which was Lucifer-centred instead of God-centred, the Fallen Nature or original sin of Adam and Eve has been transmitted to all subsequent generations (p. 52). The Fall is thus interpreted not as the result of Eve's disobeying God by eating an apple, but as the result of disobedience which involved the misuse of the most powerful of all forces, love.

The whole of history can, according to the *Divine Principle*, be seen as successive attempts by God and man, especially certain key figures in the Bible, to restore the world to the state originally intended by God and to establish His Kingdom of Heaven on earth. Ultimately restoration is possible only through the person of a Messiah who will faithfully fulfil the role in which Adam failed. But before that can happen man, having broken God's trust, has to show that he is prepared to play his part in putting things right by creating the Foundation to receive the Messiah (p. 108). In practical terms, this involves the concept of 'indemnity', whereby a good, sacrificial deed can cancel 'bad debts' accumulated by a person, his ancestors or, indeed, the whole of mankind in the past (pp. 106, 107).

Indemnity also involves a number of acts in which two or more persons symbolically 'act backwards', as it were, the sins of the past. Cain and

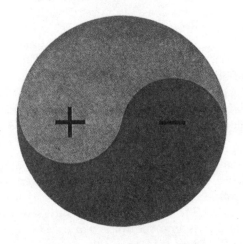

Man	man	woman
Animals	male	female
Plants	male	female
Molecules	positive	negative
Atoms	positive	negative
Particles	positive	negative

The symbol and listing both illustrate the dual characteristics of positivity and negativity. (These illustrations are taken from Outline of the Principle, Level 4, *p. 11.)*

Abel, for example, were placed by God in positions representing (relative)[16] good and evil. Cain, representing Eve's first fallen act, was in the 'position' to deal with the archangel, while Abel was placed in the 'position' to deal with God,[17] and thus it was up to Cain to fulfil the 'Indemnity Condition to Remove the Fallen Nature'. To do this Cain should have loved, obeyed and humbled himself to Abel. Instead Cain killed Abel.

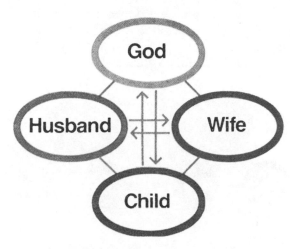

The Ideal Four Position Foundation which was meant to be established through give-and-take action centred on God. (Level 4, p. 21)

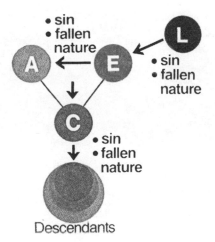

Representation of the Fall which led to Adam and Eve having a Lucifer-centred relationship and passing on original sin to their children. (Level 4, p. 47)

[This] meant that the Satanic side had struck God's side, God's efforts to separate good and evil in Adam's family had been frustrated, and the side of goodness had been lost. . . . As fallen people, we are in the Cain position to the Messiah. Therefore, by our humbling ourselves before him, and serving him, obeying him, and loving him, we attain salvation through his mediation (John 14:6, 1 Tim. 2:5). (p. 120)

Messiahship is seen as an office filled by a man born of human parents but free of original sin. Having received the First Blessing (having become a perfect, ideal individual), the Messiah must next establish the ideal family and then establish the ideal nation and world (p. 57). His children

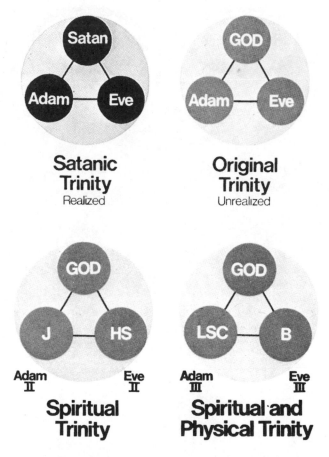

The Unification conception of the Trinity. In the lower drawing J = Jesus; HS = Holy Spirit; LSC = Lord of the Second Coming; and B = his Bride. (Level 4, p. 99)

are of an unstained lineage, as are the children of the couples whom he himself blesses in marriage and, in so doing, purifies by cleansing their blood of original sin.

The *Divine Principle* teaches that Jesus was such a man. He was born of human parents (the suggestion has been made that Zacharias could have been his father),[18] but without original sin; 'as such his value is not to be

The Holy Blessing, that is, the marriage of Sun Myung Moon to Hak Ja Han, 16 March 1960 (lunar calendar).

compared with the value of fallen man' (p. 95). By the time Jesus was born, the necessary Foundation had, according to the Unification interpretation of Old Testament history, been laid and the world could have been restored. God had told His chosen people, the Israelites, to expect him, and He had prepared John the Baptist to testify to his arrival (p. 57). Jesus, in his role of the Messiah, should, according to the *Divine Principle*, have married and thus established the Ideal Four Position Foundation as God's basis for the Kingdom of Heaven on earth.

> Christians have traditionally believed that Jesus' death on the cross was predestined as the original plan of God. No, it was not! It was a grievous error to crucify Jesus Christ. The crucifixion of Jesus was the consequence of sheer ignorance of the people of Israel concerning God's dispensation. (p. 57)

According to the *Divine Principle*, the main culprit in the story of failure of Jesus's mission was John the Baptist who, although he had initially testified that Jesus was the Messiah, did not follow him and later came to doubt that Jesus was the Messiah (p. 161):

> Now when John had heard in prison the works of Christ, he sent two of his disciples,
>   And said unto him, Art thou he that should come, or do we look for another? (Matt. 11:2,3)

Because of this, and for various other reasons, the Jews failed to recognize Jesus as the Messiah and he was murdered before he was able to marry. Through his death and resurrection, Jesus was, however, able to offer mankind spiritual salvation.

> The resurrected Jesus became the spiritual True Father by restoring the Holy Spirit. The arrival of the Holy Spirit recorded in the second chapter of Acts is the arrival of the spiritual True Mother. . . . Therefore anyone who believes in Jesus and the Holy Spirit, who are the spiritual True Parents . . . will have spiritual salvation (John 3:16). (pp. 171–2)

But God (who has to follow His own universal laws in His battle against Satan) had to allow Satan to take the physical body of Jesus to indemnify mankind's sin of faithlessness. Mankind thus lost its physical object of faith and could not receive physical salvation (p. 169). Physical restoration and the establishment of the Kingdom of Heaven on earth has had to await the establishment of a further Foundation for another Messiah, the Lord of the Second Coming.

Unlike traditional Christian theology, which has a concept of the Trinity as three persons, Father, Son and Holy Spirit, Unification theology

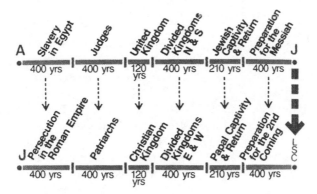

Parallels in history between the period from Abraham to Jesus, and the period from Jesus to the Lord of the Second Coming. (Level 4, p. 206)

interprets the Trinity as being of three persons, only one of whom is God. The original, unrealized, Trinity was meant to be God, the True Father (Adam) and the True Mother (Eve). Through the Fall a Satanic trinity of Satan and Adam and Eve (as false parents) was created. Jesus and the Holy Spirit were, it is said, able to take the roles of a second Adam and a second Eve and thus to establish a *spiritual* Trinity centred on God. But the world still had to await the Lord of the Second Coming (a third Adam, and the True Father) to establish (with his bride, the third Eve) the Trinity both spiritually *and* physically (p. 99).

A careful reading of history, according to the *Divine Principle*, reveals remarkable parallels between the period before the time of Christ and the last two thousand years (pp. 176–84). This, and the events of recent history (pp. 185–97), are taken to indicate that the present time is the time of the Second Coming. The separation between good and evil, which God symbolized first in Adam's family in the persons of Cain and Abel, and which was subsequently seen in terms of tribes and then nations, is now depicted as an international struggle between the two worlds of democracy and communism. From the Unification point of view, a Third World War is inevitable (p. 197). Indeed, the members believe that the current confrontation between the two world-views *is* the Third World War. God would prefer this to be fought, with as little external sacrifice as possible, as an internal, ideological battle in which Satan submits. The Moonies are, they believe, doing everything within their power to win the battle while restricting it to the ideological front. But the outcome has not yet been determined, and if the ideological battle fails, the Satanic side (communism) will attack the heavenly side (democracy), and then the heavenly side will have to defeat the Satanic side by force (p. 197). But however the battle is fought, there must, the *Divine Principle* teaches, be a fundamental ideology by which mankind can be led to the ideal world:

> Even if the submission of the Satanic world is gained through an external fight with weapons, the ideal world can only be realized through an ideology of a higher dimension, one which all people can follow freely and with joy.
>
> . . . the ideology needed must be an ideology of true love which can break down barriers between tribes and nations, and solve the serious problems among races and cultures . . . [It] must bring spiritual inspiration and a change in character and give the youth a positive viewpoint toward life. It must completely reveal the false-ness of other ideologies, especially that of the Communist ideology, Marxism-Leninism, which is the culmination of all the Cain-type views of life. (p. 198)

The final chapter of the *Divine Principle* (which is headed 'The Second Coming') is commonly referred to within the Unification Church as the 'Conclusion'. It asks how, when and where the Messiah will come again. The 'how' conclusion is that he will not 'come with the clouds' but 'must be born on earth as a substantial, physical being since he must be the example of the ideal person' (p. 203). The 'when' conclusion relies on the drawing of parallels between Old Testament and Christian history. It is admitted that the exact year of the Messiah's birth cannot be pinpointed, but the calculations indicate that he should have been born sometime between 1917 and 1930 (p. 207). The 'where' conclusion is that the land of his birth must be in the East, as stated in Revelation 7:2-4 (p. 208). Since the Messiah is to relieve the grieving heart of God, it must be a nation which has experienced the despair and suffering that God has experienced (p. 209). As the Messiah does not come to save Christians only, it should be a nation in which many religions have flourished (p. 209). It must be a nation which is the focal point of God's love and Satan's hate – that is, where the two powers of democracy and communism confront each other (p. 210). It must be a nation which has paid national indemnity by enduring suffering at the hands of a nation on the Satanic side (p. 211). And it must be a nation which God has prepared with His prophecy to receive the Messiah (p. 211).

We are told that Korea is an Eastern country whose people have neither provoked nor first invaded another nation, and yet they have maintained their own language and traditions throughout nearly five thousand years of invasions. It is a country in which Buddhism, Confucianism, Christianity and many other belief systems have flourished. The 38th parallel divides South Korea from the communist North Korea. From 1905 until 1945 'the Korean people were completely deprived of their freedom by Japan, and countless numbers were imprisoned and slaughtered and underwent all sorts of extreme persecution' (p. 211). And '[for] five hundred years Korea has . . . had a strong messianic expectation as a result of the *Chung-Gam-Nok*, a book of prophecy' (pp. 211–12). Thus the conclusion of the *Divine Principle* – a conclusion that has excited and awed thousands of people around the world – is that the Messiah was born in Korea somewhere between 1917 and 1930.

The official publications of the *Divine Principle* do not tell us who the Messiah is. *Level 4* ends merely with the injunction: 'Let us humbly listen to the voice of our original mind and search for the announcement of the Messiah. Let us calm our mind and pay attention to the hope-giving news that announces the New Age' (p. 214). There is, however, no doubt in the minds of the overwhelming majority of Moonies that Sun Myung Moon is the Messiah. In a lecture entitled 'How to be a Good Leader: Persuading People to Join and Move In', which was given at the end of a 120-day training course, one of the movement's chief lecturers instructed his listeners 'Unless people can understand Father [i.e. Moon] is the Messiah, they cannot move in.'[19]

In fact, several converts do move into Unification centres without being sure that Moon is the Messiah (a few move in without even knowing that he is the movement's leader), but when, in a questionnaire, I asked about four hundred Moonies at what point they had first accepted that Reverend Moon was the Messiah, nearly half said that they had believed it as soon as they had heard the 'Conclusion' (that the Messiah is now on the earth), and a further third said that they had believed it by the time they had joined the movement. Less than 1 per cent (three people) said that they were still not certain. There was a small number of Moonies (4 per cent) who did not answer the (admittedly deliberately loaded) question, but no one said that he believed that Moon was not the Messiah.

In addition to the *Divine Principle*, there is a further body of teaching which is intended only for distribution among the members. This consists largely of Moon's transcribed speeches,[20] and in these it is abundantly clear that Moon is referring to himself in the role of the Lord of the Second Advent. Speaking, for example, to the first American followers in 1965 he announced:

> I was born for that mission. The *Divine Principle* does not yet reveal my personal history. . . . My past sad life has been all for you, and I am here through the passage of six thousand years of history, as the conclusion of the six thousand years of history. Therefore, as the time gets nearer and nearer to the end of the age, the spirit world has to admit the truth about me.[21]

Sixteen years later, referring to himself as our Master and our Father, he told members of the French Church:

> We call him our Master, but what kind of person is he and what has he done? He is working to save the world and create the Kingdom of Heaven. The simplest thing that can be said is that he is the one who is accomplishing the will of God.[22]

> It took six thousand years for God to accomplish just the perfection of Adam and Eve, but our Father, during the course of his own life, laid the conditions of indemnity in twenty-one years; he achieved the perfection of the individual, the family, the tribe, the country and the world. Of course, not everything is completely fulfilled, but the conditions have already been set, and now it is just a question of time.[23]

Horizontal Variations

Although all the members of the Unification Church know and believe in the main tenets of the *Divine Principle*, it ought to be stressed that their knowledge of Unification beliefs and practices is by no means uniform. There are, of course, differences in understanding which arise because individuals have different kinds and degrees of interest in such matters, but there are also differences which can be related more directly to the social context. These structured differences of knowledge exist as both horizontal and vertical variations.[24] Horizontal variations are frequently traceable to the centre in which the member was first introduced to the movement. They are not variations in depth or quality of knowledge but differences of interpretation or emphasis.

It has already been mentioned that the early missionaries each brought and taught their own versions of the Principle. Not only have some of these variations persisted and been perpetuated by those who were converted by the different missionaries, but also new 'ways into' the Principle have been devised both by individual lecturers and, more officially, in new translations and study guides. One striking innovation is the production of a book presenting the Principle from an Islamic perspective.[25] In this version, quotations from the Koran are substituted for many of the quotations from the Old and New Testaments which have served to introduce the Principle to the largely Judeo-Christian population of the West. The role of Islam is given a special chapter, and the Christology plays a less important role, but the basic dogma remains the same.

A different kind of horizontal difference can be observed between

Unification fundamentalists, who accept the *Divine Principle* as literally true, and those who believe that its primary importance is that it provides a helpful myth for explaining the condition of man. The majority of this latter group accept the probability that the Unification account of the Fall is historically true, but do not consider that to be the real point of the story. Its fundamental truth lies in the recognition that it is the misuse of love which is responsible for the mess in which the world finds itself. So far as recruitment is concerned, such differences can enlarge the pool of potential recruits who could find something to attract their interest in the movement. One member responded to my remarks about the horizontal variations to be found in the beliefs with the words:

> In the end it boils down to the same thing. It's a matter of communication/language – ways to reach different cultures and backgrounds. Neat theology is indigestible to some, while it is narrowly relevant/dogmatically accepted by others. As different cultures meet, the full value of the revelation will be drawn out, not invalidating the narrowness, but showing much more than the 'theologicals' saw; not hereticizing the liberal view, but showing much more meat in the actual event than seemed possible to the liberals. We are about blending cultures!

The more theologically liberal approach typifies that of many who first entered the movement through the Oakland family – which, as indicated in chapter 2, had become the main recruiting centre in the West during the latter half of the 1970s. Unlike most other centres in America and Europe, this branch of the movement, under the leadership of Mose and Onni Durst, used neither the 'orthodox' version of the *Divine Principle*[26] nor its study guides for its introductory weekend courses,[27] but taught its own version of the Principle, a version which, on an intitial hearing or reading,[28] seems markedly different from the more orthodox text. In place of the often ponderous, translated-from-the-Korean scriptural concepts and language of the latter, potential converts are given the 'psychologically insightful', 'socially relevant', 'spiritually meaningful' (and joky) concepts and language of California – of a Californian revivalist meeting, perhaps. The style and rhetoric with which the talks are delivered is so altered that it is, at first, difficult to recognize the message as being the same as that taught in New Jersey, Manchester or Oslo. One *can* recognize the message, however, and there is no doubt that the two presentations frequently become interchangeable within the 'clearing house' of an individual person's understanding. But, at the same time, the different presentations have not only appealed to different kinds of people, they have also resulted in different interpretations of the movement's beliefs and have thus led to different kinds of perspectives and different kinds of actions, with different kinds of consequences for the members, their families and the movement as a whole.

To present, immediately after a synopsis of the *Divine Principle*, a brief account of the content of the lectures which a 'guest' will hear at a weekend workshop or 'seminar' at Boonville or Camp K is to risk appearing repetitive. My purpose, however, is to attempt to illustrate both the underlying similarities and the differences between the two accounts, and to indicate some of the ways in which the Oakland version might appeal to those whose understanding of their own and the world's problems is more receptive to social or psychological (rather than theological) explanations. And, as with the more orthodox account of Unification beliefs, I hope to set the scene for showing how it could come to 'make sense' (from a Unificationist point of view) to lead the kind of lives that Moonies do lead and how the movement itself, as an organization, rests to some extent upon the foundation of its ideology.

In Oakland the three fundamental themes of the Principle are presented to the potential convert: the true nature of Creation; men's deviation from this, and the task of restoration. First, the listener is told, we have to know what the world ought to be like if we are to recognize what is wrong and to put it right. A talk on Creation explains the principles of lawfulness, energy, beauty and love. Appeals to a combination of science, philosophy and religion and, more directly, to 'what we all really know' and 'what we all really want' lead to the emergence of a picture of the 'natural', the right and the true state of being – which is basically one of truth, joy and love in our relationships with each other and with God. But, the guest is told, if we look at human life as it is lived, we can see at once that there is something unnatural going on. Instead of love and joy, we find cruelty and unhappiness. Instead of hope, trust and loyalty, we find despair, suspicion and treachery. The three main causes of crime turn out to be inversions of three of the main forces for good: greed is self-centred hope, licence is employing freedom without compliance with the law, and lust is the selfish misuse of love. These egoistic misdirections of our love and of our natural selves we have learned and inherited from our parents, who inherited them from their parents before them. The social environment, with its corrupt and greedy institutions, reflects our false love, our ego-centred self-indulgence, unguided by lawful moral principles.

Our only hope, the guest is informed, is for us to open up our hearts and recreate ourselves. We have to begin with ourselves, and then we can change our relationships with others. By lighting the candle of ourselves we can illuminate everything around us – and, eventually, the whole world will change. But if we are alone and we do not know what course to follow, we cannot learn how to be good husbands and wives or how to create an environment in which people respect and care for each other. We need ideals and an ideology to direct us, and we need leaders to show us the way and to give us an example. And the leaders need followers to accomplish the ideals. The ideals have to be translated into a vision of practical wisdom. We have to make the most of all our opportunities in whatever situation we may find ourselves. Only a small-minded consciousness will object when we neglect some small good for a higher standard or value, when we throw away the groceries which we have collected for our neighbour in order to save someone from a fire. As the aim is to bring the Kingdom of Heaven to this world, we should, furthermore, use the means this world has to offer. Wealth, for example, should be put to good purpose in the process of the physical restoration of the world to its natural state.

Everyone, the potential Moonie is told, is meant to reach the ideal state, but since we have become separated from God, we need someone to show us how to get back to God. Jesus brought a new standard of love, but he was not fully accepted. John the Baptist did not throw his full weight behind Jesus. If he had united with Jesus, then Jesus might have been listened to more attentively. Jesus was, of course, a disruptive influence in his society – his disciples had problems with their families because they were not going home at the right time, and they were listening to Jesus instead of doing what their families thought they should be doing. But despite all his efforts, Jesus was killed before he could accomplish his mission, and people are still suffering. If we could only find the example of a true leader, we could have the opportunity to build a New Age. This is a crucial time in history. The world may be completely destroyed if we do not find the right way to save it.

Traditional, orthodox Christianity offers us an ideology but, the guest is told, this is not enough in itself. It leaves many questions unanswered, and it does not show the way forward. Religious people are often not strong enough to confront the atheistic threat of Marxism. Marxism has cost millions of people their lives. Marxists teach that power lies in the barrel of a gun. They seek warfare rather than God's love. If we have a more powerful ideology than Marxism, we can accomplish more than Marxism, in less time and without bloodshed. (At this and various other points in the lecture there may be cheers and clapping, led by the Moonie members of the audience.) The good ideals in Marxism – ideals of equality and fair distribution, for example – are God's ideals. But Satan, through the materialistic doctrines of Marxism, prevents people from recognizing that they have true value. But, the guest is urged to believe, it is consciousness, not economic reality, that is the most important force in this world. Material and spiritual reality should be interpreted together. With a proper, true consciousness we can solve the world's problems. If, for instance, we were all to fast for three days each week – if 600 million

American meals each day were 'redirected' – we should not suffer; we should receive joy from our sacrifice. We just need the heart and the consciousness to decide to do it and to begin to get rid of the problems of hunger and poverty. The Garden of Eden need not be an empty, Utopian myth.

Everyone wants the fruits, but, the guest is told, we need to work for them. We need a knowledge and love of gardening, and we need fellow gardeners. We need to create a United Nations of co-operating individuals which can be an example to the rest of the world – the coming together of an assortment of unique individuals who are united by a common ideal. The United States, with her multiracial composition, could provide such an example. The country was founded by the Puritans who, escaping the corruption of Europe, dedicated their lives to building a godly kingdom of peace. But the Puritan ideal failed because the newcomers were intolerant of the native Indians and they used blacks as slaves. The sins of America were paid for in the blood of the Civil War. Great Britain had her chance, but she exploited the rest of the world and is now having to reap the harvest she has sown.

But now, it is claimed, America has God's blessing. She has the resources and she must prove her worth by using these in the service of the world. President Kennedy had understood what was necessary when he asked young Americans to serve the world with the Peace Corps. We need to create a God Corps. The Bay Area, the Oakland Moonie proclaims, is particularly suitable for the start of such a project. What appears on the front pages in San Francisco today, appears in other papers tomorrow. From San Francisco the movement can spread throughout California, the home of the free speech movement, then to the rest of America and thence to the rest of the world. One righteous man can transform a city, a thousand righteous men can transform a thousand cities. The hope of any nation is its young people. If we can transform ourselves, we can transform our nation and, eventually, the world. All we have to do is do it!

We must, the potential convert is told, accept our responsibility. Theists, who say that God makes all the decisions, deny that He needs our help. But, the argument runs, if God had wanted to change the world by miracles, He would have restored it ages ago. Atheists, who say that everything depends on mankind, leave humanity standing alone in a vacuum. We have to understand what God's ideals are and how we can play our part in helping Him bring His Kingdom of Heaven on earth. God is responsible for most of the restoration work, but man's small role is, none the less, crucial, and he must put all his effort into his contribution.

The guest is told that everything in Creation reflects God's lawfulness, beauty and love, the best reflection of all being mankind. It is not Jesus alone who is the incarnation of the Word (as most Christians believe), but *all* human beings. God needs an object of love to respond to His love, but He is helpless unless we respond to Him. He needs our help. It is our personal responsibility to find a truthful and practical standard and to let God work *through* us. We need to be people whom God can trust, who will not give up the struggle when things get difficult. If we fail, then, according to the laws of nature, there will be disaster. It will take time to restore God's Kingdom on earth, it will take everything we have got. But the only alternative is tragedy and failure for us, for the rest of the world, and for God. We need big minds and big hearts for the big New Age. We need dedication and commitment. We must work together and respond to the challenge. All we have to do is begin!

> Unless we act to work for construction, we will surely have destruc-
> tion. So we must hang together or we shall surely hang alone.
> Now is the time for tremendous hope. We feel the darkness all
> around us. But we can also see clearly the light. The only way we
> give light and life to people is by coming alive ourselves. Only by the
> truth of relationships, by recognizing who we are, by understanding
> the movement of history, can we make the reality of history come
> true in our lives. The challenge, the task, is ours. All we've got to do
> is to recognize that it's going to take our work, our engergy, our
> dedication and our faithfulness. But that's the challenge. Our goal
> and our intentions are pure. We may make mistakes along the way,
> but there is nothing that is going to stop us. All we've got to do is to
> recognize that the Kingdom of Heaven is still at hand. If we join
> hands, and build the Kingdom, everything will be accomplished.
> Joyfully, with bright hearts and good spirits, we can accomplish all
> things.[29]

Vertical Variations

While horizontal variations in the understanding of Unification beliefs and practices are of roughly equivalent standing within the movement, vertical variations differ in the extent to which the beliefs and rituals of the Church are revealed. Generally speaking, the closer (socially) one is to Reverend Moon, the more one can share in the higher (or deeper) Unification dogma and ritual. One can identify a socially structured graduation of gnoses which range from the almost complete ignorance of those who have never visited a Unification centre, to the almost complete knowledge of Sun Myung Moon.

Non-members in the West who show an interest in the movement (be it positive or negative) are, in the first instance, unlikely to be told much more than that the movement's beliefs are based on Christianity but that they answer some of the questions traditional Christianity has failed to answer, and that the members are actively working to build a better world. There will also be talk of the beliefs and practices unifying not just Christendom, but all faiths and all peoples. If Moon himself is referred to, it will be as the founder or spiritual leader of the movement. The fact that the members believe that he is the Messiah is usually withheld from outsiders.

If his interest persists, the non-member may then learn about some of the particular problems for which the movement has a solution. Why, for example, would there still be suffering in the world if Jesus had, in fact, managed to save the world? What, moreover, is the root cause of evil? Surely not just the eating of an apple? What can we do about the situation? Moonies live their lives according to strictly moral standards. Why is this so important?

The next stage to which the non-member can progress is to be introduced to the *Divine Principle*. This is sometimes attempted in a one-hour lecture, but potential converts are not really deemed to have 'heard the *Principle*' until they have been to a two-day workshop and sat through five or six lectures which will cover the ground outlined in this chapter. In most Western centres the 'Conclusion' that the Messiah is on earth will usually be given at the end of the two-day workshop, and by then the guests will have received enough information to realize that they are meant to decide for themselves who the Messiah is. How much information the guest would be given about Reverend Moon at this stage has varied greatly. At an Oakland workshop they are unlikely to have heard his name mentioned. In many European centres, however, the first thing the guest will be encouraged to ask about is the identity of the Oriental gentleman whose picture is so prominently displayed in the entrance hall and sitting room. In other centres the display will be less ostentatious. The visitor is unlikely to be shown the 'prayer room' with its photograph of Moon and his wife, flanked by fresh flowers and/or candles on a small altar-like table (see chapter 5).

It is perfectly possible, but not very likely nowadays, for someone to become a member of the movement at the end of a two-day workshop of the kind described in Chapter 4. Those who are to become full-time members are now likely to attend seven-day or twenty-one-day courses during which they will study the *Divine Principle* in greater depth. Associate or Home-Church members, who accept the beliefs of the movement but keep an 'outside' occupation and do not live in a Unification centre, have sometimes been accorded A, B or C status, depending the length of workshop attended (A members having usually attended a twenty-one-day course – see Introduction and chapter 9).

Moon addressing guests at a banquet. Behind him is the Unification symbol: the circle in the middle represents the heart of God; the twelve rays coming from it represent the twelve gates to the new Jerusalem (Revelations); the four major rays also represent the Four Position Foundation and the unity of the four main cultural spheres (the Eastern, Jewish, Muslim and Christian religions). The two arrows forming the broken circle symbolize give-and-take (the basic principle of the universe). Above the Unification symbol is the South Korean flag.

There is no formal reason why anyone who wishes cannot proceed to a twenty-one-day course, but some individuals are prevented or discouraged from doing so because they are considered unsuitable or 'not yet ready' to receive the more detailed teachings. The twenty-one-day course does not contain much in the way of revelation that is not to be found in the official versions of the *Divine Principle*. Study guides may be used, but the 'internal literature' is not generally available. During a twenty-one-day course which was attended by long-term members (some of whom had not previously had the opportunity of attending such a course), I observed an incident in which a guest who had picked up and started reading a book which a member had left lying around was told that he could not read it – yet. The guest had studied the *Divine Principle* fairly thoroughly and was showing every sign of being prepared to join within the next few days, and the book had an editorial note which intimated that people unfamiliar with the *Divine Principle* might read it,[30] but it did contain speeches given by Moon to members, and these are not normally available to non-members. The extent to which such information is controlled varies quite widely, however: another member might quite easily have given the book to an interested outsider so long as he considered that the outsider had received enough background knowledge to be 'ready' for the further revelation.

The vertical progression is further complicated by the fact that there is a small group of non-members who know far more about official Unification dogma than the majority of Moonies. The group comprises academics (mostly, but by no means exclusively, theologians) who have attended lectures, have been given access to other 'public' writings,[31] and have discussed Unification beliefs with some of the most theologically informed members (including seminarian students and some of the early members from Korea and Japan). An interesting consequence of these discussions, and of some of the critical papers that have been written by these academics,[32] is that there has been a dialectical 'feedback' affecting not only the understanding of the members about their own beliefs, but also the re-presentation of the theology itself – for while the basic teachings have not altered over the last twenty years, the 'setting' of the beliefs is still in a state of sufficient flux for them to be translated (literally and figuratively) in a variety of ways. There is an interesting thesis on the evolution of a contemporary theology awaiting the attention of some young Church historian.

But, except for those who teach at the Unification Theological Seminary or are themselves Unificationists, few academics have been given access to the supplementary Unification beliefs and rituals which comprise the next stages in revealed knowledge – in particular they are unlikely to learn much about that branch of the theology which I think of as 'Moonology'. As, however, this book is concerned with the process of becoming a

Moonie, it is necessary only to acknowledge that there *is* more to the Unification belief system, and that this will not usually be available to the guest until he has made a clear commitment to the publicly available *Divine Principle* – and the Unification Church.

4   Meeting the Moonies

It is important to stress that the ways in which the Unification Church has made and followed up contacts with potential recruits have varied (and still do vary) considerably according to time and place. The practices in America during the early 1960s, as described by Lofland,[1] persist to some extent in parts of Europe, but generally speaking the growth and change in type of membership and the experiences of the more successful branches of the movement (particularly in Japan, and then in California) have, as was suggested in chapter 2, led to a more systematically organized approach to recruitment.[2]

Even the most sudden of conversions does not take place in isolation. We can distinguish several 'hurdles' or stages through which the potential recruit normally has to pass as part of the conversion process – although some stages will be bypassed by some individuals. First of all, initial contact has to be made, probably with an individual Moonie; next the potential convert has to be persuaded to meet the movement in a more general way, usually by visiting a centre for a meal or a (non-alcoholic) drink and chat; following this, he is likely to be asked to attend a weekend (or two-day) workshop or seminar in order to learn more about the movement's beliefs and aims. If he survives the two-day workshop, the guest will be invited to progress to a seven-day workshop, and then to a twenty-one-day course. Graduates of the twenty-one-day course will normally be invited to become full-time (or Home-Church) members.

At each of these stages there is a high level of what, from the Unification point of view, could be termed 'wastage'. Not surprisingly, the rate of wastage decreases as the guests progress along their 'Unification career'. At the start of my study I assumed that the 'wastage' would be paralleled by a 'selection' procedure so that, as it passed through the various stages towards becoming a Moonie, this diminishing group would increasingly exhibit characteristics that were shared by Moonies and distinguished it from the general population. If, for example, I were to find that Moonies were disproportionately inclined to come from middle class and/or Catholic homes, to be people who had histories of psychiatric disturbances and to have been away from home at the time of meeting the Unification Church, then I would expect to find that those who went to the workshops would display these characteristics to a lesser extent than the Moonies themselves, but to a greater extent than the population as a whole. In testing this hypothesis, however, I was to find that I had, in certain interesting respects, been mistaken.

Initial Contact

I found no evidence that initial contacts with Moonies tended to be mainly with people of the opposite sex. For the 1,000 people who attended London workshops in 1979, the frequency of introducions by a Moonie of the same sex as themselves was exactly the same as that for Moonies of the opposite sex. Even in California, where I had no means of assessing the relative frequency of this, I found a large number of Moonies who had a 'spiritual parent'[3] of the same sex as themselves.

Although initial contact can take various forms, three main 'types' can be isolated. First, there are those who are far from home, to whom, for the sake of brevity, I shall refer as 'travellers'; then there are the 'by-chancers' who meet a Moonie who is unknown to them during the course of their normal, every-day lives; and, finally, there are the 'personal networkers' who are contacted by friends or relatives who are already members of the movement.

Travellers may be filling in time before taking up or completing a university course, they may be already qualified for a job but are not yet ready to settle down or they may have steady employment but are looking for adventure or something of interest while on holiday. The traveller, usually recognizable by the knapsack on his back, can be approached anywhere. The most popular hunting-grounds have probably been the bus station and the Fisherman's Wharf area of San Francisco, but they may be picked up at the boat train terminal at London's Victoria Station. The Moonie will engage the traveller in conversation, perhaps beginning with a greeting such as, 'Hey, you look lost. Can I help?' or 'Hi! Where you from?' . . . Wow! my cousin's boyfriend (sister's room-mate, maternal grandmother) came from Pasadena (Patagonia, Plymouth-England)!' After a few further exchanges, during which the traveller will doubtless discover that he has a remarkable amount in common with the friendly stranger, he will be invited to supper to meet a group of other, like-minded young people. The traveller, who is unlikely to have any fixed plans, may well agree.

Although travellers are away from home when they first meet the

Unification Church, they are not necessarily 'on the move'. They may be *au-pair* girls or students at a language college or university, but, like the back-pack travellers, they are likely to be separated from family and friends, and may consequently, be particularly open to friendly advances from strangers.

The 'by-chancers' comprise far and away the largest group of potential members. Like the travellers, these are people who are usually approached on the street (possibly by a member who is fund-raising), engaged in conversation and invited round to a centre to learn more about the movement. But again, like the traveller, the by-chancer may be approached in some other public place, such as a university campus, a restaurant, a club or a hall where people have gathered – possibly to hear a discussion on a subject (such as spiritual renewal) which would have already drawn possible converts. The relatively small proportion of people who are first approached in their own homes has increased since the introduction of the 'Home Church' movement at the end of 1978 (see chapters 2 and 9). A few people will themselves initiate contact with the movement after having seen an advertisement or read some Unification literature; and some others may turn up at a rally, concert or lecture organized by the movement.

An interesting pattern emerges if we compare those who make first contact in the street or other public place and those who are approached in their own homes. (For the sake of brevity, I hope I may be forgiven for distinguishing between them, respectively, by the rather ugly terms 'streeters' and 'homers'). Although, as already indicated, the actual number of homers is far smaller than that of streeters, a higher proportion of homers than either streeters or networkers will go on to the further workshops and will, eventually, join the movement. It is possible that the homer finds out more about the movement than the streeter before committing himself to attending a workshop, and thus a more rigorous selection takes place at an earlier stage. It also turns out, however, that the homers produce the highest proportion of early leavers (i.e. those who join and leave within a few weeks). This could suggest that several 'homers' may form a strong relationship with their Moonie 'spiritual parent', who is able to spark off something which they can share on a one-to-one basis, but that this does not necessarily survive the attainment of membership.

Some movements make the majority of their contacts through previously existing networks.[4] This is not the major source of recruitment for Moonies, but it can, none the less, account for just under a quarter of the membership.[5] About a third of these people (more in Europe, fewer in America) will have met the movement through a relative, the rest through a friend. It is not uncommon for two or more siblings to join. More rarely, parents have been brought into the movement by their children. There is one well-publicized case of a British couple who, after making inquiries about the Unification Church when their daughter became a member, not only joined with their two other children, but also donated to the movement their 600-acre estate, valued at over three-quarters of a million pounds.[6] The daughter who had joined first, left after two months. The other members of her family are still Moonies.

A street lecture in New York.

Table witnessing in London.

Door-to-door witnessing.

Inviting a passer-by to a rally in the Albert Hall, London.

There is a sense in which the personal networkers miss the first stage of the conversion procedure. Many of them would have been unlikely to respond to an approach from a stranger, and would 'select themselves out' of the process before it started were they not persuaded by a friend or relative to look into the movement more deeply. They do, therefore, comprise a somewhat atypical group of members – most obviously in the cases of the parents who have joined. It has been suggested that people going to a workshop because a friend has taken them along could be particularly susceptible to joining because the pressures of loyalty or obligation would be greater with a friend whom one has known for some time than with newly acquired acquaintances. In fact, this does not turn out to be the case. The network may result in the potential convert's bypassing the initial selection, but it is not, by itself, strong enough to do much more than that. Networkers are *less* likely to join than those introduced by strangers, and they are, furthermore, the group which expresses the most vehemently negative appraisals of the movement following their workshop experiences. It seems clear, in other words, that after overcoming the first hurdle of a Unification 'career', it is the experiences and predispositions of the individual himself, not those of his friends or relations, that are the more significant factors in deciding the final outcome.

Guess Who Invited You to Dinner?

When I first met the Unification Church in 1974, the media had produced some stories about a new Korean 'Messiah' and his 'bizarre cult', but names such as the Unified Family, the Unification Church or the Holy Spirit Association for the Unification of World Christianity meant little or nothing to most people who had had no direct association with the movement. It was not long, however, before the name 'Moonies' was popularized, and with it were associated evaluations of a decidedly negative character. Today (1984) it appears difficult to find anyone in the West who has not heard of the Moonies.

Well over four-fifths[7] of the members who filled in my main questionnaire in 1978 said that they had never heard of Moonies before they met the movement (of course, many of these respondents had by then been in the movement for some time and had thus met it at an even earlier date). By 1979 less than a third of the control group said that they had not heard of Moonies. As I mentioned in the introduction to this book, only a few of those who had heard of them could produce any facts about the movement, but practically all of them made it clear that they knew it was a 'bad thing'. Of the 1979 workshop questionnaire respondents, just over half had not previously heard of the Unification Church.[8] Again, almost all that was known tended to be a negative evaluation. (Having attended a workshop, roughly a third said that what they had heard was not at all true, another third that it was only partly true, the rest being equally divided between those who said what they had heard was either mostly or completely true.) What is, perhaps, surprising is that about half of those who had heard about the movement said that they had heard that it brainwashed people – presumably at the very workshops that they had subsequently agreed to attend. One guest told me that the reason why he had gone to the workshop was because the Moonies whom he had met were so obviously *not* like the brainwashed zombies that he had been led to expect by the media and, he thought, only very bad or very good people could be the recipients of such a vicious press.

As they found themselves accused of all manner of nefarious beliefs and practices, most of which they considered to be the raving fabrications of a 'Fallen' media, some of the Moonies responded by becoming aggressively assertive (wearing large buttons declaring, 'I am a Moonie and I love it', or sporting T-shirts bearing the legend 'BRAINWASHED ZOMBIE'), but most became increasingly cautious about identifying themselves too readily to strangers. The point at which Moonies would disclose who they were varied enormously both within and between countries. Almost half the respondents from continental Europe claimed to have learned that they were with the Unification Church within the first half-hour of contact. Nearly all Europeans will know after a few lectures. Just over half[9] of the London workshop respondents said that they knew it was run by the Unification Church before going to the workshop, but several more said that, while they had been told that the workshop was organized by the Unification Church, they had not realized that that meant the Moonies. In Britain, however, they would certainly have found out during the course of the two-day workshop. In America a third of the seminarians said that they learned as soon as they met the movement, but 18 per cent admitted that they had not realized it was Reverend Moon's Unification Church until after they had joined.

The group with the reputation for being the most reticent in disclosing its connection with Moon, has been the Californian Oakland Family. From around the mid 1970s until fairly recently, the traveller in the San Francisco Bay Area would be introduced to the movement as the Creative Community Project. At Camp K I was told that only between a quarter and a third of the guests knew that they were with Moonies by the end of the two-day seminar. Reports from ex-Moonies confirm that this is probably an accurate estimate for the late 1970s. More recently (largely, no doubt, in response to public pressure), there has been a more open policy and potential recruits in San Francisco are now told that they are in the company of members of the Unification Church.

There was no mention of Moon or the Unification Church in the lectures that I attended in California in 1977, although on the form that we were given to apply for the seminar there was, in small print, a stamp saying 'Associated with and independent of the Unification Church'.[10] Practically all of the Oakland members whom I challenged about reports that they explicitly denied that they were Moonies, informed me that they, personally, told any guests who asked them about their affiliation (and I know they admitted the connection to at least some); they also said that they would have liked to volunteer the information to the rest of their guests (whom they 'allowed' to remain in ignorance), but, because of their bad press, people would not always listen if they introduced themselves as Moonies straight away. It was important, the argument went, to establish a good relationship first, in order to get a fair hearing (see chapter 7).

It is certainly true that on learning that they are in the presence of a Moonie most people are likely to react with fear, horror, distrust or dislike to a degree which is inversely proportional to the length of time during which they have had contact with the Moonie – up to a point, that is. Beyond that point the reaction can become irritation or anger at not having been told earlier.

In most centres a number of clues could alert the visitor to the fact that he is in a Unification house. On arrival, he may be invited to take off his shoes – but this is by no means a universal practice and it could also happen if he were to visit members of several other religions originating from the East. The guest may find himself confronted by a large picture of Moon in the hall or, perhaps, a smaller photograph of an Oriental couple in the sitting room. Copies of the *Divine Principle* and other Unification publications may be lying around, and there may be a poster or two advertising a Unification rally or portraying a Unification sentiment. I was able to find some kind of evidence that identified the movement in the 'public' rooms of nearly all the British and other European centres which I visited, although sometimes one might have had to know something about the Unification Church in order to recognize the clue. It might not be until one was looking for a mug in the kitchen that one would begin to wonder what sort of people would keep a jar marked 'Holy Salt'.[11]

Crossing the Atlantic, the clues were fairly obvious in most of the north American centres I visited – until, that is, I reached California. At Camp K it was only when I peeped through the half-open door of a room reserved for 'staff' that I saw a picture of Moon. Even if I had not already known who my hosts were, however, I would have had no doubt on that particular weekend in 1977. As I had approached the Washington Street Center in San Francisco a young man had handed me a leaflet which had a picture of Moon under the heading 'Guess Who Invited You to Dinner?' The leaflet described the Unification Church as, among other things, a secretive, deceptive movement and urged the guest to check it out by ringing 'Dan' or by asking for the Moon file at the Civic Center Library. (Although some guests may have been frightened off by the leaflet, I should be surprised if many of them would have had much success in 'checking it out'. Twice when I called Dan I was told he was not available. I was later told that the group (Eclipse) which was responsible for the leaflet had ten 'major' members who were gathering information about the Unification Church and were picketing the movement's houses in San Francisco and Berkeley, and that they had been operating for about three years. When I made inquiries at the library I practically had to produce an affidavit to persuade them that I was not a Moonie. It was only when I supplied proof of being a university teacher from England that I was allowed to go behind the counter to examine the file – which did, in the event, turn out to be quite informative.)

The Centre

Unification centres range from splendid country mansions to poky little terrace houses in smoky, industrial conurbations; from spacious fifth-floor apartments in the fashionable district of a city to the dull respectability of a suburban semi-detached house. The furnishings tend to be sparse, but there is normally at least one room which is pleasantly decorated, with comfortable chairs, in which guests can be received.

On arrival at the centre, the guest is almost inevitably offered a cup of tea or coffee. The general atmosphere is one of friendly bustle and constant, though somewhat unco-ordinated, activity. The Moonies ask the guest questions about himself, listen to his stories, laugh at his jokes, compliment him on his shirt and ask where he bought it. In Liverpool I was once – uniquely – told that I had a beautiful nose. In San Francisco I was presented with a rose as 'beautiful person of the evening'. I kicked myself for not having noticed how many flowers there had been in the vase when I arrived, but I did notice there were considerably fewer by the time I left. The guest may well feel suspicious, or at least somewhat overwhelmed, by so much appreciative attention, but he may also feel that these seem to be extraordinarily pleasant people and wonder what it is about them that gives the place such a friendly atmosphere.

After a while the conversation turns to more serious questions. Perhaps the guest is left alone with the person whom he first met or one of the leaders, or there may be a general discussion over a communal meal. In most centres he will be asked about his belief in God and whether he thinks spiritual matters are important. In California the conversation is less likely to include overtly religious issues, but will concentrate on questions (raised also in centres elsewhere) such as whether the guest thinks the world is facing enormous problems: why is there so much unhappiness in the world? What are the main causes for difficulties in personal relationships? Whom can we turn to and trust? Is there, perhaps, a chance that, although this is obviously a very dangerous period in our history, it might also be a time of great change and opportunity – if only we knew what to do about it all?

The discussion may thus bring to the guest's consciousness things that have been worrying him at the back of his mind for some time. Perhaps, it might be suggested, he has tried talking to friends about such matters, but perhaps they have appeared uninterested and have laughed or simply returned to talking about films, girlfriends, boyfriends or trivialities. Here at last, the guest may think, are people who care about the important problems of life and, it gradually emerges, they seem to be implying that they have a special message in which he too may be able to share. Another guest, however, may be vaguely interested at first but soon become bored with the serious enthusiasms; and a third guest may suspect that he has fallen in with a bunch of raving lunatics, make his excuses and beat a hasty retreat.

When the movement first came to the West, guests were told the content of the *Divine Principle* at the local centres. It was not unusual for a guest, having been invited for a lecture, to arrive expecting a packed hall and, to his confusion, find only a small house with one or two people and no other audience. It is still the practice in some European centres which are long distances from a workshop centre for all the teaching to be done at the local centre. A few potential recruits (usually those who live in remote or rural areas) will not even be given formal lectures but will study the *Divine Principle* in their own homes, making only the occasional visit to a centre before deciding to accept (or reject) the teaching and become a Moonie. But nowadays most local centres restrict themselves to preparing the guests for a visit to a workshop at a centre which specializes in providing a formal introduction to Unification beliefs for potential recruits who have been gathered from a fairly wide area.

After supper in the Bay Area the guest will hear a lecture and see some slides of Boonville, the farm in Mendocino County. He will then be pressed to take his sleeping-bag and knapsack and to spend a day or two on the farm or at Camp K as part of a seminar programme. He will be charged a small fee to cover expenses (roughly the cost of cheap hostel accommodation – I was asked for $20), but there may be offers to lend, reduce or even waive the fee if the guest insists that he cannot afford to go.

Going on to a Workshop

There is no doubt that Moonies can put a considerable amount of pressure on their guests to attend a workshop, but the fact remains that most people

Table 2 Reasons for attending workshop

| Pre-coded responses | Workshop questionnaire | | Main UC questionnaire | | |
	Non-joiners (%)	Leavers (%)	Full-time members in Britain (%)	American seminarians (%)	All Moonies (%)
Idle curiosity/nothing better to do	20	9	7	7	12	8
You thought the lectures might be interesting	18	26	20	18	9	16
You were actively seeking truth and hoped to find it	23	52	40	44	46	45
You were interested in/curious about the members	27	4	27	28	30	26
The insistence of the members made it hard to refuse	13	9	4	3	4	4

Notes: See table 1 (p. 31) and p. 150 below for details of different categories.
Because of 'rounding' the figures in this table, and in later tables using percentages, do not always add up to 100.

do not accept their invitation. Both in Britain and in California only about one in ten of those who go to a centre will proceed to a workshop.[12]

Table 2 shows responses to the question 'why did you agree to continue contact up to the time of going to a workshop?' Anticipating a later discussion, it is apparent that the non-joiners were least likely, and the leavers most likely, to be 'seekers', and the non-joiners (and the American seminarians, many of whom joined in California) were most likely to say that they had had nothing better to do. Not altogether surprisingly, the non-joiners and leavers were more likely than the joiners to claim that it was Moonie pressure that had persuaded them to go to the workshop.

As has been continually reiterated, Unification practices differ from time to time and from place to place. I cannot hope to cover all the variations but, just as in chapter 3 an attempt was made to show the similarities and differences between the more orthodox or traditional version of the Principle and the Oakland interpretation, it might be helpful to describe both a typical British workshop (which is not dissimilar to those given in the rest of Europe or most of north America) and a weekend at Camp K.

A British Workshop Weekend

The guest will arrive some time during Friday evening at a large house in pleasant surroundings. (The most commonly used venues have been houses in south London, Wiltshire and the south-east coast of Scotland and the movement's farm near Swindon.) It is quite likely that he will be accompanied by the Moonie who first introduced him to the movement.

The number of people attending any particular workshop can range from one to twenty or more, the larger numbers coming during the Easter vacation, in the summer or when 'witnessing' has been intensified by the activities of a Crusade. Most commonly, there will be between four and twelve guests who may be accompanied by four to eight members, and then there will be a staff of about four other Moonies who will be responsible for domestic arrangements and, of course, giving the lectures. A sense of sexual propriety pervades the weekend. The guest will find himself sharing a room with two, or possibly more, other guests or Moonies. (At first he may not be sure who is who.) The dormitory for the 'sisters' is likely to be in a different part of the house from that for the 'brothers', and there will probably be separate bathrooms. If any physical contact, such as hand-holding, does take place, it will only be between people of the same sex.

There will be no formal arrangements for the first night. Those who arrived early enough may go for a short walk or help to prepare the supper. After the meal there may be general exchanges as the guests and staff get to know each other, and perhaps a few songs will be sung. Songs will, indeed, punctuate the entire workshop. Three or four will be sung before each meal and before each lecture. There is usually at least one person who can strum a few chords on a guitar, (some of the members are quite talented musicians). In most centres there are copies of a song book which contains a mixture of familiar hymns, popular 'folk' songs and some special 'Family songs', including a few in Korean. If the books are not available, the songs may be written out on large sheets of paper which are hung up for all to read. (One of my more interesting – but also more uncomfortable – interviews was conducted while I was kneeling on the floor of a remote centre, copying out songs with a large, blotchy felt pen.)

Guests will be invited to choose songs, and they will soon learn the

Moonie style of singing (which is a bit like that of a revivalist meeting - hearty, with a pronounced sway and, sometimes, banging the palm of the hand against the thigh in rhythm with the music). There is also a special style for grace and the prayers before lectures. These will be given ad lib by a member in a rather breathy tone. Sometimes the prayers can continue for some time with one 'and-thank-you-Heavenly-Father-for-the-wonderful . . .' after another in rapid succession. Later, the guest might realize that 'Heavenly Father' refers to God, while references to 'Father', 'Mother' or 'True Parents' are to Moon and his wife.

Around 10.30 there will be another hot drink and the guests will start to wander off to bed. They will be woken next morning at about 7.45 to do exercises or go for a walk before a 9.00 breakfast. The first lecture will be at 10.15, followed by a coffee break, then the second lecture, with lunch just after one o'clock. The afternoon will be spent playing games, such as volleyball or rounders, going for a walk or possibly helping on the farm. There is a third lecture from 5.00–6.30, followed by supper at 7.00. Saturday evening is usually devoted to some kind of entertainment. The staff may present a homespun sketch; guests are invited, but not pressed, to do their party pieces; and again there will be plenty of singing. There will then be a further hot drink, followed by bed around midnight.

The guests are unlikely to be aware that the Moonies will rise early on Sunday morning for their 5 a.m. 'Pledge'.[13] For them (the guests) Sunday will start in the same way as Saturday, except that there may be a service in the place of the first lecture. This will consist of a few hymns, prayers, a couple of readings from the Bible and a short address or sermon by one of the members. After a short walk in the afternoon guests hear the final lecture which contains the 'Conclusion' that the Messiah could now be walking the earth. The guests will also have learned that Moon is the person who received the revelations contained in the *Divine Principle*, and they may have heard something about his early life and his work in America. Sometimes there will be a film depicting Moon or some aspects of the movement – the science conferences, the Washington Monument rally or possibly one of the mass weddings. Usually, but by no means always, the guest will have a fairly good idea that his hosts consider Moon to be the long-awaited Lord of the Second Advent. If they ask, they are liable to be told that they have to look at the evidence and decide for themselves who he might be. If pressed, most British Moonies will admit that they, personally, happen to believe that Moon can fulfil the mission of the Messiah. Around 5 p.m., after the discussion which follows the final lecture, the workshop will break up for people to go home.

The lectures form the main body of the workshop. There are at least five, and each of them usually lasts for just over an hour. The content basically follows the pattern of the written version of the *Divine Principle*.

A break from lectures during a workshop in Kent.

A game of volley ball.

Lecturers rarely refer to notes, but usually make copious use of a black-board. One lecturer may be fairly formal, quoting biblical texts by the score to support his statements; another, a talented artist, will draw cartoons and relate spiritual experiences through his understanding of the Italian masters; yet another will use the technique of continually asking his

A song with a hot drink.

A Christmas entertainment.

audience questions, then drawing out and modifying their answers as part of the lecture.

Whatever the style, it will seem evident that the lecturer has accepted the Principle as a living faith to which he is testifying, rather than some doctrinal credo that he is reciting, parrot-fashion. The integration of the

A lecture on the Fall.

A service at a workshop.

belief system with each lecturer's own personality means that each can answer questions and deal with problems as these arise – up to a point. On the whole, questions are answered (indeed ,they appear to be welcomed), but the theological output is carefully controlled so that the listener is prepared for each new revelation before it is presented. Some of the more probing queries might be sidestepped with encouraging responses such as: 'Yes, that is difficult to see – I think you'll understand better when we've done the next chapter', or 'That's a good question – it may be hard to explain it really fully over the weekend, but perhaps we can discuss it later.'

There are fairly frequent warnings that some bits of the Principle will be difficult to accept at first hearing. For example, one lecturer had been achieving considerable success with a hard-headed, analytical girl who had become very excited by the logic of the cosmology. When he had to move on to the movement's interpretation of the Fall, he prepared her for the change in epistemological criteria by saying: 'this bit is not so easy because it deals with spiritual things. Don't worry if you hear things you don't accept. Listen – don't *try* to accept, but don't deny. Up to now it's been logical, but things from now are not so easy without spiritual experience.' The next section was, however, presented in a seemingly logical, even empirical, fashion, despite the fact that the content dealt with angels. Reference was made to a Nobel Laureate whose studies, it was said, suggested that there was scientific evidence for the existence of the spirit world and life after death. Those who have had spiritual experiences are encouraged to relate these and are told that they are 'spiritually open'. 'As more people have such experiences,' they are told, 'science and religion will move closer together, and science will begin to understand the reality of the spirit world.'

During meals and the walks the guests will hear individual Moonies' testimonies. These are stories which, polished with the telling, relate how the Moonie first met the movement, the changes it has wrought in his life and how amazing it is to see what it has already accomplished. The guests will also be closely questioned about their reactions to the lectures. There are no obvious attempts to keep guests from talking to each other, and many of them do in fact chat among themselves – possibly over a quick smoke outside the back door – but the relatively small numbers and the high ratio of members to guests (usually at least one to one) mean that Moonies tend to form part of most conversations.

As the weekend draws to a close the guests will be asked whether they would like to study the *Divine Principle* in further detail. They will be told about the seven-day workshop and promised that this will provide a much fuller understanding of the beliefs and life in the movement than is possible in the short span of two days. As can be seen from table 5 (p. 146), over two-thirds of the guests do not take up this offer but some do – sometimes without any break, sometimes after a week or whenever they can take a holiday or make the necessary arrangements.

A Weekend at Camp K[14]

A workshop at Camp K is in some ways similar to those in Britain, but one *is in* California, and it is not difficult to perceive differences between the two places which have more to do with Californian culture (and weather) than with the Unification Church. The scale of the Californian workshops (or seminars, as they are more frequently called) is much larger than in Britain. There may be around a hundred people staying over the weekend, of which over half will be members. The guests will be driven north for about two hours from a Bay Area centre to Camp K, which is near Healdsburg. It may well be dark when they arrive, so it will not be until the morning that they can inspect their surroundings. The camp, which consists of several huts dotted on a wooded hillside, is visible from the main road but is separated from it by a small river, crossed by a wooden bridge. (To get to Boonville, where other workshops are held, one follows the road[15] further north. It too is situated in beautiful countryside and is about 100 miles from San Francisco. It houses guests in a couple of large trailers (caravans) which are about five or ten minutes' walk from the main road on the outskirts of the town of Boonville.)

The guests will find themselves sharing a floor with about fifteen other people, including Moonies. The lucky ones may manage to secure rather grubby mattresses on which to lay their sleeping-bags. Again, there is a strict segregation between the sisters' and brothers' sleeping and bathroom arrangements, but physical contact in the form of (albeit strictly platonic) hugging and hand-squeezing occurs frequently between the sexes. The guests may have their backs and shoulders rubbed during lectures (presumably to keep them awake) or at night (presumably to help them to sleep). I received an expert massage from one young woman while she told me about her experiences when her mother, one of the most active anti-Unification campaigners in America, had attempted to have her de-programmed.

The guests will be woken with a song some time after 7 a.m. Members will already be up, preparing breakfast (we had cheese, lettuce and mayonnaise sandwiches and orange juice). Before eating, however, the guests are asked to climb to a clearing further up the hillside and to engage in some rigorous exercising for about three-quarters of an hour. They will be asked to abstain from taking any kind of drugs, and they will be allocated to groups of about a dozen people, of whom perhaps five or six will be guests. During the course of the weekend the members of each group will get to know each other quite well. They have their meals together, and they meet in their own particular location. They also sit together in a group (guests separated from each other by Moonies) during the lectures, which everyone attends in a big hall.

The lectures follow the outline already described in chapter 3. The 'lead-up' to the lecturer reminded me of that for the star artist in a vaudeville show. He (or she) is introduced by a master (or mistress) of ceremonies; there are songs, and a band, producing many decibels, helps to whip up enthusiastic attention. Anyone who dozes off during a lecture is likely to receive a sharp prod in the ribs from his neighbour – followed by a solicitous whisper inquiring whether he is feeling all right.

After each lecture the audience disperses, and everyone joins his or her special group. Songs are also sung at the group meetings, although (to the relief of my eardrums) with the help of a guitar only. All present are invited to introduce themselves and to 'share' how they first made contact with the movement. 'Sharing' is something that is frequently expected of one in California (not just at Unification workshops). It can be unnerving for Europeans, or even for Americans from the South, Midwest or East, to sit through an unfolding 'cereal drama',[16] waiting for their turn to arrive. Most, however, find themselves following the example set by the earlier speakers (usually Moonies), and after one or two gatherings they may have disclosed not only details of their public life (where they were born, what they have studied at college), but also some of the problems that they have run into and some of their more private hopes and fears. The group members may also be asked to volunteer information about any dreams they had the previous night. These the leader may then interpret.

Despite (or, more likely, because of) the strict regimentation of the programme, the general atmosphere seems to encourage the participation of individual guests. Contributions to the conversation are generally applauded, and sometimes the group bursts out clapping at a guest's remark. The clapping can also serve to put an end to a discussion which may be in danger of getting out of hand – as can a strange chant: 'Choo, choo, choo, yeah, yeah, pow!'[17] which comes out at odd times and, with the participants holding hands in a circle, at the end of gatherings. A further 'spontaneous' response, towards the end of the weekend, is to break into song:

We love you, Eileen (or Jonathan, or Dave, or Jane),
We love you more than anyone,
We don't want you to leave us -
And we don't mean maybe!

As in Britain, the afternoon will be devoted to physical exercise. A favourite is dodge-ball, during which two teams each yell a slogan (e.g. 'Love conquers all!') while they viciously try to hit a member of the other team with a large ball. This, I freely admit, contributed to one of the hours of my participant observation that I least enjoyed.

It is not impossible for guests to exchange comments in the absence of a Moonie, but it is not easy. There is at least one member (who may or may not be of the opposite sex) who is assigned to look after each guest, and the Moonies at Camp K tend to be considerably more assiduous in this task than they are elsewhere. While a male 'buddy' does not follow a female guest into the washroom, a queue usually gathers there during breaks, so there is some truth in the oft-repeated complaint that one cannot even go to the bathroom alone. My own experience was that the toilets permit individuals enough privacy to make notes, but the washrooms could hardly be described as the ideal place for an intimate conversation. Most of my private exchanges with other guests were held after getting myself an early elimination from the games, or in whispered confidences after 'lights out'.

On the second night there will be an 'all-together' entertainment. Each group contributes a sketch or song which will have been prepared earlier in the day. These tend to display what could be called a 'we shall overcome' sentiment. At a weekend I attended Mose Durst, now president of the movement in America, but at that time the leader of the Oakland Family, delighted his audience – at least the committed section of it – by performing a solo dance to the Minuet from Handel's *Berenice*.

As the weekend draws to a close, the guest may not have a very clear idea of exactly what or whom the movement represents, but he will have no doubt that it consists of a group of very dedicated young people who are anxious that he should stay to find out more. On the whole, the approach will have been to offer a carrot, rather than to beat with a stick. Hope is tendered more forcefully than the condemnation of other beliefs or approaches; a blanket criticism of the outside world is assumed, rather than there being much in the way of specific or detailed critiques of anything which the guest may previously have held to be important. The guest is not, at this stage, told that what he has believed up to now is false; it is, rather, intimated that what he could now find out is so much more true. The constant use of phrases such as 'real warm, man' (rather than 'real cool, man'), 'close in' (instead of 'way out') and even 'rising in love' (rather than 'falling in love') are presumably meant to suggest the positive optimism of the movement. It is not difficult to understand why the Oakland Family has been accused of 'love-bombing' (see chapter 7). The attention one receives is intense, and particularly striking for those not accustomed to the California 'scene'. The welcome one is offered certainly far outstrips the friendly attentions of the British movement – but it can also be more short-lived.

Once his hosts are convinced that they cannot persuade him to change his mind, the guest who insists that he does not wish to continue to the next stage tends to get fairly sharply dropped. One girl from the East Coast who was in my group told me that she had been surprised and not a little hurt when she found that a Moonie whom she had assumed might remain a lifelong friend had lost all interest in her when she had insisted that she was going back home on Monday morning. She had, however, no difficulty in finding someone to drive her back to San Francisco when she insisted that that was where she wanted to go. Another girl in the group also went back to the city, but she had promised to return for a longer course in a week or two once she had made the necessary arrangements. The fourth non-member in our group was going to spend a 'day or so' at the farm at Boonville. How long he did in fact stay, I do not know.

Advanced Workshops/Seminars

While the vast majority of Moonies will have attended a two-day workshop (or its equivalent) before joining, whether they attended other workshops and, if so, for how long will depend largely upon the time and place that they first met the movement. Since the late 1970s it has been fairly standard practice to try to ensure that all new members in the West have been exposed to a three-week introduction to Unification beliefs and practices before they are regarded as fully committed members. Once a potential recruit goes on to a seven-day course with the Oakland Family, the lectures become more obviously religious in their orientation and, although the special Oakland perspective is still there, the relationship of the teachings to the orthodox version of the *Divine Principle* becomes more obvious,[19] but some caution is still displayed in controlling the information which is available to the guest. In a manual for Japanese leaders the lecturer is told to teach some parts of the movement's history, but under 'Points to Note', the following guidance is given: (1) It is better not to give too detailed a lecture, considering that it is seven-day workshop; (2) In this lecture, Father should be called Rev. Moon.[20]

The reason which respondents to my questionnaire most commonly gave for continuing to further workshops was that they wanted to learn more about the movement. One of the most frequently proffered reasons for not continuing (given by a fifth of the non-joiners) was that they found the workshops a boring waste of time; a marginally less frequently given reason (by 17 per cent of non-joiners) was dislike of the Unification Church. Pressure from the members was sometimes, though not very often, given as a reason for *not* continuing, but it was practically never given as one *for* continuing, even by those who did not join or who joined and then left. Only 3 per cent of my respondents mentioned other (non-

Unification) people being responsible for their not maintaining contact with the movement. About a third of the non-continuing respondents provided some contingency excuse (such as no time because of work, or having to return to responsibilities such as parenthood) which usually suggested a mild feeling that in different circumstances they just might have gone on, but to do so would have required far more effort than they were prepared to expend on the movement after their two-day introduction.

In Oakland, during the second half of the 1970s, those who stayed on for the week-long course merely repeated the same sequence of lectures and other events during the following weeks, although they would be given additional information informally, outside the routine structure. In other places, however, a twenty-one-day workshop has frequently been part of the formal process of introduction to the movement. In Britain, the twenty-one-day workshop was sometimes split into three groups, which ran concurrently, and the beginners' group might have doubled up with a seven-day course. The participants would come together for meals and some of the more general activities, but would be separated for most lectures and discussions. Several of the participants might have been Moonies who had been in the movement for some time but had joined when there were no twenty-one-day workshops or who wanted (or to whom it had been suggested that they might benefit from) a refresher course.[21]

The twenty-one-day workshop still concentrates on the *Divine Principle* but, as might be expected, in far more detail than in the shorter courses. There will also be introductory lectures to the Unification goal of 'Victory over Communism'[22] and perhaps to the more philosophically oriented 'Unification Thought'.[23] The active involvement of the guests becomes considerably greater in a number of ways. At one level the participants will contribute more to the day-to-day running of the community, helping with domestic chores; on another level not only will they be expected to listen to and discuss the lectures but also they will be asked to give lectures on parts of the Principle – a sure-fire way of finding out whether they have really grasped the niceties of ideas that seemed clear enough while they were just listening. They will be asked to apply the Principle perspective through such exercises as going into the garden and finding a plant or other object, and then talking about it (for ten minutes or so) as part of God's creation. The participants will also be expected to learn some more practical applications of the Principle by spending a couple of days fundraising and witnessing in the streets.[24]

Each day some time will be devoted to physical activities, such as walks, organized games or country dancing. As with the two-day course, there are evenings spent on homespun entertainment, with guests and members

A 21-day workshop graduation ceremony entertainment.

performing according to their talents. Everyone joins in the singing, and again whatever they do is likely to be received with encouraging applause. Sometimes party games are played, or there may be quizzes based on the *Divine Principle*. There will also be short services every day, and guests can be asked to say grace before meals or a prayer before a lecture. They will also learn more about the history of the movement and its founder. Older members will talk about their experiences: one of the original disciples in Korea may give talks (which have to be translated) about 'Father's early struggles';[25] a husband and wife may talk about their experiences as one of the 'blessed' couples.[26] There will also be some time – an hour or two each day – when the participants are left free to do what they wish. They may write letters, go for a walk or chat among themselves. The formal timetable for a British twenty-one-day course in the late 1970s is shown in table 3 (overleaf).

The atmosphere is, in one sense, much less intense at the longer workshops than it is during the shorter ones. The pace is more relaxed; everything does not have to be squeezed into so short a period. But there is also a sense in which it is far more intensely imbued with Unificationism, and the outside world seems more remote. Even those who are not going to become members will have become sufficiently familiar with the general Unification 'feel' not to jar continually with their questions. There are plenty of disagreements and arguments, but these now tend to take place within the framework of some knowledge and understanding of the movement's fundamental assumptions and principles. By the end of a twenty-one-day course, the Moonies may not have convinced the guest that he should join their ranks, but they will clearly have offered him a way of thinking and of living which is liable to be a fairly radical alternative to the future he had assumed was facing him before he met the movement. There are other, more advanced, workshops that can last for forty, 100, 120 days or even longer. These, however, are held for members only, so they need not concern us here.[27]

Table 3   Programme for a twenty-one-day workshop

Day	Morning	Afternoon	Evening
First Week: Divine Principle lectures			
Monday	Principle of Creation I	Principle of Creation II	Team meetings
Tuesday	The Fall	The consummation of history	Testimony
Wednesday	The mission of Jesus	Resurrection and predestination	Family movie
Thursday	Introduction to history: Adam/Abel	Jacob/Moses/Jesus	Talk on prayer
Friday	Parallels of history	Last 400 years	Prayer vigil
Saturday	World Wars/World affairs	Second Advent/ Christology	Family night
Sunday	Father's Life Course	*Divine Principle* test	Movie
Second Week: Divine Principle lectures; learning how to lecture; fund-raising			
Monday	How to lecture	Principles of Creation	Team meetings
Tuesday	The Fall	The Fall	Testimony
Wednesday	Mission of Jesus	Mission of Jesus	Family movie
Thursday	Parallels of history	Parallels of history	Fund-raising preparation
Friday	Fund-raising	Fund-raising	Testimony
Saturday	Fund-raising	Fund-raising	Family evening
Sunday	Lecture practice	Lecture contest	Movie
Third Week: Divine Principle lectures; learning how to lecture; witnessing			
Monday	Adam–Jacob	Adam–Jacob teaching practice	Family tradition
Tuesday	Second Advent	Second Advent teaching practice	Testimony
Wednesday	Witnessing	Public speaking	Public lecture
Thursday	World Wars/World affairs (our mission today)	Fall of Man (sin and salvation)	Family film night

Table 3 (continued)

Day	Morning	Afternoon	Evening
Friday	Foundation of faith/foundation of substance	VOC (victory over communism)	Open heart session
Saturday	Unification Church tradition	Preparation for graduation/creativity	Graduation ceremony/family night
Sunday	Service/introduction to Home Church and witnessing (sometimes Blessing talk and film of 1,800 Blessing)	Return to Centre	

Daily schedule

7.00	Rise (sometimes 6.45)
7.30	Sport
7.45	Morning Service (holy songs, reading, unison prayer)
8.15	Breakfast
9.00	Cleaning
10.00	Morning lecture or lecture practice
1.00	Lunch
2.00	Physical restoration (games or walk)
5.00	Evening lecture
7.30	Dinner
8.30	Evening programme
11.00	Bedtime

Although, as has been emphasized, the workshops differ according to place and time,[28] it is unlikely that many people, whether they be Moonies, ex-Moonies or non-joining guests, would wish to take issue with the foregoing descriptions. Nor is it likely that they would disagree strongly with the description of Unification beliefs as presented in the previous chapter. So far as they go, these are straightforward, 'external' accounts of what happens and what is offered to the guest. But these accounts do not, in themselves, go far enough in helping us to understand what *happens* to the guest. The next step is to supplement these comparatively objective accounts of the workshops with a more subjective approach by asking how the Unification Church is *perceived* by the potential recruits, and this we shall do in chapter 6. First, however, it might be helpful to take stock of the situation I found myself facing once I tried to go beyond the sort of descriptions with which I have been concerned up to this point.

There has long been a debate as to whether the social scientist should assume that the people he is studying are the passive recipients of forces beyond their control or active agents who are capable of making free choices. Is our behaviour caused, and/or do we have our own reasons for our actions? These sorts of distinction are reflected in the sociological and anthropological literature on conversion. In this study I did not want to start with a view of man which committed me to one position or another; I wanted to ask *whether* the making of a Moonie involved passive compliance or active choice. This did, however, present me with something of a problem. How was I to recognize choice or brainwashing when I saw it? I was unconvinced that this was as obvious as either the Moonies or some of their opponents seemed to think. I had to sort out what exactly it was that we might be referring to when we use such concepts; I had to decide what data I needed to collect; and I had to decide what could and, just as important, what could not be inferred from the various sources of information. In the next chapter I consider these questions and describe the model that I used to guide the collection and interpretation of the data.

5   Choice or Brainwashing?

In 1980–81 the Unification Church (or, more accurately, the then British leader, Dennis Orme) fought a libel action against the *Daily Mail* (or, more accurately, Associated Newspapers Group Ltd). On 29 May 1978 the *Daily Mail*, a mass circulation tabloid newspaper, had published an article accusing the Church of brainwashing and of breaking up families, and the article had included a story entitled 'They took away my son and then raped his mind', from which the following extracts are drawn:

> Daphne told us that David had been subjected to sophisticated mind-control techniques pioneered by the people who trained the Kami Kaze, and used effectively during the Korean war and by the Chinese communists during World War II.
>
> They included love-bombing, (constant affection and touching between groups of people), sleep deprivation, protein withdrawal, sugar-buzzing (increasing the blood-sugar level so that the brain becomes muddled), repetitive lectures, familiar music with 'restored' lyrics, and other seemingly innocent but insidious devices.
>
> David had been terrorized into believing that Moon was the second coming of Christ. . . .
>
> The Moonies we had met at the camp were robots, glassy eyed and mindless, programmed as soldiers in this vast fund-raising army with no goals or ideals, except as followers of the half-baked ravings of Moon, who lived in splendour while his followers lived in forced penury.
>
> . . . we took comfort in realizing that it was not our son . . . but a diabolical force that had been implanted in his mind. . . .
>
> David's mind, we are convinced, was raped. . . . Few people believe that mind-control is possible.
>
> It can happen. It can happen to almost anybody. David is a strong, intelligent, forceful personality. Perhaps he was in the mood, over-tired, ready to flow with the tide. . . .

David, a respected Washington journalist, warned yesterday that Moonies were as much a threat to the world as Communism. . . . 'They use hypnosis and other methods of mind-control. They operate on deception through idealism and their credibility is enormous.'[1]

The official transcript of the libel action records the following exchange:

Lord Rawlinson, QC: . . . I want you to, if you will, deal now with basic ingredients which turn a person . . . into abandoning their studies or their career, their faith, their family, and devoting themselves to going round the streets . . . selling dead flowers or dying flowers and so on. What is that? What causes this?

Margaret Singer Ph.D.: Well, it is a very well shaped social and psychological manipulation of the people coming into the organization without them being aware they are being manipulated, and that is why what the Moon organisation does as their induction process fits the definition of brainwashing. . . .

Brainwashing is a term that refers to a behavioural change technology applied to induce the learning of any new information and behaviour under certain conditions.[2]

The verdict of the jury was that the article was not libellous. The verdict was upheld by three Lords of the Court of Appeal.

What do these accusations of brainwashing mean? What is meant when an expert witness testifies that Moonies brainwash their recruits? What are parents claiming when they declare that their child is a zombie, an automaton, a robot with a 'diabolical force . . . implanted in his mind' or with 'tapes playing inside her head'?[3] Clearly, those who use such language are not merely implying that the recruit has decided to accept an invitation put to him by the Moonies in a straightforward manner; the term brainwashing is not being used in a general, we-are-all-brainwashed-by-TV-commercials sense. On the contrary, it seems clear that what is being asserted is that the recruit did not *decide* to join but that he *had* to join; he was persuaded against his will or, rather, his will – his 'free will' – was removed or bypassed by the manipulative techniques to which he was subjected. Had his brain (or his mind) been functioning normally, he would not have chosen to join the movement; but, it is claimed, he had no choice.

The Moonies, however, insist that they *did* make a perfectly free choice, that they were (and are) completely in control of their own minds, that they knew (and know) what they are doing, and that membership is what they have chosen (and still choose). Furthermore, they get extremely irritated when it is suggested that they believe that they are free only because they have been brainwashed into believing that they are free. 'How,' they ask, 'can one possibly have a sensible discussion in the face of such an accusation? Whatever we say is just taken as further proof that we are brainwashed, and nothing we can do – short of renouncing our faith – will convince our accusers that we are free human beings with minds of our own.' Admittedly, some Moonies may say that they had no choice in an *Ich kann nicht anders* sense,[4] – that is, they believe that they had to join because God guided them into the movement or that it was their duty to follow the Messiah. But this, they explain, was a *religious* or a *moral* necessity – they were not manipulated or coerced any more than Luther was compelled by anything other than his religious experience and his own conscience to stand for what he believed to be right and true.

Whose version ought we to accept? Can we decide which group is correct? On the one hand, it is not easy for someone to convince those who believe otherwise that he is acting of his own free will. The Moonies can do little more than declare that they were not brainwashed – at least that is certainly what they will say while they are still members of the movement; some who have left do say that they were brainwashed but that they did know it at the time. On the other hand, those who assert that the Moonies have been coerced will produce a wide range of alleged practices in support of their position, including kidnapping, strange diets, lack of sleep, hypnosis, trance-inducing lectures, sensory deprivation, sensory stimulation, chanting, bizarre rituals, 'love-bombing' and deception. It has also been asserted that those who join the movement often have 'serious, somewhat crippling personal disorders', are 'emotionally vulnerable' or are passing through 'very susceptible periods in their personal development'.[5]

One of the most fundamental questions with which I was to find myself grappling during the course of my research was whether or not there were independent, empirical data (upon which everyone, whether Moonie or anti-cultist, who approached the problem with an open mind would agree) that could help to overcome the *impasse* reached by one set of people who insist that Moonies are the victims of brainwashing techniques, while another set of people (the Moonies themselves) insist that they have made a decision of their own free will. Was there, in other words, an objective means of distinguishing between conversions in which the converts were responsible, active agents, and conversions in which they were the passive victims of forces or techniques beyond their control?

I believe that we can go quite a long way towards sorting out the various influences which play a part in the making of a Moonie, but to do so involves approaching the problem from a perspective different from that which is normally employed. It involves switching the main focus of attention from individuals to groups, from the isolated psyche to the social context; above all, it involves the systematic use of comparison between different individuals and groups of individuals. It involves, in other words, a sociological rather than a psychological or a medical approach. And since, as far as I am aware, no one has addressed the question which I am posing in quite the way I intend to proceed,[6] I shall try in this chapter to explain the logic of my reformulation of the problem and to spell out some of the assumptions which underlie the analysis of the data presented in the following chapters.[7] I start by introducing what I considered to be the necessary components of the investigation, but as the argument is rather complicated and involves a large number of data and concepts, and as I reject several of the conclusions which other commentators have reached, I try at the same time to clarify matters by disposing of some of the methods and arguments with which I disagree. I then proceed to a more constructive proposal.

Whose Story?

The information gleaned from observing, listening to and/or reading the writings of individuals has to comprise the raw data for any understanding of human actions. Pronouncements delivered from the distance and comfort of an armchair, without close observation of the individuals concerned, cannot substantially further the solution of our problem. But watching and talking to people is not enough. A central argument in the next few sections is that the observation or citing of individual case histories, while necessary, cannot provide sufficient information for us to hope for closer agreement on the distinction between choice and brainwashing.

Moonies' Accounts

I have already pointed out the fairly obvious fact that when we listen to individual Moonies' accounts of how they became members of the Unification Church, we shall not be told that they were brainwashed. We are, on the contrary, quite likely to be told that each Moonie has been liberated, that he has discovered freedom, and that he now feels that he has far more control over his destiny than he ever had before.[8] We may learn that he was guided by God, that he had a deep spiritual experience, that the members seemed so friendly, or the theology so logical, or any one of a dozen or more reasons; but, whatever these explanations are, the Moonie will insist that he is there because he wants to be or at least that it is he himself who decided that this is what he has to do.

Apart from the fact that we cannot prejudge the possibility that the Moonie has fallen under the power of the movement to the extent that he tells us only what his leaders want him to say (either because he is brainwashed or because he has agreed to lie), another difficulty with the Moonie's account is that it is liable to change with the passage of time (especially if he leaves the movement) because his memory and his understanding of the situation have changed. I shall return to these and other difficulties at various points, but they are mentioned briefly now in order to stress the necessity of our looking beyond the Moonies' own stories if we want to further our understanding of the process by which people become members of the Unification Church.

Friends' and Relations' Accounts

There are plenty of friends and relations who are prepared to swear that the person they knew before he became a Moonie has been brainwashed. Understandably (given the emotional involvement and, in most cases, the unexpectedness and the strength of the commitment resulting from the conversion), the reasoning behind these assertions is frequently confused, and the speaker may well jump inconsistently from one explanation to another. Some of the arguments which crop up not only in private discussion but also in books, articles and media interviews need to be elaborated briefly and dismissed, as they are frequently accepted as 'proofs' by people who, were they to stop and think, would recognize their shortcomings.

There are, for example, a number of arguments which do no more than beg the question. In their most naive form, such arguments can be reduced to the statement: 'Since Jonathan has become a Moonie, he must have been brainwashed.' This does not demonstrate that Jonathan has been brainwashed, it simply asserts it. Just as unsatisfactory is the declaration: 'Jonathan must be brainwashed because Moonies believe and do things that no one in his right mind would choose to do.' Although the fact that Jonathan now believes and does strange things might alert us to the existence of some sort of problem for which we should like an explanation, there is no logically necessary connection between the *nature of the process* by which people come to believe something and the *credibility of the belief* itself.

The slightest acquaintance with the facts of either history or anthropology will, of course, serve to illustrate the enormously diverse range of apparently extraordinary beliefs and practices which men have espoused. There are those from Eastern cultures who consider it quite incredible that there exist people who believe that the wine they sip during a particular ritual changes into the blood of a man who was born to a virgin a couple of thousand years ago.[9] Presumably the Catholic Church would wish to resist the 'logic' that all such people must, necessarily, be brainwashed. It is, to repeat, the *process* by which one comes to beliefs, not the result or the *content* of the beliefs, that must be judged if we wish to address the problem of coercion.[10] Another, slightly more sophisticated version of the an-unbelievable-content-proves-a-coercive-technique argument takes this form: 'It is not so much that Moonie beliefs are incredible, but it is incredible that Jonathan (that anyone with the sort of background which Moonies have) could believe them – unless he had been coerced'. But without further evidence which is independent of the statement itself we are back with a question-begging assertion which denies the perfectly logical possibility that the background of the Moonie aids, rather than interferes with, his decision to join the movement.

The 'it-is-too-incredible' argument for coercion depends, furthermore, upon an assumption that there are independent, objective criteria for judging the credibility of a religious belief. This is only rarely true. There is, in one sense at least, a far stronger cause for concern when (to choose an obvious example to make the point) Simon says he believes that a cup which everyone else has just observed smash to the ground is still intact on the table, than there is when Jonathan says that he believes that the Messiah is on earth, alive and well in Manhattan. There are agreed ways of showing Simon that he could be mistaken, and these are ways which Simon himself would have to accept so long as he was in full possession of his five senses. These agreed criteria are not, however, applicable in Jonathan's case. Most religious statements or world-views are patently not demonstrable or amenable to verification or refutation in the sense that empirical or scientific statements may be.[11] This means that the prounce-ment that Jonathan's religious belief or world-view is 'incredible' gives us more information about the speaker's capacity for belief than it does about Jonathan's.

Although obvious enough, this point is of crucial importance when reading some of the literature which 'medicalizes' the membership of new religious movements. For example, Dr John Clark, in an article 'Problems in Referral of Cult Members' (he had experienced difficulty in persuading colleagues to admit patients), writes: 'my working definition of mental illness was a malfunctioning of the central nervous system, causing a substantial disability because of alterations of consciousness, mood, mem-ory, perceptions, orientation, *or capacity to test reality.*' (Emphasis added).[12] I must have spoken to about a thousand Moonies, but none has ever claimed, or appeared to have, a different view of *empirical* reality from that of the rest of the population – although they may refer to a spiritual or religious reality which many of us would question.[13]

The changes wrought in the convert go beyond a simple acceptance of the *Divine Principle*, however. We frequently hear of extraordinarily far-reaching changes in his behaviour, attitudes and general vision of the world. We might learn that 'Jonathan simply isn't the same person any longer. He would never have done anything like that before. He's changed into a completely unrecognizable character. It's just not Jonathan any more.' While some people appear to change more dramatically than others, it is undeniable that something very unexpected and drastic can occur when a person becomes a Moonie. But many people undergo remarkable changes during their lives. To describe such a change may well be to provoke the question 'Why has the change occurred?', but the *description* of the change cannot, in itself, provide the *explanation* for the change. We need to know about something more than the 'before' and 'after' states if we are to decide whether the change has come about through choice or coercion.

Sometimes it is not simply the extent of the change but also the rapidity with which it has occurred that is used to justify a 'no-other-explanation-but-brainwashing-is-possible' assertion. History is full of stories of sudden and spectacular conversions, St Paul's experience[14] being but one of the most widely known. The contemporary evangelical revival in North America and Europe has resulted in thousands of 'born-again' Christians experiencing a sudden conversion, during which they claim to have received Jesus into their lives, and after which they have dramatically changed their attitudes and manner of living. If we were to accept that the suddenness of a conversion indicates that coercive techniques must have been used, we should have to assume that *all* sudden conversions are the result of brainwashing. It seems clear, however, that few, if any, of those who advocate that Moonies are brainwashed wish to adopt such a position (indeed, many of them are themselves born-again Christians) – and, even if they were to do so, they would still need to account for the fact that a significant proportion of Moonies do not undergo sudden conversions, but wait months, or even years before joining the movement.

Once we accept that neither the suddenness nor the fact of a conversion can be a necessary or a sufficient criterion for distinguishing between a forced and a genuine conversion, we may find ourselves in possession of some useful information about the sort of change that has taken place, but we are not necessarily nearer an explanation for the change.

Lest it be thought that these are purely academic considerations, let me indicate briefly some of the practical consequences of the sorts of argument that are being discussed. I am thinking in particular of the introduction of 'conservatorship orders', which enable a court to hand over responsibility for one adult to another adult. In America there have been several cases in which parents have thereby gained legal custody of their adult children for a period during which the latter may be submitted to deprogramming or counselling.[15] There is no space to discuss here the complexity of the battles which are being fought on this particular legal front, but a quotation from what became known as the 'Lasher Amendment' to the mental hygiene law of New York State may suffice to indicate the relevance of the discussion:

> The supreme court and the county courts outside the city of New York, shall have the power to appoint one or more temporary conservators of the person and property of any person over fifteen years of age, upon showing that such person for whom the temporary conservator is to be appointed has become closely and regularly associated with a group which practices the use of deception in the deprivation or isolation from family or unusually long work schedules and that such person for whom the temporary conservator is to be appointed has *undergone a sudden and radical change in behaviour, lifestyle, habits and attitudes*, and has become unable to care for his welfare and that his *judgment has become impaired to the extent that he is unable to understand the need for such care*. (Emphasis added)[16]

Ex-Moonies' Accounts

There is by now a growing body of literature, written in the main by psychologists and psychiatrists, which purports to describe Unification brainwashing techniques, the sorts of people who have become Moonies and the effect that brainwashing has upon them. The evidence adduced in these descriptions is almost invariably taken from the testimonies of ex-Moonies, and usually from ex-Moonies who have been deprogrammed and/or have been taken to the writer for counselling or treatment.[17] There is also a growing body of literature produced by such ex-Moonies themselves.[18] It is these 'victims' who are, according to Clark, 'the *real* experts (who) must be heard'.[19]

Of course, ex-Moonies can provide us with a great deal of valuable information, but the medics, psychologists and counsellors who rely so heavily (often exclusively) on such evidence are neglecting some very basic principles of research. First, someone who has left a movement is quite likely to have become disillusioned with it, and it is possible that he will regret having joined it. One way of explaining one's membership to others and, even more important, to oneself is to blame the movement's persuasive powers rather than accepting responsibility oneself. This is an option which tends to be taken up by those whose departure from the movement owed more to others than to themselves – especially when their parents have paid thousands, sometimes tens of thousands, of dollars or pounds to have them deprogrammed. It is, indeed, part of some counselling syllabuses to inform ex-cultists that they were brainwashed, since 'they don't know what happened to them, and need to have it explained.'[20] Margaret Singer, in her evidence at the *Daily Mail* trial, testified that:

> The deprogrammers, the ex-Moonies, tell the current members that are on their way out for getting this kind of information about how the process of mind-control, brainwashing, the imposed identity change, was brought about; and the deprogrammers give them a picture of how, from the moment of the meeting on the street until the new members were totally processed, it was a totally staged and orchestrated process.[21]

An analysis by Trudy Solomon of 100 questionnaires filled in by former Unification Church members indicates that contact with the anti-cult movement influences the degree to which ex-members rely on explanations of brainwashing and mind-control:

> Because the majority of evidence concerning the use of brainwashing and mind-control within the Church comes either from ex-members who have been deprogrammed and/or rehabilitated or from individuals involved in the anti-cult movement, these data begin to provide an explanation for how ex-members come to hold such notions, and how they in turn are perpetuated.[22]

The majority of Solomon's respondents had been deprogrammed, and all but seven had received some kind of formal help (rehabilitation or therapy) during or after their exit from the movement. This was due largely, no doubt, to the fact that her sample was recruited primarily through the American anti-cult network.[23] In another study Stuart Wright interviewed forty-five *voluntary* defectors from the Unification Church, the Hare Krishna movement and the Children of God/Family of Love. Only four (9 per cent) of his interviewees claimed to have been brainwashed. The other 91 per cent of his sample described their participation as entirely voluntary.[24] And in yet another study Marc Galanter compared forty-seven ex-Moonies who had not been deprogrammed with ten who had been. He found that those who had been deprogrammed were more likely to report having experienced pressure from Moonies who tried to persuade them to stay in the movement: 'In fact, the deprogrammed respondents (eight of the ten) were the only ones who, after leaving, had overtly limited the freedom of movement of other persons still active in the Unification Church in an attempt to press them to leave.'[25]

During the course of my own study I had an opportunity to talk to several former members whom I had known while they were still Moonies. Most of these left without any outside assistance, did not subsequently

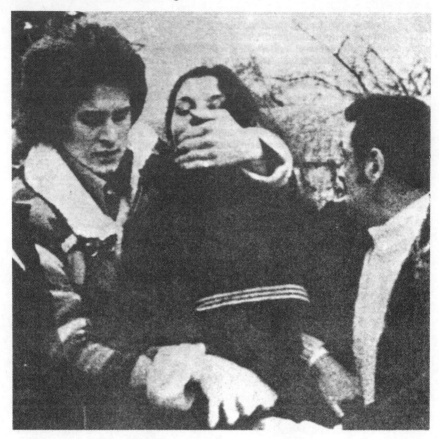

A Moonie being abducted by deprogrammers in France in 1976.

receive the services of counsellors, and made little or no contact with the
anti-cult movement or the media. With one exception, none of these
voluntary leavers said that they had been unduly coerced into joining.
They nearly all admitted that it had been difficult to leave, but most of
them insisted that they could have left at any time if they had wanted to. A
few had left, rejoined and then left for a second or even a third time. This,
of course, does not mean that these former Moonies had not been brainwashed. But, coupled with Solomon's, Wright's and Galanter's findings, it
does at least suggest that the testimonies of those who have subsequently
learned to describe Unification recruitment practices with the concepts and
perspectives of brainwashing or mind-control models,[26] cannot be taken as
proving that such concepts and perspectives provide the most appropriate
or accurate of descriptions.

Those who rely primarily on the evidence of ex-Moonies sometimes say that they have to do so because Moonies practise 'heavenly deception',[27] and that anyone who claims to have obtained accurate information from a Moonie is either deceived or deceiving. Of course, it would be as foolish to rely solely on Moonie evidence as it is to rely solely on ex-Moonie evidence, but it does not follow that observing Moonies 'in the flesh' cannot provide a wealth of relevant data, and there are numerous techniques, some of which I discussed in chapter 1, that can be used for checking and assessing the value of the information which one gains. It is also true that both ex-Moonies and those who knew Moonies before they joined the movement provide useful data (although these need to be checked as rigorously as the data provided by the Moonies). There is, however, a further, crucially important source of information that has been almost totally ignored: non-Moonies.

Non-Moonies

In chapter 1, I mentioned briefly the importance of control groups. Let me now elaborate that point. Several people have claimed to tell us about the characteristics of Moonies either before they join or after they leave the movement, but such descriptions turn out to be next to worthless when taken by themselves. If knowledge of recruits is to be at all meaningful, it is also necessary to have information about non-Moonies. We need to know whether the characteristics which we know the Moonie possesses are peculiar to Moonies, or whether he shares these characteristics with people who are not members of the movement. The information that most Moonies have ten toes is doubtless correct, but do we want to be told this?

Consider the expert who tells how he conducted interviews, which focused on their personal indoctrination experiences, with thirty patients (his word) who were former Unification Church members.[28] Claiming 'professional experience as a psychodiagnostician, psychotherapist and family counsellor', he says that he 'found that approximately 50 per cent of the cult members I have treated were psychologically normal prior to their period of cult membership'.[29] Another psychiatrist tells us that 'while a great many converts I have studied suffered emotional troubles during their earlier years and have led disordered lives, another group – about 40 per cent – have never demonstrated any signs of mental illness.'[30] And a deprogrammer assesses the stability of his subjects' 'personality profiles prior to a cult involvement'[33] as: 'highly stable 0 per cent; mild adolescent difficulties 68 per cent; serious difficulties 20 per cent; psychotic/borderline psychotic 12 per cent'.[31]

Fascinating though such statistics may appear, it has to be recognized not only that these ex-Moonies are unlikely to be representative of Moonies in general but also that we are given absolutely no clue as to what 'psychologically normal', 'signs of mental illness' or 'serious difficulties' might encompass. There is a sense in which all of us – or none of us – may be called 'psychologically normal'.[32] Unless we know what the norm is, and how many people of a similar age and background would be judged to deviate from such a norm, we are learning nothing specifically about Moonies. We do not know whether they are more or less 'normal' or whether they have encountered more or less 'serious difficulties' than non-Moonies.

To take a further example, Margaret Singer (the expert witness quoted at the start of this chapter), in a description of ex-cultists, 75 per cent of whom had left their movement because of outside intervention, has produced a list of the difficulties from which, she claims, ex-members suffer. These difficulties include depression, loneliness, indecisiveness, altered states, a blurring of mental acuity, and both an uncritical passivity and a tendency to be hypercritical.[33] No doubt Singer is accurate in her descriptions – as far as they go. But they do not go nearly far enough, and in not going far enough they could be highly misleading. First, there is no clear indication whether the characteristics she identifies could have arisen before her clients entered the cult, while they were in the cult, or as a result of their having left it. Next, we are given no indication of the *extent* to which the ex-members suffered from these afflictions – whether all of them, the majority or only a minority of them did so. Presumably Singer is not saying that the same person suffers from both uncritical passivity and a tendency to be hypercritical? In the case of those who did suffer, we have no idea whether the effects were more or less severe than when similar afflictions are suffered by those who have not had the 'cult experience'. All of us know people (including, perhaps, ourselves) who have had periods of depression, loneliness, indecisiveness, etc.[34]

A further point is that no distinction was made between the different cults from which Singer's sample was drawn; they were all lumped together and, it would appear, the most disturbing effects from each have been added to the general list without any indication of situations to which a particular effect may not be applicable. Anyone who has any acquaintance with the new movements knows perfectly well that there are some very clear differences among them. The sort of person who becomes a Moonie is unlikely to be the same type of person, or to have had the same experiences, as a Premie from the Divine Light Mission, a devotee of the Meher Baba, an *est* graduate or a one-time 'flirty fisher' for the Children of God.

At the risk of being repetitive, the point I am underlining is this: descriptions of Moonies (or ex-Moonies) do not tell us what they are like *qua* Moonies except in so far as we have some idea of what they would be like were they *not* Moonies. In the descriptions we are normally given

there is an implicit comparison which suggests that they are *more* depressed, lonely or whatever than non-Moonies. This is, however, an assumption that requires empirical investigation. We need to place our knowledge
within a comparative context in much the same way as the natural scientist
who, if he wishes to describe a particular metal as having the property of
hardness, will make the description useful only if he also gives us some
idea of its *relative* hardness – that, say, it is harder than gold but softer
than copper.

The comparative context is even more important when we come to look
for causal explanations of actions. For example, if we learn that 3 per cent
of the members of a movement had committed suicide in a particular year,
this is obviously a cause for concern, and it may well lead to an inquiry
into what it is about the movement that leads people to take their own
lives. If, however, we also know that 5 per cent of *non*-members who were
of a similar age and from a similar background committed suicide in the
same year, we might then be prompted to inquire whether there is
something about the movement which *prevents* people from killing themselves.

Such considerations led me to believe that it was essential to collect
information about a control group whose membership would have had no
contact with the movement but would be of the same age and from the
same social background as the Moonies. Just as important, I needed to
collect information from a group of people who had had contact with the
movement but had not become members.

Recruitment Practices

Sometimes a description of the events that take place at a Unification
workshop is considered sufficient proof that brainwashing has occurred.
The suggestion is that we do not have to decide between the opinions of
those who say Moonies are or are not brainwashed; we simply have to look
at what goes on from the time that the potential recruit meets the movement. Once again, however, we have to be on the look-out for question
begging arguments – that is, we need to ensure that the argument does not
rest merely on the *assumption* that attendance at a workshop is enough to
constitute brainwashing. We need to have some independent criterion for
distinguishing coercive practices from the Moonies' own description of the
workshops as 'seminars in which we tell people who are interested all
about our movement'. We need to know what the 'techniques' are, but we
also need to know how we can tell whether these constitute a process of
brainwashing rather than one of non- coercive communication.

Unification recruitment practices have frequently been compared with
the brainwashing practices to which Chinese and/or Korean prisoners of

war were subjected.[35] One of Singer's special claims to expertise on the subject rests on the fact that she spent some time working for the US Army in a unit which carried out follow-up studies on United Nations prisoners who had been repatriated from Korea. She reports that when she interviewed people associated with the cults, 'Their story of cult indoctrination methods reminded me of many of the group indoctrination methods the North Koreans and Chinese had used.'[36] The trouble with this comparison would seem, *prima facie*, to be that an undeniable element of such practices was that the victims *were* prisoners (and that they were frequently subjected to physical torture).[37] If the evidence shows that Moonies do not hold their guests as prisoners, let alone torture them, would not this suggest that such comparisons are beside the point? Not according to Singer. The special twist which she adds to her claim that the Moonies can be compared with the communist brainwashers is that they (the Moonies) are even more sophisticated than the communists because they have substituted 'love-bombing' for physical force. They lull their unsuspecting victims into believing that they are good, kind, and loving people.[38]

Of course, there will be *some* factors that are common to both the process of POW thought reform[39] and the process of becoming a Moonie. Overlaps can, however, also be found with elements of the process of becoming a Catholic, a college graduate, a woman in Muslim society or an army officer. This does not prove that the Unification Church does not use coercive measures (we shall look at the effect of 'love-bombing' in some detail in chapter 7), but arguments which rely on the fact that processes share certain common elements, while a crucial element (such as physical control) is absent, cannot be taken seriously – unless, of course, it is shown that the shared elements are in themselves sufficient, or that the missing element is unnecessary, to account for the thought reform or conversion. If this cannot be done – if the component parts of a workshop seem to bear more resemblance to other situations in which we would not infer that anything sinister was going on – then we need to look at the Unification environment as a whole and ask whether its component parts *add up to* an environment which could, by independent criteria, be labelled coercive.

How do we do this? We certainly need to find out what 'goes on' in a Unification environment, and we need to look at the various ingredients which make up the workshop. This we can do; and we can also gather as much information as seems relevant from the Moonies, from those who knew them before they became Moonies, from ex-Moonies and from non-Moonies. But, I have argued, while all these bits of information are necessary for the inquiry, none is sufficient. The next question is how can we sort out where to put the various bits of the jig-saw. How can we arrange and use these disparate data?

Reformulating the Question

Our initial question, put crudely, is: do Moonies brainwash their recruits? But this is, of course, far too imprecise a formulation. We have already seen that 'brainwashing' has been used interchangeably with a whole range of concepts (examples include menticide, mind-control, thought reform, coercion, indoctrination, conditioning, conversion, persuasion, socialization, re-education, influence or simply changing one's mind). Given this diversity, given the fact that a particular term is frequently selected simply to communicate disapproval rather than to describe precisely, and given the absence of generally agreed criteria by which we can decide which term might be the most appropriate in any concrete situation, let us try briefly to clarify at a conceptual level what it is that we wish to distinguish at the practical level.

First of all, there are two extreme positions which have to be eliminated from the discussion. On the one hand, there are those who would argue that we are *all* brainwashed – that since our behaviour is the product of heredity and environment, free will is a myth.[40] On the other hand, there are those who claim that it is impossible to brainwash anyone, except perhaps under conditions of extreme physical control and sensory deprivation in which the subject is reduced to nothing but a bundle of conditioned reflexes, is no longer capable of thought, and is, thereby, destroyed as a human being. Human beings can be influenced but, the argument runs, social conditioning is logically impossible.[41]

The trouble with both these positions is that by themselves they would seem to reduce the debate to a unidimensional level by disallowing any exploration of the *range* of personal responsibility for our actions which most of us feel can be constrained or enlarged according to the social environment. It might also be worth pointing out that the existence of free will is not an issue so far as the chief protagonists in the present debate are concerned. It is obvious that Moonies believe that they made their own decision; it is equally obvious that those who believe that a Moonie has been brainwashed are assuming that it is a very real potential (his free will) that has been removed – and that could be restored.

Given the fact that there exists a considerable body of literature which discusses the ideological changes induced in Korean and Chinese prisoners of war[42] and the changes that can occur through the use of drugs, trances, hypnosis and religious ecstasy,[43] and given the far-reaching implications and consequences of the belief, held by a large number of people that Moonies do actually brainwash their victims,[44] it would seem to be important to take the suggestion seriously and not to reject, *a priori*, the possibility that both free will and social conditioning or brainwashing can exist. Pandora's box having been opened, neither closing our eyes nor slamming down the lid will dismiss the problem.

It cannot help us to invoke free will as a *deus ex machina* – as something which mysteriously enables people to make independent decisions until it is somehow snatched away from them.[45] Nor is it helpful to enter into an argument against the position that *ultimately* everything is determined by (mental or physical) causes. What I would like to do is to side-step the issue of free will and determinism and, using what is, I believe, the more fruitful dichotomy of choice and coercion, to attempt a less ambitious but more practical set of distinctions which take into account the different *times* at which different influences act upon a person and the extent to which these different influences combine to play a role in the final outcome.

Let us begin by acknowledging that there is a sense in which our lives are, necessarily, affected by others. People are social beings. From their earliest days they will, they must, 'take in' the beliefs and practices of those around them.[46] Whether they like it or not, the society within which they find themselves will present them with both the potentialities and the constraints of their existence. How they see the world will depend, at least in part, on what others teach them to see. The child born into a Catholic home will be subjected to a different set of beliefs and attitudes from those of the child born into a Muslim home. This is one of the reasons why they will grow up as different kinds of people. It is, of course, possible that they will reject the beliefs and attitudes of their childhood, but it can always be argued that the rejection is itself caused by particular combinations of either these or other environmental (or possibly genetic) influences. How, then, can we distinguish between someone's doing something because he has been 'pushed' or 'pulled' by external influences (or his own genetic make-up) and his doing it because he has chosen to reject or accept what he has been offered by the immediate environment? It is true that the 'choice' may have been the result of a combination of both earlier influences and the present environment, but this need not prevent us from saying that it was a choice. Indeed, it would make *less* sense to say that a choice had been made if the influences which had previously contributed to a person's present personality were 'by-passed' by some kind of coercive technique. This could lead us to conclude that the philosophical anthropology (model of human nature) that seems to be most useful for our purpose is one in which people are assumed to develop, through their interaction with others, an innate capacity for reflection.[47] People can thus be seen as 'clearing houses': *in the light of* their dispositions and accumulated experiences, they can play an active role in 'sorting out' the various alternatives which are presented to them.[48]

A Working Definition of Choice

From this general perspective, we can propose a working definition of what it could mean to make a choice. A choice would involve reflection (in the present), memory (of the past) and imagination (of possible futures). A person would be an active agent in deciding between two or more possible options when he could anticipate their potential existence and when, in doing so, he drew upon his previous experience and his previously formed values and interests to guide his judgement.

How he became the person he now is, with his particular bank of memories and predispositions, is beside the immediate point. I am suggesting merely that, in so far as he can actively refer to and use his accumulated 'input', we can sensibly speak of his making a choice. If other people somehow manage to prevent his making a decision in the light of his previous experiences – or prevent his considering an otherwise available future (such as the continuation of his studies) – then we might say that his capacity to choose had been removed.

Four Key Variables

Moving on from such a definition, we can isolate four variables which must be considered if we want to judge whether someone has made a choice. First, there is the *individual* with his existing predispositions (his interests, values, hopes, and fears). Secondly and thirdly, there are the *alternatives*: in this case, these will be either to continue his life along the lines he was already following (he will already have acquired presuppositions about society and what such a future would be like) or, alternatively, to join the Unification Church. Fourthly, there will be the *social context* within which the decision will be reached. In other words, these four factors can all influence the final outcome: (1) the individual's predispositions; (2) his past experience and expectations of society; (3) his understanding of the attraction (or otherwise) of the Unification Church; and (4) the immediate environment within which he finds himself. Each could have its effect by inclining him towards (or protecting him from) joining the movement.

Having isolated these factors, we can make an important distinction between coercion and deception. If the social context were found to be the only factor relevant to the outcome – if anyone going to a Unification workshop were to become a Moonie – then we would have good reason to suspect that individual choice had been suspended. If, however, the Unification Church were to paint a false picture of its beliefs and of life in the movement, so that the convert got the wrong impression of what the movement was offering, then we could say that he had made a choice, but he had been deceived. While deceived, he could still have been capable of playing an active role in reaching his decision, although the outcome of his decision might not have been the same had he been privy to more accurate information.

The Model

Table 4 depicts nine situations in each of which the relative importance of the four variables is represented by the relative distribution of the plus signs. Coercion tends to be strongest at the top and weakest at the bottom of the table. Not all the logical possibilities have been included, but the model does allow us to distinguish, at a conceptual level, most of the possibilities that others have suggested and/or would seem to be worth pursuing. The table is, of course, only a symbolic representation. I am not suggesting that it is possible to quantify precisely the weighting to be given to each variable: what I have called 'psychological suggestibility' is not a situation in which the individual and the workshop both provide 37.5 per cent, and society 25 per cent of the ingredients which go into the making of a Moonie. Not only are social factors not amenable to such kinds of quantification, but also it is usually the *interaction* between the different factors, rather than a mere summation, that is important in deciding a final outcome.[49] It ought also to be stressed that none of these situations is likely to exist in a 'pure form' – they merely provide a model for comparisons with and between those situations which do actually exist.[50]

Table 4   Choice/coercion: a symbolic representation of the relative contribution of four variables to the making of a Moonie in nine different situations (see text for explanation)

Situation	Individual	Society	UC option	Workshop
(1) Bodily constraint	–	–	–	++++++++
(2) Brain-control	–	–	–	++++++++
(3) Mind-control	–	–	–	++++++++
(4) Biological susceptibility	+++	–	–	+++++
(5) Psychological suggestibility	+++	++	–	+++
(6) Refuge from society	+	++++	+	++
(7) Utopian promise	+	+	++++	++
(8) Non-conscious 'fit'	++	++	++	++
(9) Conscious decision	+++	++	++	+

The mind/body distinction is fraught with both practical and philo-sophical problems and it is unnecessary to pursue these here, but as there are those who offer reductionist or medical explanations of why people become Moonies, I tried, in my analysis of the data, to draw a distinction between the chemico-biological, material substance of the *brain*, and the world of meanings which are subjectively experienced and which can be thought of as being mediated through the *mind*.[51] Thus the kinds of coercion that I was to investigate were, in the first instance, distinguished at two basic levels. To begin with, there was the possibility of *physical coercion*, which could be further subdivided into the first situation indi-cated in table 4, which I have called 'bodily constraint', and the second situation , 'brain-control'. 'Bodily constraint' would not, in itself, affect an individual's ability to *make* a choice; it would merely restrict his ability to carry out what he had chosen to do (if, for example, he had *not* been successfully brainwashed and wanted to leave). 'Brain-control', however, would (through, for example, the use of drugs or hypnosis) take away a person's *capacity* to reflect – he would become incapable of initiating any choice, wherever he was, while he was in that particular condition.

The second type of coercion would not involve physical coercion so much as *mental coercion*. In its extreme form the third situation, 'mind-control', would result in a person's memories of his past experiences, and his imaginings of possible futures, being entirely reinterpreted and man-ipulated by the Moonies. Thus in the first three situations represented in table 4, the variables other than the Unification environment would be of practically no importance in explaining an individual's presence in the Unification Church. In the fourth situation, 'biological susceptibility', the workshop would again be very important, but (unlike the brain-control situation) it would have an effect only on those individuals whose biologic-al condition was such that they were unusually susceptible to factors such as an unfamiliar diet; both the individual's experience of society and the content of the Unification alternative would be irrelevant.

Just as 'biological susceptibility' describes a weakened version of 'brain-control', the fifth situation, 'psychological suggestibility', describes a weaker version of 'mind-control'. Here, certain individuals have particu-larly suggestible personalities and are unusually vulnerable to the persua-sive powers of the workshop; their experiences of society may have made them more ready than most to accept alternatives, but it will not matter very much exactly what the alternative happens to be. The content of the alternative is only slightly more important in the sixth situation, 'refuge from society' – it just has to seem less awful than any other alternative on offer. Unlike the previous situation, however, it is not an individual's weaknesses which are decisive but his experience of society which has been sufficiently unsatisfactory or unpleasant to make certain alternatives appear to be worth a try. In the seventh situation, 'utopian promise', instead of the wider society providing a 'push', it is the Unification alternative that is providing a 'pull'. This is probably the nearest approximation to the Moonies' own understanding of what is happening: they believe that the movement offers such a wonderful answer to the individual's (and the world's) problems that it would be madness for anyone not to join.

The final two situations differ according to a distinction to which the persons concerned could, understandably, object. It is, however, one which I found I needed in order to make sense of certain aspects of the processes I was observing. Approaching the distinction from my definition of choice, we could say that in both these situations the individual's predispositions and experiences of society would be *used* in the final decision, but that he would be less aware of the extent to which he was using them in the eighth situation of 'non-conscious fit' than he would be in the ninth situation, 'conscious decision'.

The Procedure

Isolating variables is much easier in theory than in practice. I was well aware that it was more than likely that all of the variables would, to a greater or lesser degree, be involved (and, indeed, interact) in any particular outcome. Nevertheless, the model which I had constructed from the four variables, in so far as it outlined a range of possible relationships between them, did seem to suggest a procedure which I could follow: first I would try to assess the importance of the social context and then, if this were found to be inadequate to account for conversions, it would be necessary to find out what sorts of people became Moonies, and in what ways they might be particularly susceptible to whatever it was that the Unification Church appeared to be offering them. To do this I would use the control groups to gauge whether Moonies might be more prone than their peers to three basic types of susceptibility: first, susceptibility to the physical or biological effects of the environment; secondly, a general susceptibility to suggestion; and, thirdly, a susceptibility to the Unification alternative. A more detailed discussion of these distinctions, and of other questions posed by the model, can wait until we are looking at the relevant data. I end this chapter with a preliminary assessment of the importance of the social context within which the decision to join is made. I shall argue that this assessment allows us to eliminate the first three possibilities depicted in table 4 in so far as these describe situations in which the Unification environment is the *only* variable of any significance; it also points to the importance of a complete absence of crucial evidence in support of the fourth situation, 'biological susceptibility'. I shall begin by looking at those situations which are concerned with physical coercion, first through external bodily constraint and, secondly, through an internal malfunctioning of the brain.

Assessing the Importance of the Unification Environment

When asked what they know about Moonies, some people have proffered the information that they do not just brainwash their victims; they kidnap them. When I have pursued such allegations, it has usually turned out that a confusion has arisen as a result of reports of activities carried out by 'deprogrammers' who have pushed Moonies into the back of vans and then locked them up in a motel room or in some other confined place.[52] Stories have appeared in the press of barbed-wire fences, guards on gates and locked doors. Whenever I have visited a Unification centre I have never had any difficulty in slipping out when I wanted to. In some of the larger centres members are expected to sign a book before they go out, but it is perfectly easy to open the door from the inside, and if it has been locked, I have always found a key hanging on a nearby nail. Although several workshop centres are located in the countryside, they are not in remote, isolated places (certainly nothing like the People's Temple hide-out in Jonestown, Guyana) but within a few minutes' walk of a main road. There have been the odd occasions when the Maccama River at Camp K has flooded, and the occupants have been cut off – unless they were to walk a mile upstream, where they could cross to the road.[53] More usually, the would-be escaper could wade across the water without wetting more than the bottom of his trousers, but it would be perfectly possible, and much simpler, for him to walk across the bridge.

The Moonies insist that their security precautions are there to keep out unwanted intruders, such as the press or deprogrammers, rather than to force helpless captives to stay inside. Throughout my researches I have been unable to find any evidence that they have ever physically prevented anyone who wished to leave a workshop or Unification centre from doing so. Furthermore, two plaintiffs who brought a case against the Unification Church, claiming, among other things, to have been 'falsely imprisoned', admitted that neither they nor any one of whom they had knowledge had ever been subjected to physical coercion, or even the threat of physical coercion, by the Moonies.[54]

The next question to be considered is whether the conditions at a workshop could affect the physical state of a guest's body to the extent that his ability to reflect in an active manner was severely curtailed

Neither drugs nor alcohol are consumed on Unification premises (unless smuggled in by a rare deviant or non-member). Potential recruits are

Preparing a meal in the kitchen of the British headquarters of the Unification Church.

Another corner of the kitchen, showing a picture of 'True Parents' – and a jar of Holy Salt.

Moonies responding to one of Moon's speeches.

specifically asked to abstain (although the occasional visit to a local pub or bar is not unknown). It is difficult to see how the evidence can support allegations that 'sugar-buzzing', trance-inducing lectures, lack of sleep or hypnosis produce such drastic impairment of the mental faculties that 'victims' are unable to function normally. The cuisine at Unification workshops is not exactly *cordon bleu*, but it is no worse than that in most college residences and probably a lot more nutritional that that which many students provide for themselves.[55] Guests at workshops are allowed seven or so hours' sleep.[56] They do not always avail themselves of this, but it is not unusual for students to have far less sleep as they prepare for examinations in which they subsequently perform perfectly well. The lectures are no more trance-inducing than those given everyday (for as many or more hours) in many places of further education. I have observed, moreover, that those who join are likely to have found the message of the lectures interesting and stimulating and to have listened in an active manner, frequently taking notes and (as is clear from questioning after the lecture) relating the content to their own past experiences. There is very little chanting at Unification workshops. Where it does occur at all (which, in the West, has been mainly in California),[57] it is of a very limited nature so far as the guests are concerned. Certainly, it is much less intense than the chanting in which one is invited to take part when one visits an ISKCON temple[58] or, indeed, that which regularly occurs in more estab- lished Hindu temples. Unificationism is not an ecstatic religion,[59] and it does not, as part of its normal practice, whip up its followers into a frenzy (although Moon and some of the more charismatic leaders can elicit enthusiastic mass responses from Moonies on occasion). As for altered states of consciousness or hypnosis, unless such terms are applied in an entirely vacuous sense, so that they are used either tautologically or to describe common, everyday occurrences, it must be obvious to anyone who has ever attended a Unification workshop that these simply do not occur.[60]

Although there are doctors who have inferred from the beliefs and behaviour of members of new religious movements that they were suffering from a 'malfunctioning of the central nervous system', there is no direct medical evidence of induced malfunctioning of the brain or central nervous system of either Moonies or their guests.[61] In the absence of direct evidence, we do have the indirect evidence that an extraordinarily high percentage of the brains subjected to the workshop manage to function with sufficient efficiency to allow their owners to decide that they do *not* want to become Moonies. If the human brain can really be rendered incapable of functioning by Unification workshops, we would need to know why the incapacitating influences work on only a small minority of the brains subjected to such influences.

Let us now briefly examine the evidence for, and implications of, a high Unification failure rate.

When someone who has been to a Unification workshop does not join the movement, his experience tends to be described as a 'lucky escape', or, more likely, to be forgotten or ignored. But such people pose a very important question. If the social context is so persuasive, why did they not become Moonies? It did not take me long to discover that such people existed; indeed, going by the apparent failure rate in the workshops I attended, and the fact that the overall membership seemed to remain remarkably small, it seemed clear that the number of non-joiners, and the drop-out rate amongst the members themselves, could be pretty high.

When doctors want to indicate the efficacy of a treatment for an otherwise terminal disease, they might talk of a 70 per cent success rate. This is not meant to be taken to mean that all the patients get 70 per cent better; it means that 70 per cent of the patients get better and that the other 30 per cent die. When one goes to a Unification workshop one either becomes a Moonie or one does not. If we look at *individuals*, the treatment or technique can be described only as a success or failure. Unless there is a 100 per cent success or failure rate, we cannot assess the extent to which different individuals' characteristics could affect the outcome. By describing a *group* rate we can.

Thus, if I wanted to make an objective assessment of the effectiveness of the social context within which the decisions to become a Moonie were made and of the relative importance of the individual characteristics which were brought to that context, an accurate knowledge of the ratio of joiners to non-joiners was crucial. By laboriously working through membership lists and mounds of application forms for numerous workshops (and further checking these data with notes from interviews with members and parents and my own attendances at workshops during that year), it was possible to chart what might be termed the 'Unification career' of each of the original 1,000 or so applicants for a two-day workshop in the London area during 1979 (see chapter 1 for details). This is summarized in table 5.

Although the 1979 London group was the only one for which I am confident that I obtained an accurate rate, what information I have gleaned of other times and places in Britain suggested that it enjoyed a higher rate of joining than other workshop cohorts. Certainly, so far as absolute numbers are concerned, the Unification Church in Britain had never had (and has not had since) as much success in recruiting new members as it had in 1979.[62] The only other study of which I am aware that has systematically followed the fortunes of a group of potential converts is that carried out by Galanter with 104 persons in the Los Angeles area.[63] As can be seen from table 5, his findings were remarkably similar to my own. Unfortunately, estimates concerning the success and failure rates of the Oakland Family workshops, particularly in Camp K and Boonville, but also in other centres, have tended to conflict with each other quite markedly.

It is, of course, easier for Moonies (and others) to remember people who stay than those who leave, and some of the exaggerations are undoubtedly due to unconsciously selective memories. It is also the case, however, that both Moonies and anti-cultists have a vested interest in making the success rate look as high as possible (the former for the purpose of morale boosting, the latter for evidence of brainwashing). Where no records are available the most reliable source for accurate figures is probably the ex-Moonies who left of their own free will and who have not subsequently been active in the anti-cult movement. Independent visitors rarely stay long enough to calculate the rate for more than a few workshops, which could well be atypical. But, even taking seriously the estimates of contemporary Moonies, ex-Moonies (deprogrammed and otherwise) and students of the movement, it seems that during the course of a year, of those who got as far as going to a two-day Oakland workshop, no more than a quarter, and possibly as few as one in twenty, would end up as full-time Moonies.[64] I strongly suspect that the reputation which the Oakland Family has enjoyed of being the most successful Unification recruitment centre in the West during the late 1970s, has had more to do with the *number* of people it introduced to the movement than its success *rate*.

Table 5   Unification careers

	London, 1979[1] (N = 1,017) (%)	Los Angeles, 1978[2] (N = 104) (%)
2-day workshop		
Start	100	100
Finish	85	
7-day workshop		
Start	30	29
Finish	25	
21-day workshop		
Start	18	17
Finish	15	
Agree to affiliation to UC (all types: i.e. including 'Home-Church members' and students continuing full-time study)	13	—
Actually join for more than 1 week (all types)	10	—
Still affiliated after 1 year	7	—
Still affiliated after 2 years	5	—
Still affiliated by 1 January 1983	4	—
Join as full-time member for more than 1 week (i.e. living in UC centre and working full-time for UC)	8	9
Still member after 4 months		6
Maximum percentage still full-time UC after 1 year	5	—
Maximum percentage still full-time UC after 2 years	4	—
Maximum percentage still full-time UC on 1 January 1983	3.5	—

Notes: [1] Based on all those attending two-day workshops in the London area throughout 1979.
[2] M. Galanter, 'Psychological Induction into the Large Group: Findings from a Modern Religious Sect', *American Journal of Psychiatry*, vol. 137, no. 12, 1980, p. 1575. Four of the workshop attenders and one of the joiners in Galanter's study were removed by relatives.

The data depicted in Table 5, and the very fact that the numbers of full-time members in the USA seems never to have risen above a few thousand, rule out some of the more spectacular 'no one is immune' claims;[65] and if, in the light of these data, we consider the role of the workshop as a social context which brainwashes, manipulates or coerces young people into becoming Moonies, it is clear that it is not as terrifyingly efficient as has sometimes been suggested. It would appear to be at least 90 per cent *ineffective*. The 'at least' has to be stressed since a heavy selection process takes place before people agree to attend workshops[66] – if *everyone*, including successful, happily married businessmen in their late forties, were to go to the workshops, the failure rate would undoubtedly be much, much higher.

If we start our calculations from the number of those who get as far as visiting a Unification centre, a generous estimate suggests that no more than 0.5 per cent will be associated with the movement two years later, and by no means all of these will be full-time members. In other words, it is just not true that anyone can be brainwashed by Unification techniques: it seems quite clear that factors *brought to* the workshops by the potential recruit are crucial to the outcome. If we are to understand why someone becomes a Moonie, we need information about what sorts of people are most likely to join and how their character, their predispositions and their experience of life could respond to what the Unification Church seems to offer them.

It is also perfectly possible that those who have joined did so because they came to the workshop with a highly susceptible biological make-up. But how are they to be differentiated, except *ex post facto*, from the other workshop guests? I have been unable to unearth any evidence that anyone has ever noticed that those who join the movement were, *before* they met the movement, unusually susceptible to physical changes wrought by such things as diet, sleeping patterns, sitting through lectures or participating in energetic exercises – none of which would seem to be vastly different from similar phenomena in non-Unification situations and all of which leave the majority of guests unaffected. In other words (to conclude the discussion concerning physical coercion), a 'brain-control' explanation of recruitment can be dismissed on account of the high rate of non-joining, and a 'biological susceptibility' explanation would have to depend, question-beggingly, for its evidence upon the final outcome, when it assumes the very thing which it is claiming to demonstrate: that those who become Moonies must do so because they are differentially susceptible to changes in diet or what-have-you, while those who do not become Moonies cannot be similarly susceptible.

I am not suggesting that people who attend Unification workshops do not sometimes feel tired or that their resistance may not be lowered through an unaccustomed diet. I am arguing, however, that there is no evidence that they are rendered significantly more physically incapable than they might be in other, fairly normal, contexts. In other words, were they in another situation at that time and in that state, we would consider them perfectly capable (as far as bodily functioning was concerned) of choosing between options in accordance with their personal interests and their past experience.

But this does not mean that the workshop is not important. In almost every case it is a necessary precondition for someone joining the movement to have spent some time in a Unification environment. While there is no evidence that the conditions at Unification workshops have a *direct* effect on the brain, it is still possible that they may have an *indirect* effect. Of course, the guests' brains must be affected inasmuch as they continue to allow their owners to react to the environment. But even if the potential Moonie has a brain which is physically capable of making decisions, his capacity for choice may still be severely curtailed because he is being coerced at the *level of meaning*. He may be seeing the situation in the way that those around him want him to see it rather than the way in which he would see it if he were to think the matter over in another environment. He could, in other words, be physically capable of going through the process of decision-making, but, in fact, it could be the Moonies who are interpreting the present options and reinterpreting his past experiences to the extent that it is they who are in control of the final outcome. The next two chapters address this possibility.

6   Reactions to the Workshop

Having found no evidence to suggest that physical coercion (in the forms of 'bodily constraint', 'brain-control' or 'biological suggestibility') was responsible for a person's becoming a Moonie, my next question was whether there was evidence that any kind of mental coercion was involved.[1] It will be remembered that 'mind-control', the third type of situation portrayed in table 4 (p. 138), was defined as one in which the Moonies at the workshops would be able to manipulate their guest's vision of reality so completely that he would interpret it only in the ways which the Moonies wanted. The fact that the vast majority of guests did not join the movement suggested that Unification techniques of persuasion were not as powerful as this extreme situation would imply. It also suggested that the 'utopian promise' of the sixth situation was not as irresistible as the Moonies themselves would have liked to believe. It suggested, instead, that something that the guest brought to the workshop (his character, predispositions, memories and experiences of society) would play a significant role in deciding why some people joined and others did not. I did, however, want to gather information about how the workshop *was* interpreted by the guests.

At one level potential recruits will see the Unification centres and workshops as I described them in chapter 4. But while their perception will certainly depend in part on what is objectively 'out there', it will also depend upon the selection mechanisms of their own personalities and their previously developed expectations, hopes, fears, likes and dislikes. The guests will not just see the smiling faces; they will also experience these as signs of friendliness or of dissimulation. They will not just hear the lectures; they will interpret these as an exciting new truth or a boring load of rubbish. They will not just pass a weekend with a group of young people; they will experience the thrill of a new challenge, a dreary, embarrassing or mildly amusing two days, or a threatening claustrophobia.

By asking a group of people who had shared roughly the same objective experience (that is, a workshop in the London area during 1979) what their reactions were, I was able to record the diversity of the subjective responses and this diversity can give some indication of the relative importance and influence of the character of the individual guests in their interpretations of the alternative offered by the Unification Church.

Just to clarify the terms I shall be using in this chapter, unless otherwise stated, 'Moonie' will refer to a full-time Moonie; 'leaver' will refer to someone who joined the movement but left within a short period (a few weeks at the most);[2] 'non-joiner' will refer to someone who attended at least part of a two-day seminar or workshop, and possibly the whole of a twenty-one-day workshop, but never actually joined the movement; 'control group' refers to a group of people who were of a similar age and social background to Moonies but who had had no direct contact with the movement; 'European' will refer to continental Europe, excluding Britain. Where there are clear differences between British, American and/or European Moonies these will be mentioned; otherwise it should be assumed that while the 'hard' data refer to Britain, the findings do not conflict with my somewhat less systematic research into the movement in the rest of Europe and North America. The analysis does not refer to the situation in Asia, Africa or Latin America.

Given the dangers (discussed in chapters 1 and 5) of selecting responses which can then be assumed to be either more or less typical than they actually are, it is important to have some idea of the *relative distribution* of responses to questions asking for assessments of the workshop. This is given in table 6. As can be seen, the responses, even those from the non-joiners, were remarkably favourable. It is, it seems, perfectly possible to spend (at least) a couple of days with Moonies and end up both without joining and without believing that either they or the movement are insufferably awful.[3]

One would expect those who joined to have believed that the lectures contained the Truth, but it is clear that by no means all the joiners thought them to be the whole truth straight away. I have talked to Moonies who admit to having had (and, in several cases, to still having) serious doubts about certain aspects of the Principle. One Moonie was probably speaking for several of his fellow members when he said that at the time of joining he had thought that the *Divine Principle* made more sense than any other set of beliefs he knew, but that there were some things which he had decided to put in what he called the 'pending tray', to think about and sort out later. Such 'pending' matters may be resolved with 'greater understanding', but they may be forgotten, or they may nag away at the back of a member's mind, gradually to be joined by further doubts which, eventually, lead to his leaving the movement.

Table 6   Reactions to Workshops

	Non-joiners (%)[1]	Leavers (%)	Full-time joiners (%)
What did you like most about the 2-day workshop?			
The lectures	24	57	52
The people	31	11	31
The general atmosphere	34	35	35
Everything[2]	5	4	6
Nothing[2]	5	—	—
Other	9	—	2
What did you like least about the 2-day workshop?			
The lectures	43	32	16
The people	15	5	5
The general atmosphere	14	5	11
Nothing[2]	8	26	46
Other	20	31	20
How would you rate your reaction to the following during the 2-day workshop?			
(a) *the lectures*			
You thought they were the truth	9	44	63
Quite a lot of truth, but you couldn't accept it all	40	44	30
Interesting, but you did not accept their truth	43	8	8
Boring and uninteresting	4	—	—
Nothing but a load of rubbish	5	4	—
(b) *the members*			
Really nice people whom you liked a lot	53	60	84
One or two you liked, others not so much	27	36	13
You found them rather strange and peculiar	18	4	3
You did not like them at all	2	—	—
(c) *the general atmosphere*			
Friendly and homely	52	68	61
Stimulating and exciting	8	12	31
Quite pleasant, but not really your cup of tea	29	20	8
Oppressive, claustrophobic, frightening	12	—	—

Notes: [1] Figures do not add up to 100, as some respondents coded more than one option.
[2] 'Everything' and 'nothing' were not pre-coded options, but there were enough responses to create a separate category for coding.

The Non-Joiners' Experiences

While not all joiners accepted the *Divine Principle* in its entirety, it is perhaps surprising, in the light of the widespread belief that Moonie doctrines are gobbledegook,[4] that practically half the non-joiners should have said that they thought the lectures contained quite a lot of truth, 9 per cent believing they *were* the truth. One non-joiner said that she had had quite a frightening experience when what she had come to believe was the truth was revealed to her. She wrote:

> I feel that people condemn the Unification Church because they will not admit that what the members say makes sense, probably fear is in most people's minds. The members have answers to all questions, answers that are so real that one does tend to get a little fearful. Most people like to pop along on a Sunday evening and say a few prayers and sing a few hymns and they think they have done their duty. I am the worst culprit, I don't even do that! Most people are not dedicated enough to join this church. Some won't even listen, they are too busy trying to persecute them. . . . I am aware (acutely) of God's presence, in my life. I know what I ought to do but I do not do it. It is too much for me to comprehend, I feel. The Unification Church DO know the answers, there is NO doubt in my mind on that, and there are very few things that I can say I am not doubtful about.
> P.S. They have not brainwashed me by the way!

Another respondent, admitting that it was for selfish reasons that he had not joined (he had put 'not being able to smoke inside' as the thing he had liked least about the workshop), wrote:

> I thoroughly believe in the UC and that the other churches are both ignorant and arrogant towards the UC. The UC has God in their hearts and not just in their mouths.

At the other end of the spectrum there were those people who were violently opposed to the movement. There was, for example, the man who had converted to Christianity at the age of 15. It had, he said, meant something for a little while, 'but cooled off as I faced new temptations of sex and drugs and rock and roll which seemed to offer greater excitements and fulfilment'. About the Unification Church he wrote:

> The UC is evil. I hate everything about it. I don't blame the members – they are victims of some dark satanic force. I'm glad I was challenged, and was able to resist. People shouldn't be subjected

to this sort of thing. We should be free to walk down a street without being emotionally assaulted by these Moon-worshippers.

A Jamaican woman who was lonely and had thought that the Unification Church was a debating society where she could have interesting discussions and make new friends, dismissed the experience with the words,

> I thought it was a load of intellectual clap-trap. I couldn't accept the written philosophy. It seemed pseudo-intellectual.

The majority of people, however, fell between the extremes of complete acceptance or rejection. They were more inclined to show some respect for the status of the teachings, although they themselves would not embrace them, a common position being that they were as believable or unbelievable as most other theologies. One fairly typical response came from a Malaysian who said that he did not continue to the seven-day course because he 'couldn't find the time. Besides I can't live for seven days with so much holiness.' He wrote:

> I find the UC's belief is much more logical than others and has better solutions to some problems. Like others they believe in love and peace. But they certainly try and have a good way of achieving it. Of course I do find some of their 'theories' 'unbelievable'. If you get to *understand* more religions, you'll find it hard to tell which is the truth!

Another respondent said that he had not continued to the seven-day workshop because it was 'too expensive [£15], also tedious to listen to things one could not accept when they would not argue constructively'. He commented:

> The Moonies did not seem to have lost their rationality except that they fervently accepted Moon's doctrine. To me an Anglican vicar appears equally irrational except his arguments are based on more serious scholarship and study of the Bible.

Several of the evaluations of the theology gave clues as to the kinds of 'protection' with which the respondents might have come to the workshop. There was the tolerant indifference of the lapsed Catholic who wrote:

> Nothing wrong with it, if you like that type of thing. I was bored.

And there were those who were already confirmed in their beliefs – beliefs which could take various forms. There was a Marxist community worker who declared the movement to be:

a capitalist venture camouflaged in a kind of religious revelation. Mr Moon thinks of himself as a second Christ which is rubbish. Waste of time.

There was a French atheist:

They are not stupid. I find the ideal of brotherhood fine. But it is difficult to approve such beliefs when you don't believe in any deity. On the whole [the members are] sensible people, agreeable, nice, open to other people's ideas etc. But I wouldn't like to share their way of life. I want to achieve my spiritual fulfilment myself.

There was a 77-year-old inveterate searcher:

So far Theosophy is the nearest to satisfy me. But I search and keep an open mind on other teachings.

And there was the 'real' Christian:

Boring, very claustrophobic and I found no truth at all. The truth was not there. In one month they could turn your mind into a cabbage. . . . The members have *no* longer minds of there (*sic*) own. Their beliefs are of the mind but not of the hard (*sic*). The church and its practices is *just* for money. . . . My faith is in God and *Christ said blessed is he who hears my word and keeps it*, and he who keeps the commandments shall have eternal life.

(*Above and opposite*) *Scenes from a workshop at the Moonies' farm in Wiltshire.* (*It is not difficult to distinguish some of the guests from the Moonies.*)

As will already be apparent, many of the respondents found themselves liking or admiring the members – sometimes feeling rather sorry for them perhaps, but generally acknowledging their commitment and dedication. A few respondents talked of individual Moonies whom they had not liked, and one or two dismissed all Moonies as brainwashed zombies, but the most frequent criticisms levelled against the Moonies were that they were *too* nice and *too* dedicated. The following comment came from a young woman who had a Moonie relative:

> Well the members are nice people and most of them, like X, are truly believers in the beliefs, but who knows what there is behind the organisation? . . . Why are they so kind? Too kind.

Another respondent was put off by the general lack of realism which he found in the movement:

> I think that its beliefs are too 'positive' to have any significance on the every-day life of today. Their values and practices cannot possibly be relevant to present-day society. The members seem to me to be on cloud 9 trying to escape reality on the whole! To me they are too 'nice' and 'good' and 'obliging' for me to be able to relate to them as real people.

A fairly typical 'traveller' was the African who had been in the country for only three months and who said that he had not found himself fitting into the society. Despite the fact that he had heard that the Unification Church was 'a sect not unlike the Reverend Jim Jones's catastrophe in Guyana', he had agreed to go on the seven-day course because he 'got bored staying at home and it was a chance to see places outside London and live on a farm'. He got as far as starting the twenty-one-day course but did not finish it because:

> It was too much time to waste on a thing the essence of which I don't agree with and I got bored with the lectures. I don't agree with their teachings or the methods employed; they stress too much on making people feel guilty and since they dogmatically believe in their Principle the people themselves become boring to talk to. . . . The members themselves are nice and fraternal people but rather boring and uninteresting to talk to because they are enthusiastic about one subject only – their *Divine Principle*.

Some respondents, like my fellow guest at Camp K, reported feeling rather hurt or disappointed when they found it difficult to maintain a friendship with a Moonie once they had made it clear that they were not going to join, but several others said that they still kept in touch, often claiming to have sustained a deep, spiritual relationship with one or two of their Moonie friends. One fairly extreme case was that of the Briton who confessed:

> I must be honest that I fell in love with one of the members and had decided that I had met the perfect match. Even though I am extremely anti-Unification Church I still keep in touch with her in her own country. It is my conclusion that she being involved in the Church has moved away from her family and therefore comes more

to rely on the Church. After a recent programme on the Church I got in touch with her, trying to tell her the truth, but to no avail.

A more commonly cited experience was:

> Within two weeks of my becoming acquainted with one of its members I realized that my hope of making friends on a social basis was quite unrealistic. Since this was the reason I had agreed to go to the workshop, I decided fairly quickly that I could not benefit from its superficial overflow of joy for mankind. Most of its members were so happy on the surface that people like me were forced to adopt a cynical attitude if only because it was impossible to reconcile what we had heard from the press with our present experiences. In spite of this initial turn-off I was still very impressed by the dedication of many of its members. I still receive regular letters from the person who introduced me to the church. . . . Instead of sending stereotype forms asking you to contact them they send very personal messages about their hopes, fears and spiritual desires. This very positive attitude towards thinking about themselves. . .and the fact that many of them travel worldwide to spread their news. . .really does deserve my admiration (even if I do not agree with everything they say).

The most commonly proffered reason for rejecting the Unification Church was that the guest did not believe the *Divine Principle* to be the truth, the stumbling-block most often mentioned being the idea that Moon could be the Messiah. There were also fairly frequent references to the wealth amassed for Moon by his followers. One respondent who had agreed to join and then decided not to (partly because of parental pressure wrote:

> I still think a great deal of them, although all contact with them is over. They really are lovely people from all accounts trying to make a better world. But the question of Reverend Moon comes into it and I cannot accept him; and of course if you can't accept him that destroys the whole argument. Unfortunately with the Moonies it's all or nothing. Which is a shame, as they are wonderful people.

Another respondent agreed to join as a Home Church member but then changed her mind:

> There were parts of the teachings that I felt some doubt about, and felt that to be a UC member I needed to give 100 per cent of myself but I was not willing to do so – my career etc. I think more people should look at the UC because some of their ways and ideas are good.

> When I decided to not join full time I was not pressurized to stay but allowed to do what I wanted to do.

But another frequently mentioned 'put-off' was the authoritarian attitude of the movement:

> I generally do not like being told what to do and the Moonies were very much into telling people how they should live their lives.

Several people objected to the movement's anti-communist stance, and others (including a couple of homosexuals) complained of its strictly puritanical standards of morality.

Curiously enough, many of these aspects of the movement were also among those which other guests declared to be its main attractions. The questionnaires made it abundantly clear that one man's meat is another man's poison. For every respondent who praised the excellence of the cooking, another would complain that the fare was dull and stodgy; the guest who had loathed the enthusiastic group activities would be matched by one who had found them delightful and stimulating. A few people said that they hated everything about the movement and had loathed the workshop; other non-joiners said that it was one of the best weekends they had ever spent.

The teachings produced not only a variety of intellectual responses – some found them excessively boring, others found them incredibly stimulating – they could also result in very different emotional responses. For a young woman whose husband had been killed in a car accident, the opportunity to talk about the spirit world and life after death had, she said, brought a feeling of immense relief: 'For the first time in my life I have met people who did not think I was strange to talk about such things'. But the experience of another woman who was to join and then leave the movement was far more disturbing (it was, indeed, the most disturbing of all the responses to the questionnaire). She wrote:

> When I went to London to work about two years ago, I became very interested in spiritualism. I had always felt there was more to life. Spiritualism answered a lot of questions for me, e.g. was God really a condemning God, the true meaning of Heaven and Hell. Man's free will and karma. I also had a deep feeling for Jesus Christ. Who was he really – was he meant to die? In the [Unification] Church I studied the mission of Christ. The results of the deep study upset me very much. Everything became acutely out of proportion. I felt that man was so evil, that I was better off taking my life than living in this world. . . .
>   At the time I joined I felt I had something worth living and working for. . . . After I left the workshop, I saw everything

from a completely different viewpoint. . . . Everything seemed very evil. . . .

I left the movement about five months ago. At first I really didn't think that I was going to survive. The Unification Church strips you completely of your ego. You become very frightened of life. I left with X. He has suffered the same reactions. Since then we both feel more able to cope, although there are of course occasions when we both revert back to this childlike fear and acute depression. Our faith in God and the spirit world has not been completely destroyed.

The questionnaire itself made no explicit reference to brainwashing, mind-control or undue pressure (the nearest suggestions being in the final, precoded responses in tables 4 and 6), but several of the respondents made a point of volunteering the opinion that they had not been put under any pressure to join and insisted that they had certainly not been brainwashed. Roughly the same proportion (about a quarter) mentioned (some with little more than mild irritation) that they had felt under some sort of pressure – that they had felt uncomfortable because they were always being watched or (less frequently) that they had been made to feel guilty. None of the non-joiners claimed that he himself had been brainwashed, although one person did express some uncertainty and wondered whether what he was told in the lectures might have subconsciously affected the way he thought, and a couple more non-joining respondents were worried that others, more vulnerable than they, could have been in danger of being manipulated. A few of the *leavers* did, however, suggest that they could have been subjected to some version of mind-control, and several more respondents (both non-joiners and leavers) expressed concern that the Moonies, whom, on the whole, they regarded as genuinely dedicated and sincere, were brainwashed or acting out of misplaced idealism, or were misguidedly allowing others to direct their activities. The most forceful statements on the subject came from four of the leavers, one of whom I have already quoted. A second wrote:

> The more I learned the more amazed and disillusioned I became – I couldn't take the pressure being put on me or the eternal 'wicked-ness' of my soul. . . .
> In a nutshell, the Unification Church members are basically good and sound people being totally led up the garden path. If the spiritual energy expounded by these people was channelled into a Christian movement (instead of 'fake Christian' movement) the world would truly benefit from their work.

The third, a graduate in her forties who had become a Home Church member and then left, wrote:

I came to feel that I could become liable to indoctrination which made me pull out quickly - the seemingly genuine affection for people generated by Unification Church members is a powerful weapon – but it did seem to be genuine. Many aspects I disliked intensely – e.g. fund-raising, self denial, arranged marriages, the loss of self-identity, the unquestioning acceptance of Reverend Moon and all he said.

The fourth leaver who felt that the movement had a frightening influence wrote:

As an ex-Moonie I am not bitter towards the members but astounded, rather, at my own gullibility. I think if I had not left when I did it may possibly have been too late. After making the decision that I had to get out or sink because I could no longer swim with the movement I truly found myself doubting my sanity.

Consequences for the Unconverted

Like the Moonies, the researcher's primary interest in the outcome of a Unification workshop tends to focus on whether or not people end up by joining the movement. Unintended consequences can, however, be as interesting as intended purposes, and I soon realized that while the non-joiners may not have been converted, it did not follow that they had remained unaffected by their contact with the Moonies. There was, indeed, little doubt that the workshop had been more than a passing non-event in the lives of most of the guests, even if they did not become members, although one inveterate seeker did claim that since he had been to so many of these sorts of thing, he was not sure that he could remember which had been the Unification Church. A third of the non-joiners claimed that they had changed in some way as a result of attending the workshop, and a further quarter said that perhaps they had changed.

Curiously enough, it is probable that the Moonies are more successful in promoting rival beliefs than they are in promoting their own. Well over half the non-joiners who said that they had changed claimed that they had, as the result of attending a Unification workshop, become more convinced of the truth of some religious belief other than that of the Unification Church e.g. 'I have become stronger in my Catholic religion'). A quarter reported that they had actually discovered God or that they had been given a renewed experience of God: 'Now have a very firm belief in God'; 'I now can talk deeper about God and know more things about him'; 'My faith in God has grown stronger'; 'More stable in my religious belief'. Disbelief also could be reinforced: '[I now] hate everything to do with religion and my past values and beliefs were greatly strengthened'. By some the *Divine Principle* was seen in positive terms as the source of inspiration for their growth in understanding of religious questions and beliefs; for others, increased religious consciousness was the result of a negative reaction to Unification teaching: 'It has made me more aware of false Christs as prophesized in Revelations [New Testament] . . . and has made me look at the Bible more closely. . . . it has been a marvellous education and confirmation of the one and only true Bible.'

Turning to more secular changes, 15 per cent of the non-joiners claimed that they had become happier or more contented in some way: 'I came out of my depression and no longer take tablets. I am bright and alert as never in my life before'; 'More optimistic'. On the other hand, 11 per cent claimed that they were unsettled or unhappy: 'Bad tempered sometimes, unsure of life in general, edgy'; and a further 11 per cent reported that they had learned to be more careful in future: 'Less naive – more cautious about this sort of thing'; 'I used to be very friendly and trusting. Now I am more suspicious.'

Several people felt that they had learned how to become better people as a result of the workshop: 'I seem to look at things differently. I still pray. I had morals anyway, but they have been upheld even more strongly'; 'I feel I can discipline myself much more – and care for more people unselfishly – plus many personal changes.' Quite a few respondents claimed that they had become more open-minded or that they now recognized the need for open-mindedness: 'Now appreciate more other people's beliefs'; 'I think a lot more and question most things'; 'Opened my mind to religion, but not blinded my view. For I can see both sides of the coin, unlike some who only see one'; 'Opened my eyes to unexplored avenues'; 'The workshop did not change me to the extent of making me want to join but made me more aware of the need for a greater understanding and a greater fellowship between churches.'

It has already been intimated that some of the most severe critics of the movement were to be found among those who joined for a short time and then left. This was not altogether unexpected. What was perhaps more surprising was to find that the majority of the leavers still saw the changes that the movement had wrought in their lives in positive terms: 'I (now, because of the UC) believe in God, the Bible, Jesus, spiritualism and the probability that Rev. Moon is what the UC claims him to be. I have a guideline by which to set my life morally and feel more capable of responsibilities of my life.' Another person who had left wrote: 'I feel I think more deeply – to a degree I feel my morals are higher.' Another claimed: 'My views on relationships between people have altered. I find I am trying not to be so self-centred. Perhaps I am still searching to find the truth.' Another concluded: 'I understand better why I should love other people and the need for helping others less well off than me.' Finally, another leaver wrote: 'I became more sensitive generally about life and more open-minded.'

The Conversion Experience

Those who became members and were still in the movement at the time they filled in the questionnaire (or were interviewed) displayed almost as much diversity in their reactions to the workshop as the non-joiners. The question of why they had joined was approached from several different directions. The first question on the subject in the main questionnaire was open-ended; that is, it did not suggest any particular answers but just asked the respondent 'What were your reasons for deciding to join the Family at the time?' The majority of answers focused on the truth of the teachings as their main reason, using words like 'I knew that the *Divine Principle* was true.' Several wrote about the change that hearing the lectures had made to their vision of reality: 'My mind became clear, my confused thoughts of life became like a beautiful picture. History became (*sic*) to have a purpose. I knew this was God in my heart.' For some, hearing the teachings seemed like the end of a long search: 'I felt God was finding me and wanted to show me his truth. I was always searching and asking questions and for the first time my questions were being answered.' Several respondents suggested that their lives had been given purpose, meaning, direction or hope: 'I could see that through the Family I could help restore the world and establish the kind of relationships with people that I longed for.' A few seemed to be joining for rather negative reasons – because there was no other hope: 'I couldn't see any other way in life that could lead to a better tomorrow. My other experiences in life had really made me aware of that.'

There were a few who were less than certain that the Unification Church would inevitably restore the Kingdom of Heaven but felt nevertheless that it had something to offer them. One respondent (who has been in the movement for eight years) said that his reasons were

> Basically self-centred. . . . I wanted to experiment with a 'God-centred life'. Not convinced at that time of the truth of the Family. Is it true or not?

Another man who expressed uncertainty, was persuaded by the greater uncertainty of the alternative of *not* joining. He wrote:

> While visiting the centre I kept working and I was in my everyday

life. I could see the difference clearly. I wondered, 'If it is not true and I join, I waste my life. If I don't . . . well, the life is already a waste – But if it is true. . . .' I thought it over for a long time till I made up my mind.

As well as those who expressed cognitive relief, there were quite a few converts who talked of the psychological or emotional relief and comfort which they experienced when they found an atmosphere in which they felt 'at home'; many said that it was the friendliness or the show of love that had made them want to join:

I wanted to become loving and giving and joyful like all the family members. They had purpose in life, which I had not.

A highly qualified 29-year-old electrical engineer who joined with his wife said that he had been influenced by

the logical explanation of God and His plan for the world, and realizing that we had been prepared for this mission in life in many different ways. God had protected us and was now asking us to 'take up the cross' and follow His plan, which we understood through the *Divine Principle*. . . . *Divine Principle* explained many of the misunderstandings from traditional church doctrine, and explained a way of life which would enable us to perfect our marriage relationship, centring on God and also [to] follow God's dispensational course and bring sinless children into the world.

A number of the respondents who mentioned having feelings of release or freedom when they accepted that the *Divine Principle* was the truth, were aware of a slightly paradoxical aspect of this kind of freedom. One convert said that he had experienced 'a feeling of great responsibility coupled with great elation and that a great burden had been lifted.'

I suspected that many (though by no means all) of the converts emphasized the importance of the teachings at the expense of the influence of the Moonies themselves. From talking to converts it seemed that this was because the Moonies were seen primarily as the vehicles through which the converts learned of the teachings which provided their 'real' reason for joining. Two of the pre-coded questions that I asked did, however, result in more weight being given to other factors. Table 7 shows the results of asking the respondents to use the numbers 1 to 5 to assess the *relative* influence of each of five factors but to put 0 beside any category which had been 'definitely of no importance in influencing you to join'. The responses from the American seminarians (several of whom joined in California) are included, as these differ slightly from the British responses. The (continental) Europeans were less likely to emphasize the importance

Table 7 At the time of joining, what do you remember as having made most impression on you?

		British members (%)						American seminarians (%)					
		1	2	3	4	5	0	1	2	3	4	5	0
The community life of the Family	1st	9						6					
	2nd		10						17				
	3rd			26						22			
	4th				25						25		
	5th					10						11	
	none at all						20						20
The members themselves	1st	22						26					
	2nd		31						23				
	3rd			23						25			
	4th				9						15		
	5th					3						—	
	none at all						12						11
The political position of the Family	1st	1						—					
	2nd		4						2				
	3rd			5						6			
	4th				5						2		
	5th					27						22	
	none at all						57						69
The Conclusion (that the Messiah is on earth)	1st	46						32					
	2nd		24						17				
	3rd			14						18			
	4th				10						8		
	5th					2						2	
	none at all						5						24
Any of the rest of the *Divine Principle*	1st	16						29					
	2nd		25						31				
	3rd			21						15			
	4th				21						12		
	5th					5						2	
	none at all						12						11

of the members, but more likely to place the 'Conclusion' (that the Messiah is on the earth) high in their list of priorities.

Table 8 records the relative impressions accorded to different parts of the *Divine Principle*, both when the respondent first heard the teachings,

Table 8 Which particular part of the *Divine Principle* made most impression on you when you first heard it; and which part is most important to you now?

		British members		American seminarians	
		Then	*Now*	*Then*	*Now*
		(%)	(%)	(%)	(%)
Chapter 1 (the Cosmology	Then	17		27	
and God's Plan)	Now		19		25
The Fall	Then	13		12	
	Now		14		20
The History	Then	15		28	
	Now		8		9
The Mission of Jesus	Then	23		22	
	Now		8		19
Spirit World	Then	2		3	
	Now		2		—[1]
The Conclusion	Then	28		8	
	Now		44		27
All[2]	Then	2		—[1]	
	Now		5		—[1]

Notes: [1] Less than 1 per cent. [2] Not a pre-coded option.

and at the time of filling in the questionnaire. Although I am not concerned in this book with the operation of the Principle once the converts have actually become Moonies, one reason why I have included these figures is in order to show how the importance of the 'Conclusion' significantly increases *after* joining. This, furthermore, supports my impression that, despite a wide-spread assumption to the contrary, people rarely join the Unification Church because of any charismatic qualities which Moon is personally perceived to have. Only a tiny handful of the converts had seen Moon before they joined the movement. Once they become members, however, it is, I believe, possible to detect a process, which I have come to think of as 'growth charisma', during which the members *learn* to see Moon as a charismatic figure.[5] In those cases in which the 'Conclusion' *was* considered particularly important at the time of joining, the reason was usually either an acceptance of the belief that the Messiah (rather than Moon as a charismatic leader) was on the earth and could help to bring the Kingdom of Heaven to earth or took the form of gratitude towards Moon for having revealed the *Divine Principle* and having suffered on our behalf, rather than a *personal* commitment to Moon – that came later. It is also interesting to note that the British (and other Europeans) were, and remained, more likely than the Americans to stress the importance of the Messiah, despite (or possibly because of) the fact that Moon is a more distant figure for those on the eastern side of the Atlantic.

It is possible that the relative importance of the *Divine Principle*'s

Moon in a relaxed mood.

chapter 1 (and the 'History') for the Americans reflects the stress on the social, rather than the religious, which is to be found during the early stages of initiation to the *Divine Principle* in California. Another interesting pattern in table 8 is that nearly a quarter of the respondents said that

Members expressing delight in watching 'Father'.

'True Parents' with two of their daughters and Mrs Choi (centre).

the Unification interpretation of the mission of Jesus had made the most impression on them when they first heard the Principle. Several members (particularly those who had been brought up as Catholics) have told me that they had always been worried about why Jesus had to die, because if he had brought salvation to the world, why were things still as bad as they were?

As can be seen, a significant minority of the converts were affected by the story of the Fall as an explanation for the troubles of the world. For some who had always tried to preserve strict moral (sexual) standards it was a relief to find others who shared their disgust at the permissiveness of the rest of society; for those who had been attempting to gain happiness through sexual relationships, the Principle's account of the Fall seemed to explain why they had not succeeded in achieving what they had sought. One young man wrote:

> I had heard the *Divine Principle*, but I was unaffected. Several days afterward I was engaged in a deep discussion with a girl with whom I had been living for one year. We had been very unhappy and several times had tried to find out why. On this occasion I felt very strongly that there was something important that we were both ashamed to talk about. I brought the subject into the open and realized the parallel with the UC teaching on Original Sin. I was dumbfounded, and then became intensely happy, with a sense of freedom. I felt

intoxicated. (This) experience caused me to join the Unification Church and gave me the strength to remain in UC despite many difficulties.

Over half the Moonies claimed that they had had a conversion experience which was often of a deeply religious or spiritual nature, and that it was this which had convinced them that they had to commit themselves to the movement.[6] For most of them the experience had lasted for between five minutes and half an hour, but for some it had lasted only for a few seconds, and for a few it had continued for several days. Some of the converts had had the experience while they were alone, but it was most likely to have occurred while they were listening to a lecture.

It is difficult to select examples of conversion experiences because they cover such a wide range of incidents and emotions. Some sound very dramatic in the telling, others much less so, but by the converts themselves these are all seen as important turning points in their lives. The first example is of a fairly typical 'quiet' experience which a British recruit described:

> When I first met someone from the Family in the street I decided to go to the centre that evening. I felt drawn to go there. When I arrived at the centre I felt very welcome by the members. I went upstairs to the lounge and heard a lecture on the first chapter. I immediately felt a deep peace and joy. I could accept the teachings in heart. When I went home I felt incredible joy and happiness and somehow I just knew God existed. I remember laying down in bed and didn't want to go to sleep in case the feeling would go away. The next morning I could still feel God's presence with me. I have never had such a wonderful experience in my life and it is on that basis that I could accept the existence of God.

Another British man wrote:

> When I actually heard 'conclusion' for the first time I had a rebirth experience completely intoxicated in love and joy – I even inspired my parents about God – in fact the whole week after the rebirth all I was talking about was God – my parents thought I'd gone crazy. But actually I was just so full of spirit, happy, singing, full of love. Amazing experience – I still feel it to this moment.

An American who had been praying for guidance for a 'sign' as to whether the movement 'was God's will for me', wrote:

> I was deep in prayer with my eyes firmly closed and my head touching the earth, then there was a flash of white light (it was a very

cloudy day) and I felt great peace, tranquility, as if my prayer had
been heard. Another brother who was also praying experienced the
same at the same time and felt the same way.

Not all the experiences were entirely pleasurable. Some felt that something was definitely happening to them, but they were unsure just what or
why it was. One convent who said 'The "Conclusion" made me want to
run away. I was scared', declared that during the experience of conversion
'I felt like I was falling off a cliff and couldn't see whether I was going to
land on soft or hard ground. So I just closed my eyes and reached out for
my spiritual parent.'

Quite a number of converts say that they dreamed about Moon, and that
it was this that had made them decide them to join. There were also a few
who claimed to have dreamed about him before they knew about either
him or the Unificatio Church. One American convert described the
following experience:

before meeting Rev. Moon . . . I had another dream of Jesus. He
was standing behind Rev. Moon. Rev. Moon's head was covered in
white clouds, but now I know it was him because I know the way he
is built. Anyway, he opened up his arms and spiritually directed me
to come to him. He embraced me, and for the first time in my entire
life I felt like I had found my true home. I woke up crying because of
the love I felt.

As I mentioned in chapter 1, Moonies have sometimes told me that
there was little point to my research because the real explanation for their
presence in the Unification Church was that God, or the spirit world, had
guided them there. I do not question the contention that those who report
undergoing a religious conversion have, in fact, had an unusual experience. There is, however, no way in which I can know whether or not it was
God who was responsible for their experiences or for 'guiding' their lives
in the way that the majority of the members claimed to know that He had.
But I would like to make the point that although Moonies may believe that
their experiences directly accounted (or had previously prepared them) for
their conversion, this does not preclude the possibility that the *interpretation* of their experience has been strongly influenced by others. Indeed,
one interesting finding which resulted from my asking non-Moonies about
their spiritual experiences was that when those who had been members of
a religious group at the time of the experience but had since left were
asked for their explanations both then and now, a significant number of
respondents admitted that they had believed at the time that they were
having a religious experience, but had subsequently come to the conclusion that it had been their imagination or the result of some mundane

trigger. Conversely, those who had *since* become part of a religious community were more likely to say that they had dismissed the experience at the time, but now realized that God had been talking to them. Such findings do not, of course, imply that people believe only what 'fits into' a particular social context. Some people clearly cling to beliefs that are, socially, extremely uncomfortable to hold. But the fact that the people concerned *can* alter their own understanding of God's role in their lives, and that a substantial number (though by no means all) of the ex-Moonies now deny the Unification interpretation of their experiences, suggests that there remains a case for investigating the strength and efficacy of social pressures in such matters. It is, in other words, at least possible that someone who believes that he is being guided by God is, in fact, being guided or even coerced into that belief by others.

Sometimes it is the suddenness and unexpectedness of a conversion experience which, on the one hand, convinces the Moonie that it must have been the result of God's intervention, or, on the other hand, convinces those who knew him before that it could only have been sophisticated brainwashing techniques which were responsible for the recruit's 'snapping'.[7] As I suggested in chapter 5, I am not persuaded that either of these arguments necessarily follows.

One 'sudden conversion' which I witnessed occurred quite early on in my study, but I was already priding myself that I had become fairly adept at distinguishing the 'possibles' from the 'no-ways'. Although she had confided in me that she was unconvinced by the *Divine Principle*, I had selected Mary as the most likely 'possible' and had been carefully observing her reactions for two days. Then, during the final lecture which revealed the 'Conclusion' that the Messiah was on earth, I suddenly felt convinced that she had 'seen the light'. 'Mary's gone?', I scribbled in my notes. She was sitting bolt-upright in her chair, transfixed, as though in another world.

At the end of the lecture she said that she had had a strange experience: suddenly everything had fallen into place and she had realized that she was hearing the most wonderful truth. She insisted that she knew the precise point in the lecture at which the realization had occurred. I was surprised to find that this had been as much as fifteen minutes *after* I had noted my observation. On two subsequent occasions I have thought I saw 'something' happening and subsequently learned that the guest had experienced a sudden conversion around that time – or, rather, a few minutes after I had noticed the transformation.

I cannot explain this phenomenon, but I am unconvinced that sudden conversion is as discontinuous as it might appear. First of all, there appears to be a very definite 'lead-up' to the experience, even though the converts themselves may not be aware of it; secondly, those who undergo sudden conversion appear to have more characteristics in common with other (non-sudden-conversion) Moonies than with the non-joiners; thirdly, there is an observable period of consolidation after the event, during which the gaps in the new vision are filled in.

The range and distribution of the responses to the workshop questionnaire mirrored the range and distribution of responses that I have observed at workshops. In sum, the vast majority of the guests considered that the members were pleasant, dedicated and sincere; but they also thought that the Moonies were misguidedly giving up their lives for a belief system which, although it possibly contained quite a lot of truth, should not be swallowed in its entirety – especially with respect to its messianic belief and its millenarian promise. There were also two minority groups, one accepting what the Unification Church seemed to offer and joining the movement, the other rejecting it completely with accusations that the movement was evil and dangerous.

These data suggest a need to put into perspective some of the more sensational reports by people who boast of how they 'felt themselves being drawn into the Moonies' clutches, but just managed to escape in the nick of time' or allegations that 'no one is immune to their psychological coercion'.[8] It can be argued, quite legitimately, that not all the guests will have attended *exactly* the same workshop. Different guests and, to a lesser extent, different Moonies will be present on different occasions. Such variations, however, cannot account for the systematic diversity of guests' reactions to the workshops. I hope that the descriptions and the arguments which I have presented will, by now, have convinced the reader that several of the reasons adduced by their opponents to show that Moonies brainwash their victims are little short of fatuous. But there are some accusations which do deserve more serious consideration. The next chapter is devoted to a closer look at the effects of environmental control, deception and 'love-bombing'.

7 Environmental Control, Deception and 'Love-Bombing'

In the last chapter we saw that the Moonies clearly could not control all, or even most, of their guests' interpretations of their workshop experiences. It is, nevertheless, possible that they could deprive certain people, who brought certain characteristics to the workshop, of at least some of their capacity to make an active choice in the light of their predispositions and past experiences. While there did not seem to be any evidence to support the existence of differential *biological* susceptibilities to the physical effects of the workshop, differential *psychological* susceptibility to the social effects of the workshop might yet explain why some guests joined while others did not. We shall turn our attention to the kinds of susceptibilities which the converts seemed to have in chapters 8 and 9, but in this chapter we shall look a bit more closely at some of the ways in which the workshops might have had a coercive influence on at least some of the guests.

First, to highlight the practices with which I shall be particularly concerned, let me quote part of a 'testimony' which was given by a girl who had been involved in the recruitment practices in Oakland. Her remarks are followed by the comments made by Ken Sudo, the then Director of Training at the Barrytown International Training Center, who was in charge of the training course in which the girl was participating.

> Onni taught us that we have to be happy-makers. She said that the purpose of life is joy so you must be very joyful all the time and in Oakland it is that way when you walk in the house. Everyone is very joyful. We sing songs and we sing them three times faster than you do here [in Barrytown, New York]. She emphasizes not so much the truth at first, but that you must really love people. You must 'love-bomb' them. Onni has a staff of about twelve people who are the best 'love-bombers' in the whole world. Sometimes when I would be having trouble with one of my guests – they were not responding – I could give one of them a look and they would come

over. Their ability wasn't in anything they said but it was in loving that person. Finally the person's heart would melt and he or she would sign up for a training session. Onni . . . would assign one person to each new member [sic] and we had to do everything for that person: we couldn't leave them for a second. We even followed them to the bathroom and back, and we did everything for them first. So many members never really came because of me but mostly because of the things that Onni taught us. The kind of love she showed us and the kind of standard.

MR SUDO: What she described is the key to success in witnessing and it has been put into practice in Oakland. . . . Love must have been the secret of success. Love is more important than truth. How to be the source of love is a big job and it takes a long time. It is difficult to be like Onni immediately. Her secret is love for Father.[1]

Most of us have probably had the experience of not being able to make up our minds over some tricky issue – perhaps how we should vote at a meeting – and have found ourselves swayed one way or the other according to the person who has last spoken. Most of us have probably also felt discomfort at being the odd one out when everyone else seems to be seeing things in a different light. We may have begun to suspect that we were wrong.[2] However, some of us have occasionally experienced the sudden amazement of realizing that a particular perspective which we had taken for granted throughout our lives might not, after all, be the only way of looking at things (perhaps because no one in our previous environment had ever questioned it).

There can be little doubt that the Moonies are successful in controlling the environment of their workshops. It is, after all, their home ground. They do not put decisions about the day's timetable to the vote. Everyone is expected to attend the lectures and other activities; if the guests do not want to fit in, they are asked to leave – not to find a friend with whom to make alternative arrangements for the afternoon. Guests seldom have the opportunity to get together to reinforce each other's doubts. The near-constant presence of enthusiastic Moonies means also that conversations are kept from becoming too critical or from wandering too far off the point, and, in California especially, it also ensures that the lectures and other activities are met with such seemingly unanimous 'Isn't-this-all-wonderful?' responses that it can be difficult for the guest not to feel exhilarated and drawn into following the example of the Moonie 'cheerleaders' – an effective practice, but by no means one which is unique to the Unification church. David Taylor aptly describes this aspect of the Boonville seminars which he attended as 'the choreography of Total Participation'.[3] Furthermore, by asking the guests to write down comments, and by taking them on one side to ask them what their reactions are, the Moonies can, on the one hand, discover and try to deal with negative responses and, on the other hand, find out what appeals to each particular guest so that positive reactions can be reinforced and 'objectified'.[4]

The intensity of contact and the speed with which converts join are, generally speaking, greater the further west one travels, the Scandinavians being most likely to deliberate by themselves for some time, and the Californians having the minimum non-Moonie contact between meeting and joining the movement. Despite the fact that some people take several years of private study before deciding to join, it is clear that the vast majority of Moonies join after a remarkably short, intense exposure to the Unification Church – most members having joined within a few weeks of meeting the movement,[5] and about a third (more in America, fewer in Europe) having very little or no time to consider the situation in a different social context or to discuss it with others.[6] Nevertheless, about half the Europeans and Americans and three-fifths of the British Moonies did discuss their decision to join with someone outside the movement. Most commonly this was with parents, but often it was with a friend, and sometimes it was with several people. The reason most frequently given for not discussing it was that it was the individual's own decision and that he had to make up his own mind. A fairly typical explanation was: 'I felt it was something which I had to work out for myself. Actually I felt a great responsibility to join the Family – we [the young of today] have to make a move in order to make any changes in this world.' Others said that no one would have understood; quite a few said that they had never even thought about telling anyone else; and 9 per cent said that they were too far from home to make contact. However, it is probable that quite a few guests were actively dissuaded from contacting friends or parents by the Moonies, especially those who met the movement in California where they could have been told that other people 'wouldn't understand', or, if contact was made by telephone, there could have been a 'staff member' nearby to 'support' the guest as he tried to explain to his worried parents that he would be staying for just a bit longer with 'this wonderful group of people I've met'.

Those who *did* talk to others generally met with negative reactions which ranged from horror, fear, amazement and disbelief to mild concern. One in ten claimed that the people whom they had told were delighted; and just under one in ten said that their parents (or other contact) had expressed misgivings, but had also added that they trusted the respondent to know what he was doing; but most of those who did discuss it were advised not to join the movement. A small minority reported having received threats of reprisal if they joined; and a few (five of the British

Moonies) said that they had been subjected to physical coercion in an attempt to prevent their joining. Not surprisingly, it was parents who were most likely to have tried to dissuade their children, but attempts were also made by friends, other relations or clergy and, in 6 per cent of the cases, by a spouse or girl/boyfriend. A fairly typical account of a convert's experiences with his family comes from a French member who was a few days off his twenty-sixth birthday when he joined the movement:

> About three weeks after joining the family I met my two brothers, my sister-in-law and a friend in my brother's apartment near Paris. . . . One of my brother[s] is [a] priest and came from the south especially to see me. They tried to dissuade me about my decision. I stayed about three days with them. . . . Of course they showed me a lot of negatif [*sic*] articles about the family life, the brainwashing method. None of these articles I could really relate to. I explained to them how I met the family, the reasons I joined. . . .

As it is a feature which affects life *within* the movement rather than the conversion *to* it, I do not discuss the 'totalism' of the Unification ideology in any detail in this book. It must, nevertheless, be acknowledged that in so far as the potential recruit finds his environment controlled by Moonies in such a way that he cannot (or at least finds it difficult to) 'check out' what he has been seeing and hearing with people who would put forward an alternative point of view, he will undoubtedly be under pressure to see things from the Unification perspective. But, as we have already seen, this is not pressure which the majority of people cannot resist. The vast majority of people *do* resist it. In the next chapter we shall be asking what kind of susceptibility it is that seems to differentiate those who become Moonies from those who do not, but first let us look more closely at those aspects of the Unification environment which have come to be known as 'heavenly deception' and 'love-bombing'.[7]

The concept of 'heavenly deception' is one which causes considerable embarrassment to most Moonies. It is not part of the official theology of the movement, but some members have undoubtedly become persuaded that the end can justify the means in a number of areas, including recruitment. The justification which is most frequently quoted is the biblical account of the deception employed by Jacob when he stole Esau's birthright.[8] So far as recruitment practices are concerned, I would like to distinguish between (1) deception which involves suppression or denial of the fact that the proselytizers are members of the Reverend Moon's Unification Church, (2) deception concerning the beliefs and practices of the movement, and (3) deception with reference to 'love-bombing'.

As we have seen, Moonies have not always disclosed their connection with the Unification Church to potential recruits. Although by no means complete on the subject, my data suggest that during the late 1970s, roughly a third of the guests had learned of the Moon connection immediately on meeting a member; another third found out within a comparatively short space of time (within half an hour, or at least by the time that they had heard a lecture), but the final third did not realise that they were with Moon's Unification Church until they had heard several lectures or, in some (mainly Californian) cases, until they had actually joined the movement. The question that concerns us here is not one of straightforward, moral condemnation (although I certainly do condemn deception), but in what ways the evasion of revealing the Moon connection could contribute to the success of Unification recruitment.

Returning to the language of our model, an individual might make a different choice between the two alternatives (joining the movement or continuing as before) according to whether or not he knows he is with the Moonies. As I indicated in chapter 5, if the guest has not been told, we could say that, although he had been deceived, he is still *capable* of making up his own mind. In practice, however, it does not necessarily follow that, once the truth is revealed to him, he will simply change his mind in much the same way that we would expect a man to get off a bus as soon as he finds out that it is not going in the direction in which he thought it was at the time that he decided to board it. It is, after all, possible that the man might, in the meantime, have been persuaded by his fellow passengers that the direction (the route and the terminus – the way and the end) was preferable to the direction in which he had (possibly without much enthusiasm) originally intended to travel.

It has frequently been suggested that the deception provides time during which the guest will become so affected (or infected) by the Unification alternative that when he does eventually find out it is too late for him to be able to change. From the Unification point of view, it is the media and the movement's opponents who are the main perpetrators of misinformation. Moonies, or at least some of their number, will argue that the guest will not have been 'brainwashed' in the interim – he will, if anything, have been 'deprogrammed'; he will, they argue, have had the time – the opportunity (which would otherwise have been denied him) – to discover for himself what the Unification Church is *really* like, and that the scary stories which he had been told about the movement are either unfounded or grossly exaggerated.

Either, or even both, of these arguments may contain some truth, but, without any clear, independent evidence that the guest was either capable or incapable of making a choice at the time he discovered who his hosts were, the 'he-was-deceived-therefore-he-was-brainwashed' hypothesis is in danger of becoming no more than another question-begger. We have yet to explain why the majority will still leave after they have discovered the truth, and why yet others will join without ever having been deceived. While just over half the non-joiners said that they knew of the Moon connection before attending a workshop, nearly two-thirds of the joiners claimed that they had known; and, while it might be suspected that Moonies would be more likely to claim that they had known when in fact they had not, this could hardly be said to apply to those who left, yet exactly the same proportion of the leavers also said that they had known. This might lend support to the position of an East Coast Moonie who told me that she always insisted that those in her charge should reveal who they were and the kinds of things they believed in, not just because she happened to disapprove strongly of any kind of deception, but also because one could waste a great deal of time with people who were not really interested. It was, she said, better to sort out the sheep from the goats as quickly as possible.

In other words, the fact that a guest does not at first know who his hosts are might mean that (like the 'networkers') he pursues the path towards Unificationism further than he might otherwise have done, but there is no evidence that, once he has found out what the movement seems to be offering, he is any more likely to become a Moonie than those who are not so 'helped' – it is, in fact, possible that he is one of those who are less likely to join (having been 'falsely selected' in the first place). I am not suggesting that the deception itself will make him *less* likely to join (although this could occasionally happen – see p. 102): on the contrary, I argue below that extra time used for, and gained by the creation of friendships *can* make a difference. I am, however, suggesting that such 'extra time' can 'work' only in those cases where the guest would have joined had he not been deceived, but had previously never heard of the Unification Church or its leader. My argument is that the negative publicity which the movement has received could stop someone from becoming a Moonie (and deception might bypass such an obstacle); but this particular type of deception will not, in itself, *result* in his joining the movement.

Thus far I have been talking about deception which occurs when members have not revealed that they are Moonies. A different form of deception can lie in a failure to disclose the true nature of the movement to potential members. Moonies are unlikely to present their guests with statements such as, 'Moon has had at least two, and possibly as many as five wives. He lives in the lap of luxury, and has control over an enormous amount of money', or 'The movement has been the subject of close scrutiny by various government agencies', or 'A large number of our members become disillusioned and leave.' Nor is the guest likely to hear about the whole spectrum of Unification beliefs and practices. Some information is for members only. The potential recruit might be allowed to think that the food distribution to deprived people in California or the medical assistance given to the sick in Zaïre is more extensive than is in fact the case. He is unlikely fully to understand the amount of time that he will be expected to spend on fund-raising; and while Moonies will certainly tell their guests that building a better world demands blood, sweat, tears and toil from those who have accepted the responsibility, this can be made to sound like an exciting challenge rather than a gruesome warning for those who have become convinced that the Unification Church can achieve such a goal.

It is also true, however, that it is not only Moonies, but believers of all sorts of religions who are anxious that others should be privy to their own particular brand of Truth, who will present their beliefs in ways which they feel are most likely to 'get through' to those whom they can persuade to listen. One rarely finds evangelists of any faith eagerly divulging the more esoteric or the less edifying aspects of their ideologies, their institutions or their leader's lives. Most religions have some skeletons in their cupboards and, at least in the early stages, they tend to hold to certain inner gnoses. It is not uncommon for the poor and needy to receive only a small proportion of the money raised by various religions (and secular charities) which concentrate more on the task of evangelizing[9] or looking after their own.

Even a thousand wrongs do not, of course, make a right, but leaving aside for the moment the question of 'love-bombing', and given the far from perfect standards which generally prevail (and, indeed, have prevailed throughout history) when those of a particular persuasion wish to gain the sympathy and acceptance of others, it is probably true to say that the factual information which Moonies give their guests is usually a fairly accurate account of what the overwhelming majority of members do *themselves* believe to be the truth. Even deprogrammed members who have come to believe that they were brainwashed, will usually attest to the sincerity of most rank-and-file Moonies and concede that, on the whole, the workshops give a correct (albeit a selective and somewhat rose-tinted) account of Unification theology and the goals which the members are hoping to achieve. Whether the beliefs are in fact true, and whether the goals are actually attainable by the means which the movement espouses, are, of course, completely different questions.[10] It is, however, the case that a considerable proportion of Moonies leave once they discover that they no longer believe that the Unification alternative lives up to its promise. Some of these leavers will say that they were deceived; others will say that it was not so much deceit as a genuine but subsequently unfulfilled hope, that had led them first to join and then to leave the movement.

There can be no doubt that Moonies shower their guests with an unusual degree of friendliness. The question is, does this friendliness constitute, or contribute to, coercion? In our society being nice to people is generally considered a virtue rather than a vice; loving one's neighbour is a – if not *the* – fundamental social principle underlying Christianity. What about love-bombing one's neighbour?

There are, of course, instances in which one becomes suspicious of too much friendliness, especially from people whom one does not really know but has reason to believe have an interest in gaining one's confidence. In such instances over-effusive overtures can be counter-productive. The gushing sales assistant is unlikely to sell me anything once she has informed me how elegant I look in a dress which is two sizes too small. But most of us do, none the less, feel more relaxed and trusting in what appears to be a friendly, caring environment; we are, other things being equal, more likely to have our defences down and to be open to new suggestions – and many Moonies have testified that it was the smiling faces, the happy atmosphere or the loving community which first attracted them to the Unification Church (see table 7, p. 164).

Before considering the possible effects of love-bombing, there is a red herring which ought to be cleared out of the way: this is the suggestion that the Moonies manipulate their guests so that the guests are actually *coerced into* responding with affection. Most of the literature on the brainwashing of prisoners of war has included comment on how the prisoners have sometimes developed feelings of affection towards their captors, and how this contributed to their eventual conversion.[11] It is, however, quite obvious that the kind of treatment to which the prisoners were subjected was totally different from that to which the guests at a Unification workshop are subjected. Prisoners do not agree to be locked up because they think that their captors are rather nice or interesting people; their initial reactions to their captors (and what they stand for) are, typically, fear, resentment and/or hatred; the affection is not manifested until *after* the prisoners have been reduced to a state in which they have experienced the emotions of helplessness, hopelessness and loneliness.

Various explanations have been put forward to account for this surprising phenomenon of loving one's persecutor. According to Sargant, for example, the prisoners have been pushed to a state in which 'abnormal brain activity' has been induced;[12] another theory is that 'human beings need warmth and attention from at least someone, and if the interrogator is the only one around to provide it, then his will have to do.'[13] It is obvious, however, that such explanations rely on the decidedly unloving behaviour that was previously meted out to the prisoner. If a guest at a Unification workshop were to be in such a state that he was literally forced to accept the friendship which the Moonies offered him, then it would have to have been his experiences *before* he attended the workshop that had reduced him to such a desperate plight.

However, as I mentioned earlier, it has also been argued that the Moonies' recruitment techniques constitute extra-super-plus-brainwashing because of the very fact that they *start* by overwhelming their guests with affection. Just how effective is this practice? It has long been recognized that the existence of an 'affective bond' can play a crucial – some have claimed a necessary – role in the process of recruitment. Lofland and Stark, in their analysis of conversion into the Unification Church in the early 1960s, wrote:

> If persons. . . are to be further drawn down the road to full conversion, an affective bond must develop, if one does not already exist, between the potential recruit and one or more of the. . . members. The development or presence of some positive emotional, interpersonal response seems necessary to bridge the gap between first exposure of the [Unification] message and accepting its truth. . . . Final conversion was coming to accept the opinion of one's friends.[14]

Can this be said to constitute some kind of coercion?

Returning to the earlier discussion of what choice (or lack of choice) might entail, we now have to ask whether love-bombing could remove or diminish the guest's capacity to draw on his own experiences and dispositions; could his new-found friends be acting as reinterpreters to the extent that he has become incapable of seeing things in the way he would otherwise see them? The key word is, of course, 'incapable'; and the key question is, how can we determine whether someone has lost the capacity to draw on his past experiences because he has been love-bombed?

As we have already seen, the affection displayed at the Unification workshops has produced a variety of responses. On the one hand, some guests have reacted quite forcefully against what they saw as the over-effusiveness of the Unification approach; on the other hand, there have been guests who were attracted by (some even believed that they had fallen in love with) Moonies, yet, despite this, they decided not to join the movement. In other words, it seems clear that love-bombing is not an irresistible technique which inevitably secures conversion – even in those instances in which the affection is both accepted and reciprocated. There were, furthermore, some joiners who strongly denied that their conversion had been influenced by the members. One man described a religious experience in which he had heard the voice of God about a month before he met the movement. He claimed that God had told him that he would work for the Messiah to realize the Kingdom of Heaven. He had given up the career he had planned and was trying to find out about various religious movements. It was, he said, the 'Conclusion' which decided him to become a member: 'I wasn't so impressed by the people, I still am not

Happy Family games on a Holy Day.

Enjoying Creation.

(there [*sic*] probably not so impressed by me so it's mutual). I have been previously very individualistic and it was the DP that struck me most. The Truth. In the Family the ideal still has to be realized. The members are not perfect. This is obvious.'

At this point we ought, perhaps, to rehearse a couple of arguments

INTERNATIONAL ONE WORLD CRUSADE

••••MAKING REAL
THE FAMILY OF MAN

An IOWC leaflet promising the realization of the family of man.

which were discussed in chapter 5. First, we must, once again, be careful not to lapse into tautology: as conversion can be defined as 'a radical reorganization of identity, meaning, life',[15] we cannot just observe a radical change and conclude, without further evidence, that it has come about merely because the convert has been love-bombed. Secondly, we have to bear in mind that there is a sense in which our very existence as social beings depends upon our acceptance of the perspectives of others. Generally speaking, the younger we are, the less we question other people's (usually our parents') view of the world. The maxim attributed to Ignatius de Loyola ('Give me a child to the age of 7, and I shall have that child all his life'), while not infallible, has enough truth in it to make a telling point when one considers the relative likelihood of successfully influencing a person's beliefs at different periods in his life. As we grow older and alternative perspectives become available, we learn to accept or reject fresh ideas, usually in the light of our previously formed dispositions. There are many different reasons why we may find one alternative more attractive than another, one reason being that someone whom we like, admire or respect happens to see things in a particular way, and we decide to trust that person's judgement. The person may, of course, be unworthy of that trust; he may be deceiving us into thinking that he believes or feels something which he does not; or he himself may be misguided and may have faulty judgement which appears to us to have a more forceful backing than it has, possibly because of the sincerity with which his belief seems to be held.

Converts who admit to having been influenced by the affectionate attention showered upon them at the workshops say that they were prepared to trust the Moonies because they looked so happy together. They seemed to have answers which worked, and even if they did not have *all* the answers, at least they seemed to know how to create a loving, caring community. If one had the opportunity of becoming part of such a community, then, the guest might be prompted to think, why not go along with the general perspective which seemed to generate such a good and happy environment? One such instance was reported by one of my interviewees:

> When I got there it was very late on a Friday night and, although they were clearing up from a huge dinner, the girls in the kitchen stopped everything to make me a meal. That was a very nice kindness, not out of duty because they had to, but because they wanted to. I can't really explain it. I just knew. It was no one thing. I just felt inside that that was what I wanted, that this was what I want to do. I can honestly say I didn't understand the teaching, but the history – I could see that there was a purpose or plan working through history. I had tried other ways and I knew that they wouldn't work, and although I didn't understand the teaching completely I felt that I wanted to try it out. At least give it an

opportunity to work. I didn't realize then what I realize now. In a way it was a leap of faith for me to join.

Not that he was entirely without misgivings:

Basically I felt a great love and warmth from all sides and I couldn't understand why they were so loving and warm. Why were they so serving? At times I found it a bit oppressive, it was too much for me at some times. I couldn't understand why they were doing it because I'd never met Christians like that before. They were talking about changing the world. Other Christians always talk about the Bible and believing in Jesus Christ and believing faith would do it – and I believed that that wasn't going to do it at all.

There seems little doubt that many such potential recruits have been influenced by similar attentions, and that the friendly atmosphere can be a major factor in persuading people to join the movement. But, we may still ask, can this be classified as undue coercion? About a year after our interview, the Moonie whom I have just quoted left the movement, mainly because he no longer found that he was getting along with the members, and he had become disillusioned with several of the leaders. Could it not be argued that it is perfectly reasonable to *choose* to join a group of people who seem to be unusually friendly and loving - and, if one were later to discover that the members were not noticeably more loving or lovable than other people, equally rational to decide to leave?

In fact, the story is not quite as simple as that. Although I do not believe that we need to resort to theories of brainwashing or mind-control to understand why someone could be attracted to a life in which there is more happiness and love, we might be sceptical about whether the Unification alternative really does consist of a life of more love. We may well want to know whether the love-bombing is a deceptive device, used to trick the unsuspecting recruit into developing emotional ties from which he will find it difficult to extricate himself. Finding out about the movement's connection with Moon, or even about its beliefs and practices, involves a fairly straightforward 'know or don't know' act of cognition. It is possible that the 'deception-allows-Moonies-time-to-hook-their-victims' argument has most cogency when it refers to a period during which friendships are developed. Finding out what a relationship really means to the other person, or what one is prepared to do for the sake of perpetuating that relationship, can be a process fraught with ambiguity and ambivalence. As Unification theology itself declares, love is a very powerful force – and the misuse of love can be just as powerful.

As one might expect, the genuineness of the affection which the

Moonies display at workshops varies from individual to individual. Moonies – especially those who joined the movement because of the loving environment which they themselves had experienced at a workshop – tend to be people who set considerable store by the value of love and friendship (see table 14, p. 230). Unification theology exhorts everyone to try to look at other people from God's point of view in order to find what it is that He would value in even the least obviously attractive of His children, and there is no doubt that many Moonies do try hard to do this in their relationships with others. It is also true, however, that the Unification Church considers its primary goal to be the restoration of the Kingdom of Heaven on earth, and while this is certainly seen to involve loving and caring for one's fellow humans, it also involves having to secure certain scarce resources – in particular, the movement has to rely upon the non-Moonie world, which it is hoping to transform, for new recruits and for economic viability.[16] Thus while the Moonies are certainly expected to make potential recruits (and influential people) feel loved and cared for, they are not expected to 'waste' too much valuable time on those who show no interest in the work of restoration. God may see something of value in everyone, but for the committed member of the Unification Church those who have the most value are those who are prepared to sacrifice their lives for His sake – which, in practical terms, means accepting the truth of God's divine Principle, and, of course, following the leadership of the Messiah.

It is always difficult – even for the person concerned – to know what the 'real' motive behind any action is. There are undoubtedly some, particularly those in leadership positions, who calculate the effects of love-bombing merely in terms of increasing membership figures which, in turn, are calculated in terms of increasing the number of fund-raisers in the field. The potential recruit becomes a potential means by which to achieve the millennial goal; love of individual men and women is reduced to a method of establishing the Kingdom of Love for Mankind.[17] Another factor that ought to be mentioned is that there is a certain amount of status attached within the movement to acquiring 'spiritual children'. Those who bring new recruits to the movement, and thereby become spiritual parents, are assumed to learn to grow in their capacity for love as they look after their spiritual son or daughter. It is, indeed, a rule (in theory, if not always in practice) that a blessed couple cannot 'start a family' (that is, consummate their marriage) until each partner has at least three spiritual children.

Most Moonies would, however, be genuinely shocked at the suggestion that they are being deceptive when they offer their guests affection. They would not only protest that they *ought* to love them as people (and many undoubtedly do develop a genuine affection for some of their guests), they would also be convinced that it is in the guest's own interests (as well as the interests of the world) for him to become a Moonie. The Moonie might, furthermore, argue that offering affection to a potential convert is less wrong and certainly no more manipulative than Calvinist parents or Catholic nuns frightening children with stories about hell fire and eternal damnation,[18] and that the picture which Moonies present to their guests of a loving community is not all that different from – possibly even less extreme than – the exuberant enthusiasms displayed by some born-again Christians.

Not surprisingly (for those of us who are not Moonies), life as a member of the Unification Church is far from a bed of roses. I have argued elsewhere that there is an apparently inexorable 'socio-logic' whereby the actual practice of 'doing love' is, in a number of ways, counter-productive.[19] For example, the more the Moonie tries to change the world to the ideal of unified units of God-centred families, the more he finds himself disrupting his own family life. This is a discussion which takes us far beyond the brief that I have set myself for this book, but there are two more points which I would like to make that do assume some knowledge of life within the Unification Church. The first of these is merely the obvious one that it is perfectly possible to believe that the Unification alternative does not 'work' in the way in which most Moonies expect it to without necessarily believing that all, or even the majority of Moonies, are being deceptive in their belief that it does or could work if only they (and others) tried harder. The second point is more substantial. It is that, although the evidence clearly indicates that neither the love-bombing nor any of the practices of the workshop is sufficiently effective to ensure that 'anyone' can be made into a Moonie against his will, and although I would be more inclined to apply the label 'mistaken' than that of 'deceptive' to the majority of rank-and-file Moonies, it is none the less clear that friendships formed at the workshop can play a role which is crucial to some conversions, and thus provide a path to membership of a community which differs decisively from the pluralistic environment of most of Westerns society. Like many religious orders, the Unification Church is an organization within which there is only one prevailing world view and some of the features of the 'total institution' can be observed.[20] This in itself can be an attraction to people who might choose to be a member of a (relatively) 'closed' community, rather than coping with the uncertainties of the wider society; but such organizations can also limit the options available for those who, were it not for the existence of some kind of 'affective bond', might well prefer to inhabit a more 'open' environment.

In other words, there are those who choose (in the light of their dispositions and previous experiences) to become members of the Unification Church because they are attracted to the 'loving community', but who will leave once they discover that Moonies can be as unloving as other people; but there are also those who, through their freely chosen acceptance of the loving community, find themselves bound to the movement by feelings of being needed and of not wanting to let down their friends, the Church, or God. The rhetoric – and the reality – of friendship and loyalty can be used to exert considerable pressure upon the Moonie to fall into line. In much the same way as 'ordinary' love can blind someone to faults in his loved one, so sometimes will Moonies close their eyes, at least for a while, to at least some of the practices which would probably have kept them out of the movement had they not already been attracted by the vision (and, indeed, the experience) of love and friendship which they had encountered at the workshop. Allied to this process is the one in which loyalty to individuals can be translated into loyalty to the group, especially when the group is as tightly bound as is the Unification Church.[21] These, however, are phenomena which one cannot hope to observe, or even begin to understand, if one has already committed oneself to the theory that Moonies are unthinking, insensitive robots who are wound up each morning before being sent out on their current mission by an omniscient and omnipotent master.

As I have already intimated, we cannot expect to understand the ways in which an organization like the Unification Church functions (or fails to function) unless we first understand something about the human resources with which it has to operate, and, as I have sought to argue in the last three chapters, we need to take into account the previous experiences and previously formed dispositions of the guests if we are to understand why some people are attracted while others remain immune to the Unification alternative. In the next two chapters we shall turn our attention to the 'raw material' of the potential recruit in an attempt to discover the kind of susceptibility which the convert 'brings with him' to the workshop.

8 Suggestibility

The discussion in chapter 5 probably made it clear that, as a sociologist, I believe that the social environment has a very important role to play in influencing the behaviour of men and women. People who find themselves in one social context will behave very differently from people in another. Furthermore, people who *come from* different social environments will react in different ways when placed in the same social environment. Once that is acknowledged, however, we still have the problem of deciding *which* environmental influences are in operation at any particular time.

Let us return for a moment to our definition of choice. I suggested that 'a person would be an active agent in deciding between two or more possible options when he could anticipate their potential existence, and when, in doing so, he drew upon his previous experience and his previously-formed values and interests to guide his judgment' (see p. 137). From this I argued that we would have to consider four variables if we wanted to judge whether someone had made a choice: (1) the individual concerned; (2) and (3) the alternatives (in this case remaining outside or joining the Unification Church); and (4) the social context within which the decision was reached.

Thus far, I have argued that the suggestion that the social context is the exclusively important variable in deciding whether or not someone becomes a Moonie just does not stand up to the evidence. The high rate of rejection and the enormous variety of responses to the Unification workshop point to the importance of variables *brought to* the immediate situation. It is possible, none the less, that, although the persuasive techniques of the workshop are not such as to prevent most people from making a choice, the techniques are such that they *take advantage of* certain individuals who *already* have a severely limited capacity to 'be an active agent in deciding . . .' This chapter is thus concerned primarily with the situation that I labelled 'psychological susceptibility', but also, to some extent, with the 'refuge from society' situation. But, first, let me clarify some of the distinctions between these and the final two situations characterized in table 4.

Some Unification (or Unification associated) publications.

Information or Persuasion?

The Unification workshop has, in effect, two major functions. One (stressed by the Moonies) is to inform; the other (stressed by their opponents) is to persuade. Given that we have to explain a differential rate (why some people become Moonies and others do not), we can now ask whether what the joiners bring with them is an unusually high *susceptibility to persuasion*, or an unusually high *susceptibility to the information*. That is, do people become Moonies (1) because they are more open to suggestion than non-joiners (and would join practically anything in such a social environment), or (2) because they are more attracted to the alternative which the Unification Church offers them?

Of course, the distinction can be only a theoretical one. A few people might join the Unification Church whatever its beliefs and practices, and some people have joined after months of studying the *Divine Principle* by themselves, but the majority of Moonies are likely to have been influenced by a combination of both the beliefs and the persuasiveness of the environment. How, then, can we unscramble the sort of susceptibility which Moonies are most likely to have brought to the workshop?

For reasons which have already been presented, we cannot rely on the opinions of individual Moonies or non-joiners, nor on their subjective reactions to the workshops if we want to find an answer to this particular question. We also have to recognize that the *post hoc* statement 'Because Jonathan became a Moonie, he must have been particularly suggestible' is no less question-begging than the statement, 'Because he became a Moonie, he must have been brainwashed.' The first statement merely allows that Jonathan's susceptibility is not necessarily universal; it still denies, without any independent evidence, the possibility that Jonathan may have found the Unification Church alternative more attractive than any other, and that he may have made an informed, free (active) choice to join.

One way in which we might try to assess the relative strength of the two variables (the attraction of the Unification Church alternative and the persuasiveness of the social environment) could be to conduct an experiment in which one control group was presented with a variety of non-Unificationist beliefs during a Unificationist-type workshop, and another control group was presented with Unificationist beliefs in a variety of environments controlled by, say, Catholics, academics, the military, friends and relations – or no one at all. But, quite apart from the well-nigh insuperable methodological problems which would be encountered, I do not believe such an artificial experiment would be very helpful because the distinction can be only analytical – it can be made only in theory. In practice, it was, I suspected, normally the two factors working *together* which resulted in conversion. It was seeing, or believing that they saw, the beliefs in *operation* in the Unification environment which convinced potential Moonies that there was something worthwhile in the Unification alternative – that the beliefs actually worked.

Is it possible, then, for empirical research to take us further than this, perhaps rather obvious position? I believe so. What I tried to do was to draw as clear a distinction as practicable between, on the one hand, those characteristics and experiences which would, as *criteria independent of both the workshop and the final outcome*, suggest that a person was particularly susceptible to persuasion *per se*, and, on the other hand, those characteristics and experiences which could suggest that the person was particularly receptive to the kind of alternative which the Unification Church seemed to be offering.

Taking into account the earlier argument, we cannot look at the Moonies in isolation if we want to discover the extent to which they are particularly vulnerable to either or both of these dimensions of susceptibility. This is because nearly everyone will exhibit both sets of characteristics to some degree and we have no means of assessing, for any particular individual, the relative balance of one set of characteristics against the other set. We cannot judge whether Jonathan's inability to resist love-bombing is more or less decisive than his desire to play an active role in restoring the world. We need to discover whether Moonies are more or less susceptible than others to active and/or passive persuasion. My task was thus to compare, along both dimensions, Moonies with non-Moonies – the latter group being further divided into the sub-groups of non-joiners, a control group, and the general population – and the 'leavers' who, it turned out, yielded some especially interesting data. But before we turn to the data, let me elaborate further the distinction I have drawn between active and passive receptivity to persuasion.

The *passively susceptible person* is one whom we should probably think of as rather inadequate or pathetic – someone who cannot really cope with life. It may be that he is not very intelligent, or he may have suffered from unpleasant or traumatic experiences. Depending on the environment within which he finds himself, he could as easily drift into petty crime, drugs, the Punk scene, the Hare Krishna movement or born-again Christianity. Any motivations which he might experience in changing from one 'scene' to another will tend to be *negative* – changes will be 'escapes from' rather than positive 'attractions to'.

By way of contrast, the *actively susceptible person* will not normally be thought of as either inadequate or pathetic. He may fall into the general category of 'seeker', and he might not be very sure exactly what it is that he wants to do, but although his character and previous experiences may have left him susceptible to certain kinds of influence, he will be open to only a limited range of alternative options. He will be unlikely to drift, and he will be unlikely to be persuaded to change his way of life merely in order to escape from what he already has; but he could be tempted by a carrot which seems, in a *positive* way, to promise something that is 'just what he was looking for'.

The Psychoanalytic Approach

During the time I have been studying the Moonies, numerous colleagues, friends and acquaintances have generously given me the benefit of their opinions as to why people join cranky groups like the Unification Church. Most have never met a Moonie, but from their general knowledge of the world and human nature they have felt sure that the 'real' explanation must be that the Moonie was a 'rather pathetic screwball' to begin with; something must have been lacking or not quite right; perhaps the Moonie had had an unhappy childhood, wasn't very bright or (least helpfully of all) was 'just the sort of person who would become a Moonie'. The more psychoanalytically oriented have hazarded suggestions that Moonies must have suffered from severe birth traumas, rejection at the breast or an unpleasant encounter in the woodshed. It is more than likely, I have been informed, that the Moonie was really looking for security, for an omnipotent-father symbol; that he was, fundamentally, a sexually hung-up, rationalizing, sublimating, transferring neurotic who was unable to come to terms with the realities of life and his own crazy, mixed-up self.

Perhaps. But how can we check whether this is, in fact, the case? 'Easy,' comes the reply. 'All that is necessary is for the patient (the Moonie) to be analysed over a period of time, and the analyst will bring to the surface the deep-seated problem(s) which led to his joining the movement.' I do not for one moment doubt that analysts would indeed turn up with such an account of the Moonie's personal history. But then I am also fairly confident that most of them could find equally excellent reasons in our psychical histories to explain why I, the Pope, Jerry Falwell, Jane Fonda, John Doe, or you, the reader, should have become a Moonie – had any of us done so. Rather like the Moonies, psychoanalysts have their own way of seeing and interpreting the world. I am not denying that their (various) visions may not be in some ways helpful to the believers, nor am I suggesting that there is no truth in their (various) interpretations. What I am saying is that such analyses are useless in our present quest. They do not allow us to distinguish – except *ex post facto* – between joiners and non-joiners, and they certainly would not allow us to distinguish between 'active' and 'passive' susceptibility.[1]

Psychological Tests

At the other end of the reliability[2] spectrum, there exists a whole battery of tests which psychologists have designed to assess the mental health or psychological condition of their subjects. I did not administer any such tests in my research, partly because I was not entirely convinced that the tests really measure all that they claim to measure, but also because I already had my work cut out collecting and analysing data which I believed to be more central to the questions in which I was mainly interested. There have, however, been others who have administered tests with some results which ought to be reported.

One such set of tests was carried out by Wolfgang Kuner on German members of the Unification Church (and other groups). He reached the conclusion that no support could be found for the public image of the movement being 'a pool of mentally ill youngsters'; in fact, there was a higher proportion of 'not-normal' cases among the control group of students (nine out of 125) than there was among the Moonies (fifteen out of 303). Kuner did, however, report that members of the Unification Church, Ananda Marga and Children of God all showed evidence of 'narcissistic traits' and a need for social appreciation.[3]

Marc Galanter found that a sample of American Moonies scored less well on a psychological general well-being scale than a control group which was matched for age and sex[4] but which was not matched for other social variables that could have influenced the outcome.[5] Galanter's later study of a Unification workshop in Los Angeles has already been referred to (see table 5, p. 146). In the course of this, he administered the same well-being test to the guests. He found that the original control group scored highest (had the greatest 'well-being'); next came the non-joining guests who dropped-out after the two-day workshop and who had practically the same score as the long-standing Moonies in the earlier research; the lowest scores were achieved by the new joiners from the workshop. Galanter hypothesises that this could indicate that Moonies are people who have enjoyed less psychological well-being than their peers, but that membership of the movement could help them to ameliorate this situation.[6] This may be true, but it is a pity that Galanter did not follow the fortunes of the admittedly small number of new joiners for a further month or so in order to see whether early leavers could account for the discrepancy – as my data suggest they might have done.

A Preliminary Checklist for 'Inadequacy'

Turning to my own study, I had, in the early stages of the research, found myself collecting a checklist of characteristics and experiences which are frequently taken to indicate that the person concerned will be particularly vulnerable to passive suggestibility and, thus, to the 'lure of the cults'. The checklist included things like the immaturity of youth; a history of mental disturbances, drug abuse and/or alcoholism; poor and/or erratic performances in school; divorced parents and/or an unhappy childhood; lack of ability to keep friends; being in a transitory state and/or having no clear prospects or direction in life; and a tendency to be indecisive, and/or to drift from one job and/or girl/boyfriend to another.

I must admit that many of the notes which I made on the transcripts of my interviews drew attention to such things as the existence of a stepfather or a near-rape experience during childhood. Rather like my psychoanalytically oriented friends and the popularizers whom I condemn in chapter 1, I assumed that such experiences would turn out to be particularly typical of Moonies, and that they could be pointed to in order to explain membership.[7] When, however, I came to look at the control group, I discovered that my explanation was not going to be that simple; and when I came to look at the data concerned with the workshop attenders (whom I had presumed would fall somewhere between the Moonies and the control group), I was to discover an even greater complication.

'True Parents.'

The Moonies did score slightly higher than the control group on some of the characteristics on the checklist, but on others they scored slightly lower, and on yet others there were more similarities between the British Moonies and the (British) control group than there were between the British and European or American Moonies. In other words, national or cultural differences were often more obvious than Moonie/non-Moonie differences.

'Health' and 'Normality' of Family, Mind and Body

It was quite clear from the study (through the questionnaire, and interviews with both the members and their parents) that Moonies do *not* tend to come from poor or obviously unhappy home backgrounds. Slightly more of the Moonies (13 per cent) than the control group (8 per cent) had parents who had separated before they reached the age of 21, and 15 per cent (compared to 5 per cent of the control) had a step-parent, but only 5 per cent of the Moonies described the relationship as a poor one. If the parents were separated, the Moonie had usually been brought up by his mother; a mere 1 per cent had been brought up in a foster or children's home. When asked to assess their parents' marriage, the British Moonies and the control group gave an almost identical set of answers, about half saying that their parents were either 'happy' or 'very happy', a quarter that they were 'all right', an eighth saying 'just bearable', and another eighth claiming that their parents' marriage had been 'miserable'. American and European Moonies were less likely to say that their parents' marriage was very happy, but practically all the respondents said that they believed their own parents' marriage was a lot better than most. Fewer Moonies than members of the control group had mothers who worked when they were children, and if mothers had worked, only 15 per cent of them (compared to 27 per cent of the control) had done so before their children started school.

Given the fact that most Moonies were in their twenties, it is hardly surprising that they tended to enjoy good or excellent physical health (the Europeans reported more illnesses than any other group). The only health difference that could be detected between the control group and American or British Moonies was that the latter were slightly more liable to report having suffered from some kind of respiratory illness such as asthma, which, they not infrequently claimed, had cleared up since their joining the movement.

Turning to mental health, 7 per cent of both British Moonies and the control group reported having sought medical help for some kind of psychiatric problem (which was serious in the case of 3 per cent of the

Moonies and 1 per cent of the control). Only one of the Moonies who filled in the workshop questionnaire reported having sought help for a psychiatric problem, but this had been a serious case, involving hospitalization; however, 8 per cent of both leavers and non-joiners had sought medical help, exclusively for serious illnesses in the case of the leavers. There were also several reports of mild psychiatric disturbances or depressions. The numbers for these were still very low, but what differential there was turned out to be interesting: 95 per cent of joiners, 85 per cent of non-joiners and 83 per cent of leavers reported no psychiatric problems at all.[8]

Some mention of suicide was made by 6 per cent of the British and American Moonies and 16 per cent of the Europeans. In absolute numbers this involved one British, one American and two European Moonies and one member of the control group reporting that they had actually attempted suicide before meeting the movement; one British and two European Moonies indicated that they had considered it since joining the movement. In the other cases the respondents reported that they had only thought about taking their own lives, but that they might have gone on to do something about it if it had not been for the Unification Church. A small number of Moonies and control reported having been raped or having had an extremely unpleasant sexual experience, and one or two respondents appeared to have strong guilt feelings concerning sex, but these came to less than 3 per cent of all the Unification Church respondents.

Drug-taking and alcoholic consumption were instances in which differences between the groups were more closely correlated with national background than with membership of the Unification Church. The majority (58 per cent) of Americans had taken drugs at some time (these were mostly soft drugs, but one in ten of them had taken hard drugs); by way of contrast, a quarter of the control, a fifth of the British Moonies and 15 per cent of the Europeans had taken drugs, British Moonies being the most likely to have tried hard drugs (6 per cent). On the other hand, Americans were the least likely to report heavy alcohol consumption. British Moonies were more likely to have been either complete abstainers (11 per cent) or very heavy drinkers (6 per cent) than the control, but two-thirds of both these groups said that they scarcely ever drank or else that they were only light social drinkers. There was no difference between the proportion of Moonies and control who had been vegetarians; Moonies were more inclined to give a religious explanation such as 'sacredness of life', while the control were more likely to give a Utilitarian 'cruelty of slaughter' reason; the Americans were most likely to say that they had given up meat for reasons of health.

There was little evidence that the Moonies would be particularly suggestible to persuasion because of a lack of basic intelligence. Two-thirds (more than either the non-joiners or leavers) had continued their education beyond the age of 18: over four-fifths had reached at least the General Certificate of Education Ordinary-Level standard (or its equivalent); an eighth had degrees; another eighth were at university; and a further quarter had taken some other post-school examination. The Moonies tended to be considerably more consistent in their academic performance, though with a smaller proportion of excellent grades, than the control group. Leavers were the most likely to be erratic, and a higher proportion of non-joiners than Moonies had poor grades. Over half the Moonies held some sort of qualification for a job, half of these being professional qualifications. Thus, like the Moonies, the leavers and the non-joiners were much better qualified than the general population; but, when one looked at the statistics in more detail, it emerged that these two groups (the non-joiners and the leavers) contained both more of the better educated and better qualified, *and* more of the less well educated and less well qualified of the workshop attenders.

The Most and Least Suggestible were not Moonies – for Long

This pattern, in which the non-joiners and (even more clearly) the leavers displayed a wider 'spread' than the joiners,[9] was one that I was to find with respect to several of the characteristics which I was checking in my search for susceptibility to social persuasion. It appeared that the non-joiners and leavers were liable to have among their number not only people with characteristics which would make them 'less suggestible' but also those whom one might have expected to be *more* suggestible than the people who actually joined and stayed in the movement.

The more I analysed the data, the more it seemed that, in the course of recruitment to the Unification Church, what economists call a 'negative marginal utility' could come into operation so far as factors which are presumed to characterize suggestibility are concerned. That is, a certain amount of susceptibility would seem to increase the likelihood of a person's becoming a Moonie – but only up to a point. If the 'susceptibility-to-persuasion' characteristics were too strongly represented, the workshop attender would be *less* likely to join; and although some of the 'most susceptible' people might join, there was a very high probability that they would then *leave* within a very short time. At the same time, it appeared. that there was another group of early leavers who could have been attracted by the Unification Church alternative but who turned out to be possibly more strong-willed or less susceptible to accepting everything than were those who stayed in the movement for a longer period.

Looking, for example, at average (mean) age, it might have seemed that the younger guests were more vulnerable, as the average age of those who join the Unification Church was 23, while the average age of those attending the two-day workshop was 27, and this dropped to 25 for those going on to a twenty-one-day workshop. If one looked at the age distribution *within* each group, however, it seemed that those who were to become Moonies were particularly 'ripe' between the ages of 22 and 24, and a larger proportion of the guests who were *under* that age did not join. The leavers tended to be older than those who stayed in the movement. It could be that, being older, they found it easier to leave – as indeed do several of the younger recruits when they have become a bit older. There was, however, also evidence to suggest that some of the leavers were habitual seekers who had grown older while trying out various different lifestyles without success. They were far more likely than either the Moonies or the non-joiners to have looked into other organizations for a short period of time; and the non-joiners were more likely to have been (or still to be) associated with another religious, spiritual or political group. Only a few Moonies had explored many other alternatives.

While it is true that those who are away from home, in a transitory stage, or unsettled in their careers were quite likely to have agreed to attend a workshop, this too turned out to be a characteristic more frequently found among the non-joiners than the joiners. It has been suggested that those without work might be more vulnerable, yet only 3 per cent of the Moonies, compared with 7 per cent of the non-joiners and 16 per cent of the leavers, had been unemployed at the time of attending the workshop. Over half the British Moonies had been settled in steady employment for over two years, and two-thirds for more than one year. Only a few of the respondents had been in their present occupations for a short time: a third of the Moonies and non-joiners, and half the leavers had been in their current jobs for two years or more, and about half of all the workshop attenders had expected their current situation to continue for at least another year; but there were 7 per cent Moonies, 8 per cent non-joiners and 13 per cent leavers who had had no definite prospects and not much hope or who were feeling pretty desperate, not knowing what the future might hold.

It is sometimes thought that students are particularly vulnerable, and, indeed, 41 per cent of those who went to the two-day workshop were students, but the figure dropped to 27 per cent for the twenty-one-day workshop, and less than a quarter of the joiners (including CARP members)[10] were students. Although the number of 'travellers' attending a workshop was fairly high, they tended to drop out at a faster rate than the 'by-chancers' (see chapter 4). The percentage of guests who were British rose from 40 per cent at the start of the two-day workshop to 52 per cent at the start of the twenty-one-day workshop, to 60 per cent of those who became full-time members of the movement in 1979. The proportion of CARP members who were British was lower (44 per cent), but many of the travellers returned to their own countries – sometimes as Moonies but frequently as apostates – once their studies had been completed. (Thus if one analyses the *current* membership of those who joined in Britain, 78 per cent of those who had joined in 1978 and 1977 and over 80 per cent of those who had joined in 1976 and 1975 are British.)

Representations of Self

Asking people months or even years after an event what feelings or emotions they were experiencing around the time that the event occurred is, of course, fraught with difficulties. However honest someone may try to be, he is likely to have selected for memory whatever seemed, in the light of subsequent events, to be of particular importance.[11] Obviously, the Moonies see their joining the Unification Church as a significant turning point in their lives, and it is quite possible that they will exaggerate the differences between 'before' and 'after' states of mind. Indeed, there were some Moonies who seemed to wallow in what I think of as the 'bum-to-saint' syndrome – a pattern familiar enough to those who have ever had to listen to born-again testimonies in which the convert explains what a miserable sinner he was before taking Jesus into his life. Where it was possible to compare what parents had told me (or my own knowledge of the person) with the questionnaire responses, there appeared, however, to be a reassuringly reliable correspondence between the assessments of the Moonie and those of the other person.

Throughout the questionnaire I approached the questions which relied upon subjective information in a variety of different ways in an attempt to assess the consistency of the responses. One of the most revealing questions (which, unfortunately, was not included in the much shorter workshop questionnaire) asked respondents to write down six key words or phrases to describe themselves during different periods in their lives.[12] These self-descriptions were analysed from various points of view, one being for expressions of general emotion. There was not a great deal of difference between the control group and the Moonies, but Moonies were slightly more inclined to use introvert expressions to describe both their happiness and unhappiness (e.g. 'withdrawn' or 'content/secure'), while the control group was slightly more likely to use words like 'rebellious', 'lively'. The control group was less likely to report extremes (of either happiness or unhappiness) the most extreme unhappiness ('dead', 'depressed') being reported by a small number of Moonies for the period six months before they had met the movement.

Both the Moonies and the control tended to express mild approval of themselves (e.g. 'balanced', 'honest', 'friendly'), which was sometimes coupled with mild criticism (e.g. 'immature', 'complacent'). Moonies were, however, slightly more inclined to project greater self-concern than the control group. Very few of the respondents expressed self-hatred, disgust, or severe self-criticism. The sharpest contrast between the two groups was that the Moonies (particularly the Americans) were more likely to appear disproportionately self-congratulatory by using words like 'clever', 'sincere', 'popular' or by writing down more than three 'mild approvals' for a particular period. This was least apparent in the period just before meeting the movement, and most apparent for the 'now' period.

The 'Late Dip'

The respondents were given the opportunity to express their assessment of their happiness (and other states) more directly in a pre-coded form (which facilitated comparisons both between groups and over time for members of the same group). Even when one recognizes the limitations of self-descriptions and retrospective memories, it is interesting to see how very few Moonies claimed to have had an unhappy childhood.

Table 9 gives the detailed responses, but it is also interesting as an example of another pattern which emerged with respect to several other variables (and which I shall discuss further in the following chapter), the pattern being that not only did the Moonies tend to 'dip' just before they met the Unification Church but also that many of them *started* being unhappy *later* in their lives than the control group. Although they were likely to drop from a 'very happy' childhood to being 'happy' or 'all right' during their teens, only 22 per cent of the joiners reported being unhappy up to the period six months before meeting the movement, by which time over a third were unhappy. By way of contrast, nearly a third of the control said that they were unhappy during their early teens, but this had fallen to 12 per cent by by their late teens and/or early twenties. This pattern actually shows up more clearly when looking at individual responses (as some of the 'dips' cancel each other out when a whole group is taken together). In fact, a third of the Moonies (but only about a fifth of the leavers and control group) dipped by at least one point on the scale (e.g. from 'happy' to 'all right') in the period just before meeting the movement, but 15 per cent of the Moonies said that they were actually happier then than they had been in the previous period. The leavers were the most likely to have *remained* unhappy for a longer period and, as can be seen from table 9, it was they who were most likely to have had an unhappy early childhood.

Table 9   Happiness as assessed by respondents

		Up to 10 years old (%)	11–16 years old (%)	From 17 years old to six months before meeting UC (%)	In six months up to UC (%)	Now (%)
Moonies		32	6	5	5	52
Leavers	very	30	13	—	4	17
Non-joiners	happy	33	16	10	14	21
Control group[1]		28	13	22	36	
Moonies		40	31	37	31	36
Leavers	happy	22	29	22	13	22
Non-joiners		35	35	32	25	27
Control group[1]		38	28	37	36	
Moonies		24	41	38	27	11
Leavers	all right	26	33	52	58	52
Non-joiners		25	35	39	38	38
Control group[1]		22	29	30	24	
Moonies		2	16	16	24	—
Leavers	just	17	13	26	17	—
Non-joiners	bearable	6	9	16	20	8
Control group[1]		8	22	8	3	
Moonies		2	6	5	13	2
Leavers	miserable	4	13	—	8	9
Non-joiners		1	5	3	3	4
Control group[1]		4	8	4	1	

Note: [1] The periods for the control group were (a) up to 10 years old (b) 11–16 years old (c) from 17 years old to six months ago (d) in last six months.

A roughly similar pattern emerged when the Moonies and control group were asked to assess their spiritual well-being, the Moonies tending to 'droop' progressively up to the time of meeting the movement, claiming their spiritual well-being was 'now' (since joining) much, much better than average.[13] Both Moonies and control group tended to consider that they had enjoyed average or above-average material comfort throughout their lives: even after joining the movement, Moonies still tended to consider that their material well-being was 'about' (47 per cent), or 'above' (37 per cent), average.

Still on the look-out for that elusive character 'passive suggestibility', and in an attempt to pick up the general 'feel' of responses to the longer questionnaires[14] from someone other than myself, I asked my two research assistants,[15] who were doing the coding, to assess each of the respondents for a number of variables. They were unable to detect any significant differences between the Moonies and the control group for such character- istics as popularity with friends, shyness, feelings of loneliness, feelings of being loved or feelings of being unattractive. However, in their overall impression of each of the respondents, the coders classified 13 per cent of the Moonies (and 4 per cent of the control group) as 'rather sad and pathetic', and they thought that 5 per cent of the Moonies (2 per cent of the control) were in some way psychopathic; they designated an equal proportion (11 per cent) of the Moonies and the control as 'religious maniacs', 4 per cent of the Moonies (5 per cent of the control) as 'self- righteous bores' and 14 per cent of the Moonies (9 per cent of the control) as 'mildly strange'. They also said that 10 per cent of the Moonies (20 per cent of the control) seemed unusually attractive people whom they would like to meet and have as friends. The rest were classified as 'ordinary boy/girl next door'. Of course, these were highly subjective judgements, but, considering that the research assistants were relying solely on ques- tionnaire responses, they do correspond, to an uncanny degree, with the sorts of diagnosis I could have made after talking to a thousand or so Moonies in the flesh.

In conclusion, taking all the evidence into account, including that which I elicited in interviews and through participant observation, it would seem that while a small proportion of Moonies could be classified as inadequate, and a slightly larger (but still small) proportion could be classified as slightly sad or pathetic, most Moonies do not differ significantly from their peers with respect to characteristics which could form independent criteria for assessing whether or not a person could be classified as prone to 'passive suggestibility'. In fact, the evidence suggested that while people who were exposed to the social context of a Unification Church workshop included those who, prima facie, would seem to be *more* as risk than the control group, these were the very people who did *not* join, or, if they did, they were among those who would leave pretty quickly. It also seemed clear that while some of the Moonies had suffered the sorts of experiences which might make the 'refuge from society' situation seem a plausible one to explain their membership, it was only a limited number whose experi- ences were markedly worse than those of their peers. Again, the evidence suggested that there was a group of workshop attenders who appeared to have had more traumatic or unpleasant experiences than members of the control group, but such people tended to be among those who either did not join or left soon after having done so.

It does not, however, follow that the majority of Moonies do not have certain characteristics which suggest that they could be more 'actively susceptible' to the Unification Church. In the next chapter I shall describe some of the predispositions and social experiences which might explain why those who join can be persuaded, upon exposure to an environment controlled by Moonies, that the Unification Church has something positive to offer them.

9 Susceptibility

In chapter 8 I argued that there is not much evidence to suggest that Moonies-to-be are substantially more inadequate or pathetic than their peers, but that this does not mean that it is impossible to detect characteristics and experiences which could make them susceptible to the Unification alternative. In this chapter I attempt to map a profile of a typical Moonie, largely in terms of his social history in so far as this could contribute to his developing such a susceptibility. Returning to the model depicted in table 4 (p. 138), I am now considering evidence of characteristics that might contribute to either of the final two situations: 'nonconscious fit' and 'conscious decision'.

At first glance some of the characteristics which I shall describe might seem to be better classified as constituting a 'passive' suggestibility (or susceptibility to persuasive techniques) – particularly those of love-bombing. My reason for including a description of such characteristics in this chapter rather than the previous one is that they tend to be characteristics which would not normally be considered grave disabilities or inadequacies in someone who does *not* become a Moonie, and/or they are the sorts of characteristics which could provide a fairly rational explanation for someone's choosing (rather than passively accepting) the Unification alternative. In other words, these are previously existing predispositions and/or experiences which the recruit could draw upon or use in his decision to try out the Unification alternative, although he might not be aware of the influence of such characteristics at a very conscious level.

Moonie and Non-Moonie 'Bundles'

I hope that at this point the reader will bear in mind what has already been stressed several times: that there is a considerable diversity of people, beliefs and practices to be found within the Unification Church. No two people will ever have had exactly the same experiences, and there is no one set of characteristics that is either necessary or sufficient to account for someone's becoming a Moonie. There are, rather, *bundles* of experiences, attitudes and desires which, when more (rather than less) present, are likely to predispose a person towards joining the movement. And, just as significant, there are other bundles of characteristics which are more likely to 'protect' their owner from becoming attracted to the Unification alternative. It is the broad distinctions between these two bundles that I shall be attempting to draw. For those wishing for a more statistical account, I have published elsewhere further details of the differences that I found between Moonies and non-Moonies.[1]

Age, Sex, and Class[2]

One of the best-known characteristics of the membership of the new religious movements is that it tends to consist largely of middle-class youth. The Unification Church is no exception. Its membership is certainly young – though not as young as is sometimes supposed. Almost no one[3] joins under the age of 18, unless, of course, his parents have also joined. The average age of joining has remained fairly constantly around 23 years.[4] In 1976 nearly 80 per cent of the British membership was aged between 19 and 30; in 1978 the average (mean) age of full-time Moonies in both Britain and America was 26;[5] by the beginning of 1982 the average age of the British members was 28. It has, naturally, risen since then, but it does not rise by nearly as much as a year each twelve-month, since there is a high turn-over rate[6] and the new recruits continue to be mainly in their early twenties. Of course, if one were to include second-generation Moonies, the average age would be reduced quite considerably, but as we are concerned in this book with those who are recruited (rather than born) into the movement, I have excluded them from my calculations.

The sex ratio in Britain and the United States[7] is two to one in favour of men. (This is not a pattern which is repeated in all European countries, however.) Both the sex ratio and the age distribution are markedly different from those to be found in the more established Churches where, in both Britain and the United States, women are more likely to attend church, and the early twenties are a time of diminished church attendance.[8] It is comparatively easy to understand why the Unification Church would be unlikely to attract older people as full-time members, if only because of the hectic life-style and degree of commitment which is expected. I have no clear explanation as to why more men than women are attracted to full-time membership. One possibility is that women tend to get married earlier than men, and marriage is one of the greatest 'protections' from membership. (Some, but not all, of the 'selection' for marital status seems to have occurred before people get as far as going to a workshop, since the non-joiners were more likely than the joiners, but less likely than the control group, to be married.) Another possible explanation which occurred to me was that the Unification Church is decidedly unsympathetic towards modern ideas of female emancipation (although there are a few feminist members who have spoken out quite strongly against what they see as the movement's sexism), but I had to abandon this as a plausible explanation when I went through the thousand-odd application forms for a two-day workshop and found that only a third of these (and of the application forms for the twenty-one-day course) were from women, and potential recruits would have been unlikely to know much about the movement's attitude towards women at that stage. Other possible explanations for the sex differential (such as the different 'career structures' which exist for the two sexes) have occurred to me, but they cannot, I regret, be more than mere speculation. I was unable to detect any clear differences between the sexes in *their* reasons for joining the movement, except that the women were (somewhat to my surprise) more likely to give theological reasons (mentioning particularly the 'Conclusion') or to say that they had been given a sense of purpose, while the men were more likely to mention the appeal of the love, or to rate the importance of the community life more highly. When asked what was the greatest sacrifice that they had made in deciding to join, the men were slightly more liable to mention freedom or their careers, while the women were more likely to mention their family or boyfriends; but such differences were so slight that little ought to be read into them.

The class background of the British Moonies, the non-joiners and the British population as a whole is shown in table 10, but by themselves variables such as age, sex or class cannot help us to *understand* why someone becomes a Moonie; they help us only in the initial stage of mapping the Moonie population. We need to look in more detail at the social institutions which would have had most influence on the potential recruit, and

Table 10   Class backgrounds of workshop attenders (according to father's occupation)

	Upper-middle (%)	Middle-middle (%)	Lower-middle (%)	Upper-working (%)	Middle-working (%)	Lower-working (%)
Joiners	7	24	15	24	26	5
Non-joiners	14	25	29	6	18	8
Leavers	5	32	—[1]	11	26	26
General population[2]	5	18	12	38	18	9

Notes: [1] Less than 1 per cent. [2] Male population of Great Britain over the age of 15. These are not strictly comparable with the other data, since I coded several occupations as middle-working class which the Registrar General classifies as upper-working class.

these, given the age of the Moonie population, are likely to have been the family, the educational system and probably, since we are trying to understand a religious movement, organized religion. I shall then report some of the general responses that I got to questions about the future of society, before ending the chapter with a consideration of the ways in which Moonies seem to have been active 'seekers' before they met the movement. First, however, I would like to touch on the Home-Church membership whose characteristics resemble more closely those of the church-going public as a whole.

Home-Church Membership

Home-Church (or Associate) members are converts who do not move into a Unification centre but remain in their own homes and continue with their own work, although they may visit the centres fairly frequently and participate in activities such as occasional fund-raising drives. In other words, they are people who, while unable or unwilling to become fully *committed* to the Unification way of life, are none the less prepared to declare that they have become *converted* to Unification beliefs.[9]

By May 1980 there were 140 Home-Church members in Britain, most of whom had joined during the previous eighteen months. Geographically,

A Home-Church Rally. Dennis Orme is standing on the right of the picture and Doris Orme is fourth from the right; in the foreground are members of the Go World Brass Band.

A Home-Church gathering in Birmingham.

they were clustered in areas with active centres, a third living in London and the South-East and nearly a quarter in South Wales. Educational achievement for Home-Church members is not as impressive as it is for full-time Moonies, and although 14 per cent had degrees, nearly half had not continued studies beyond secondary-school level. This is related partly to the fact that while 80 per cent of the full-time Moonies were under 30 years of age, 80 per cent of the Home-Church members were over 30, and a half were over 40 – although they were least likely to join while actually in their forties.

The most noticeable difference apart from age (although related to it) is that while less than 7 per cent of the full-time members had been married before they joined, only a fifth of the Home-Church members had *not* been married. Half the latter were still married; 17 per cent were separated or divorced; and 11 per cent were widowed. Two-thirds had children, frequently quite a large number, and a few were unmarried mothers; 12 per cent were introduced to the movement by their own offspring. Rather than being weighted towards men, the sex ratio of Home-Church members was 56:44 in favour of women. One quarter put housewife or mother as their occupation; 13 per cent were nurses or midwives. Others were in secretarial, clerical or semi-skilled work. While over a half were in the middle classes, their occupations reflected a bias towards the lower middle or the middle working class.

The existence of the Home-Church members indicates that the Unification Church can appeal to a constituency wider than that from which the full-time Moonie is drawn, but that it succeeds in doing so only as long as it does not demand the kind of unquestioning devotion and sacrificial life style that the young, unmarried Moonie is prepared to give, and which is, in certain respects, more like the commitment expected of a monk, nun or priest rather than of 'ordinary' members of a congregation. None the less, Home-Church members often gave the impression that they had been, and perhaps still were, leading lonely or unsatisfying lives; they were anxious to be involved and of help – indeed, one of their most frequent complaints was that the movement did not make enough use of them.

Just to bring the numbers up to date: early in 1984 the membership in Britain, broken down by the new classification,[10] showed about 750 'Associate members' (which included over forty parents of 'Full Centre members'), about sixty 'Practising members', and about fifty 'Full Home members'. There were also about 250 Full Centre members in Britain and around the same number of members who had joined in Britain, but were currently overseas, mostly in the United States. The number of British members who had joined overseas is difficult to estimate but is possibly around a hundred.

Institutions and their Influence

Family Background

Returning to the analysis of full-time members: in the previous chapter I suggested that the theory that people become Moonies because of an unhappy family background does not stand up to the evidence. But this does not mean that people become Moonies *in spite of* a happy family background; they are, I believe, quite liable to join *because of* one. That is to say, in so far as Moonies are looking for the warmth and affection of a secure family life, this is unlikely to be because they have never known one; they are far more likely to be hoping to return to one. They are not likely to be turning to the Reverend and Mrs Moon as 'True Parents' because they have never known parents whom they respected and loved; they are much more likely to be responding to the idea that those who are in the 'parental position' can legitimately claim respect and obedience because they have grown up respecting their own parents (perhaps so much so that they were particularly disillusioned or disoriented when they recognized that their parents, like other human beings, have certain frailties and are not entirely omniscient). Furthermore, Moonies do *not* appear to be rejecting the values that were instilled into them during their childhood; they appear, on the contrary, to have imbibed these so success- fully that they are prepared to respond to an opportunity (which society does not seem to be offering them) to live *according to* those very standards and ideals.

My initial analysis of the class backgrounds of the workshop attenders showed that they were even more disproportionately middle-class than the Unification membership. (That is, more non-joiners than joiners had fathers in non-manual occupations.) What, I wondered, was it about middle-class youth that made them particularly prepared to go to workshops but less likely than the other guests to become Moonies? Several plausible hypotheses came to mind, but, with a more detailed analysis of the data, two interesting patterns emerged which suggested that I was asking the wrong question, or at least that I was approaching it with the wrong assumptions. First, although more non-joiners than Moonies came from middle-class backgrounds, the non-joiners were more likely to have fathers in lower-middle-class occupations (such as routine clerical work), while the Moonies' parents were more likely to have been holding highly skilled and/or responsible jobs (such as foremen) in the upper-working class. Secondly, a 'horizontal' analysis of occupations showed that the Moonies' parents were less likely than the non-joiners (or control group) to be in jobs which were specifically orientated towards making money (financiers, stock brokers or businessmen) and were more likely to have jobs which are usually associated with the values of duty or service, either to individuals (e.g. doctors, nurses, teachers) or to their country (e.g. the armed services, police, colonial service).

A further clue that emerges from the Moonies' descriptions of their family background (and, indeed, from discussions with many of their parents) is that Moonies tend to have come from what could be called conventional and highly 'respectable' homes in which traditional values of family life, morality and 'decency' were upheld – or, at least, in which it was generally acknowledged that they ought to be upheld. I noticed that several (but by no means all) of the parents to whom I talked had very 'black-and-white' ideas about the world. One father told me that he could not for the life of him understand how his son could have been brainwashed into joining such a group: 'We brought Nigel up always to stand up and be counted for what was right, never to bend according to the way the wind was blowing.' I also formed the impression that quite a few Moonies came from homes in which values and standards were taken for granted rather than discussed at great length. It was *assumed* that certain actions were wrong and others right, rather than there being much in the way of 'working it out'. Disagreement was not so much forbidden as not expected.

The majority of all the respondents said that they had had good relationships with their parents; Moonies were slightly more likely to have been 'friendly' than 'very close', and more of them than the control said (particularly about their fathers) that the relationship was 'all right but distant'; less than one in ten claimed to have had a poor relationship with his parents during the period just before he met the Unification Church (although about half of them had not seen their parents for more than a month). Quite a large proportion of the Moonies believed that they were their parents' favourite child.

When I first looked at the faith in which British Moonies had been brought up, I was puzzled as to what might account for the disproportionate number who had been brought up as Roman Catholics (21 per cent compared with 12 per cent of the British population), and why an even higher percentage (35 per cent) of the workshop attenders were from Catholic backgrounds. Even more intriguing was the fact that the workshops reflected the same proportion of Nonconformists as the general population (12 per cent), but twice as many of the British Moonies (25 per cent) came from Nonconformist backgrounds (most frequently Presbyterian and Methodist). Further analysis revealed, however, that once again I was asking myself a question which was based on a misleading assumption, and that the explanation was likely to lie not in any intrinsic differences between the different faiths but in the facts that, first, a disproportionate number of workshop attenders came (or their parents had come) from a Catholic country, particularly Ireland, and that several of these were 'travellers' (students or *au pair* girls from countries such as France) who, as I pointed out earlier, were more likely to be interested in meeting people or 'doing something' for a weekend than in actually joining the movement. Secondly, and even more important, it appeared that religious *involvement* was a more significant predictor of eventual membership than was the *kind* of faith in which the involvement had occurred (so long as it was, in Britain, within the Christian tradition).[11] Although over two-thirds of the adult English population will claim to be Church of England, only about one in twenty are actually members of the Anglican Church.[12] 'Church of England' tends to be a rather vague label which frequently implies more of a cultural than a religious commitment; and Moonies do tend to have been brought up in families that could be described as more religious than the rest of the population.[13]

As the control group had been selected with an intentional bias towards people from a religious background,[14] I could expect it to provide only a limited number of comparisons on the subject. In the event it turned out that the respondents in the two groups (Moonie and control) produced a remarkably similar distribution of assessments of the importance of religion in their parents' lives. Despite this similarity, however, it seemed clear that the Moonies had had a far greater exposure to organized religion than had the control group – and, indeed, that the Moonies had had quite a lot more exposure than the non-joiners or the leavers, although these latter groups had still had considerably more exposure than the rest of the population.[15]

The most striking difference was in church attendance. This was particularly high during the Moonies' early childhood.[16] As they passed into adolescence the differences between the Moonies and the control group became much less marked, but at all periods in their lives the non-joiners and, especially, the leavers were much less likely than the joiners to have been frequent churchgoers. All the groups were more polarized than the general population (in that they tended to worship either frequently or not at all), although more of the control group and the leavers would go to church a few times a year or for special occasions such as Christmas or Easter. In other words, the pattern that emerged from the Moonies was that churchgoing had been particularly important during early childhood; later they were unlikely to drift into a casual relationship with a church, but would have decided either to keep to regular worship or to discontinue contact with institutionalized religion altogether. Another finding was that an unexpectedly high proportion of Moonies (43 per cent) had parents whose denominational affiliations differed – one parent being, for example, a Catholic while the other was a Methodist. This, taken with the fact that religion was important for the parents, could suggest that Moonies are people who had been prepared to look for religious answers to problems, but they will not inevitably have learned to look exclusively to one particular faith for such answers.

In the previous chapter I mentioned that, at some point in their lives, most respondents had had a temporal 'dip' (in happiness, feelings of well-being, self-confidence, etc.), but that those who were to become Moonies were liable to claim to have enjoyed feelings of happiness and security for longer than the other respondents and, therefore, to have experienced their 'dip' later in life – sometimes not until after they had left home. It seems as though many of the problems and the questionings that are normally experienced throughout adolescence came later for Moonies than for their peers. Many Moonies seem, for example, not to have experienced much difficulty with personal relationships (boyfriends and girlfriends) until relatively late in life, and they also tend to have doubted the existence of God at a later age than usual. Although this certainly does not apply to all Moonies, it does seem that a fairly high proportion of them were protected from the problems of life for longer than their peers. Despite (in some cases possibly because of) the fact that they were often intellectually advanced for their years, Moonies have sometimes been emotionally immature. This does not mean that they have been plucked from their mothers' breasts. While they were more inclined to have stayed home for longer than the control group, only a quarter still regarded their parents' home as their permanent residence at the time they had joined the movement; well over half had left their parents' home more than a year beforehand, 38 per cent having left more than three years before joining.

What I am suggesting is that several of those who had had a happy, secure home background had been ill-prepared to cope with the disappointments, hurt and disillusionment which they experienced around the time that they first ventured out into the world, and that such people might experience considerable relief on meeting a group of friendly people who appeared to share the same values and to believe in similar standards. It is not altogether surprising that many Moonies have told me that their immediate reaction on meeting the movement was: 'I felt I had come home'. This is not to imply that Moonies simply wanted to return to their home. Most of them had felt the need to be independent of their parents long before they had met the Unification Church. Usually this was no more than part of the normal pattern of growing up, but there was a small, yet none the less recognizable, group of Moonies who had desperately wanted to escape from parents whose care and devotion had, they felt, been suffocating. Sometimes it was the father who expected his son (or, occasionally, daughter) to follow in his footsteps or to do even better than he had – and 'better' was often defined as succeeding in a career which had little attraction for the child who had felt himself being pushed along an educational production line in a direction which he himself had not chosen and which may well have seemed to prevent his being able to fulfil the very ideals that his parents had instilled into him during his childhood.

Another kind of suffocation was due to mothers who had selflessly devoted their lives to looking after their children but who did not wish to let go; they had reached a point where their need for their child's dependence was greater than the child's need for them. The child (who might by now be in his early twenties) felt that he had to make a stand and choose his own way of life, but at the same time the fact that he had been brought up in an environment in which he had felt cherished, and in which decisions had been made for him, could make *his* decision to stand on his own two feet more liable to be a decision to do so within another 'we-love-you-and-we-have-got-all-the-answers' environment.

One can recognize a further group of Moonies who, while having been brought up and protected with the same feelings of love and care, and having been subjected to roughly equivalent values, are likely to have found their parents not so much overbearing as over-liberal. Such parents would, perhaps rather suddenly, have expected their child to make his own decisions ('now you are grown-up'), but the Moonie may have felt inadequately prepared for the choices and difficulties he encountered as he experienced his 'late big dip'. For those who have been carefully protected, the psychological discomfort of too much freedom can be as great as that caused by too little freedom.

There are some Moonies who have come from unhappy homes, and there are those who have had early experiences of pain and suffering. Generally speaking, however, a happy, protective and caring family background in which decency, duty, service to one's fellow men, one's country and/or one's God were taken-for-granted values, is likely to be part of the bundle of experiences which the potential Moonie will bring with him to a Unification workshop.

The Educational System

Although it is rare for the educational system to be explicitly mentioned in Moonies' testimonies, it can nevertheless be recognized as having played a significant role in predisposing young people to join. This is not only because it happens to be one of the institutions of which potential converts will have had most experience, but also because of its organization, its values and the role that it plays in modern society. In order to 'get on' in the world today, it is necessary to have the correct qualifications; and the correct qualifications – at least in the industrialized West – are usually bits of paper distributed to those whom the educational system has judged to have reached the requisite academic standard. It is a standard which is based mainly on a comparison with one's peers. The system produces a pyramid-type structure of paper-holders, quite a large number of people getting the less valued certificates and relatively few getting those which are more valued. Many of the young people who join the Unification Church will have made a promising start well up the slippery slopes of the pyramid. As a group they have, as we saw in the last chapter, achieved much better results than the national average.

There can be little doubt that most Moonies' parents believed that their children's performance in the education system was important for their future achievements; about a quarter of the Moonies (compared with about 5 per cent of the general British population) went to fee-paying schools. Thus not only will the potential Moonie have done better than his peers by *objective* criteria, he is likely to have been encouraged to think of himself *subjectively* as an achiever, and he will have started to define himself in such terms, accepting the criterion of academic success as the pathway to success in general. This showed up quite clearly in the interviews, and in the questionnaires when the respondents were asked to use key words to describe themselves at various periods during their lives. Although the question made no mention of education or academic abilities, the majority of respondents did, at some point, define themselves in terms of achievements which were themselves measured in terms of the values of the educational system (e.g. 'studious', 'academically ambitious', 'doing well at school'). While there was no obvious pattern for the control group, Moonies were liable to use such self-definitions during the earlier years of their lives (until they were in their late teens), but they then put in an entry which suggested that they had redefined themselves as no longer being a willing part of the educational system, even though, objectively speaking, they may still have been in it. This rejection was sometimes blamed on the system, and sometimes on the self. The kinds of entry one now found were 'lazy', 'uninterested in school work', 'searching for alternative values to academic rat race', 'bored with study'. In other words, the Moonie had started by identifying himself as one of those who had the ability to rise through the main channel that is available for 'getting on' in the world today, but he had then found that he could not get on as far as he had assumed he would, and/or else (possibly, but not necessarily, as a consequence) he had come to the conclusion that either the means and/or the goal were not worth pursuing.[17]

It is not only Moonies who have experienced the contemporary West as a society in which competition is rife and academic success is demanded from an early age. There are plenty of educationalists who have frequently complained that hasty decisions have been thrust upon or squeezed out of children who have had little time to contemplate at their leisure what they might really want to explore. Subjects have been chosen according to whether they were likely to yield good examination results rather than because they offered any intrinsic satisfaction. Indeed, having accepted the system, one might well be so busy trying to achieve that one does not know what *could* give satisfaction. It is not difficult to believe one has been cheated of time to stand and stare. All are given equal opportunity to succeed – or so the conventional wisdom goes, at least within the lore of the conventional middle classes from which a large proportion of potential converts are drawn. Failure, it follows, must be the result of personal failure. But, of course, it also follows that for all but the very bright (or perhaps the very lucky) there must, at some stage, *be* failure. The further up the pyramid one climbs, the keener the competition. The goal that the system offers is to reach the top. To achieve less is, within the definition of the system, to *be* less. If Tom is first, Dick can only hope to be second, while Jonathan will be a failure in third place. Is it all worth it? At least some of those who were eventually to join the Unification Church had already decided that it was not.

The Religious Factor

It was argued in chapter 3 that, in order to understand how the Unification Church 'works', one has to approach it as (among other things) a religious movement. This is certainly necessary when trying to understand the attraction which it holds for some people and which it does not hold for

Table 11(a) Did you believe in God at the time you went to the workshop?
(data from workshop questionnaire)

	Joiners (%)	Leavers (%)	Non-joiners (%)
Yes, definitely	61	68	50
Yes, probably	33	24	24
No, not really	6	8	18
No, definitely not	—	—	8

Table 11(b) Do you sometimes doubt God's existence now?
(data from main Unification Church and control group questionnaires)

	American seminarians (%)	European UC (%)	British UC (%)	Control group (%)
No doubts whatsoever	76	87	76	26
Sometimes have slight worries, but no serious doubt	21	12	18	20
Occasionally	2	2	6	10
Quite often	2	—	—	15
Do not believe in God[1]	—	—	—	29

Note: [1] Not pre-coded in Unification questionnaire.

others. It has already been said that Moonies tend to come from homes in which religion was important. Table 11 (a) and (b) suggests that disbelief in God provides the workshop guests with a pretty effective immunity to the Unification Church, at least in Britain.[18] Furthermore, the somewhat surprising fact that so many of the control group did not believe in God would suggest that atheism and agnosticism could account for a considerable number of people of a similar age and background to the Moonies 'selecting themselves out' before they had reached the stage of attending a workshop.

When they were asked what faith they held at the time that they first met the Unification Church (or at the time of filling in the questionnaire in the case of the control group), the majority of all of the respondents declined to name any particular denomination, saying that although they believed in God, they rejected, or did not feel able to align themselves with, any one religion. Indeed, one of the tendencies to emerge most forcefully from the research was the disillusionment that *all* the young people were experiencing with the more traditional churches. Generally speaking, the Roman Catholic Church elicited the most accusations of hypocrisy, although the word frequently recurred (in a variety of exotic spellings) with reference to all the established religions; the Nonconformist Churches were the recipients of slightly milder expressions of ambivalence or rejection; and the Church of England was most likely to bask in contemptuous indifference. The control group was the most vocal in both its criticisms (especially among the Catholics) and, in some cases, its approval (especially among the Nonconformists); those who were to become Moonies were more inclined to have lost interest in the church in which they had been brought up and to say that they had been looking for some alternative.

Although almost all the Moonies said that they had had some kind of spiritual or religious experience after meeting the movement, well over three-quarters of them claimed to have had such an experience *before* meeting the movement.[19] The most common form that the experiences took was a sense of the presence of God or Jesus or some other person, but quite a few claimed to have had visions or to have heard God or Jesus speaking to them; other experiences included improved or enhanced senses, and a strong sensation of being at one or in harmony with the world or with nature. Most of the respondents who had had such an experience reported that it had altered their outlook on life in some way: usually they had felt happier or more secure, about half the Moonies (a third of the control) saying that it had given them some sort of religious meaning, direction or hope. A further fifth of the Moonies (7 per cent of the control) claimed to have dedicated their lives to God as a result of the experience.

Yet, despite the importance which the experience had had for so many respondents, nearly half the Moonies (over a third of the control) had not told anyone what had happened. While the control were more likely to say that they had remained silent because they wanted to keep it to themselves, the Moonies were more likely to say that they had felt that no one would have understood, that they were afraid of being thought peculiar, or that they had not wanted to risk allowing anyone to make fun of the experience.

In fact, my respondents were not nearly as unusual in this respect as they, and perhaps others, might believe. About a third of the total population in both America and Britain will admit to having had such experiences, and the figures are higher for the better educated.[20] David Hay obtained an affirmative response rate of 65 per cent when he asked 100 postgraduate students whether they had had such an experience – a percentage which was marginally higher than the one which I obtained from my control group. Hay also reported that a large number of his respondents were reticent about talking about their experience, quoting as a characteristic response: 'No, I've not told anyone. For the simple reason, there's such a lot of disbelievers about, and they'd ridicule you, like.'[21]

Members studying the Divine Principle.

A prayer meeting.

I do not, therefore, want to suggest that Moonies are unique or freakish because they will (very probably) have had some kind of religious experience; I do, however, want to point out that they find themselves in an environment in which they (and, indeed, others) *believe* that such experiences are uncommon occurrences and that those who have them can be considered slightly (or very) nutty. Reading through the responses of both Moonies and the control group, I began to feel that had Freud been studying present-day students in Britain rather than late nineteenth century matrons in Vienna, he might have concluded that it was spiritual rather than sexual repression which lay at the root of many current frustrations. It is, after all, often quite acceptable for a student to tell his friends whom he slept with the previous night. He is far less likely to tell them that Our Lady appeared while he was saying his prayers.

Even, perhaps especially, the established Churches have a tendency to frown on direct, personal experiences with God. One can easily be given the impression that such things are not *comme il faut*; members of a jealous priesthood are liable to insist that it is they alone who ought to be the mediators of all communications with the transcendental, and that it is arrogant, perhaps even dangerous, to explore the Beyond unless one is an established (an institutionally qualified) expert. Few of the respondents in any group had talked to priests or other members of the clergy about religious questions either in depth or very frequently. Moonies were most likely to say that they had tried but had not got anywhere; they were also likely to give the same reason for reticence in discussing religious questions with their parents and their friends. Although a third of both the Moonies and the control did say that they had discussed religious questions often and in depth with friends, it was clear that most of them had not found modern, secular society an easy place within which to explore, let alone live, a religiously orientated life. One woman, describing the state of her faith in the period just before she met the movement, wrote: 'Very deeply questioning. Dissatisfied with Catholicism. I knew religion was meant to be a way of life not just a belief.'

By way of contrast, the Unification Church offers potential recruits not only permission to explore religion but also the concepts with which, and the context within which, they may do so. The *Divine Principle* provides a religious language and a religious perspective through which the world can be interpreted. The movement itself offers an environment in which not only is the existence of God not questioned but also one can dedicate one's whole life to fulfilling His most cherished desire – one has, the members believe, the opportunity of contributing towards the restoration of His Kingdom of Heaven on earth.

Visions of the Future

The potential Moonie is not a drifter; he is a '*doer*'. While the big decisions in his life may have been made for him, he is an active person who, as already mentioned, is likely to have experienced achievement. He may, like thousands of others, have thought of himself as a special person who was going to be or do something important, but at the same time he may not have been sure exactly what this would be. (This does not mean that he will not have had any ideas about his future – more Moonies than control had a definite idea of what they were going to do when they left school.) He is unlikely to have wanted to run a bank or even to run the country, although a few Moonies will have seen themselves as potential leaders; but he is likely to have wanted to make a definite contribution to the society in which he lives.

He may, however, have found that, unlike his family, society is rather uninterested in him. Having been a big fish in a little pond, both at home and, perhaps, at school, he is liable to have become a little fish in a big pond once he went to university or sought employment. Modern, bureaucratic society may be willing to *give* in an impersonal, welfare-state kind of way, but it is unlikely to want to *take* anything very much. Organizations like Voluntary Service Overseas tend to be highly selective, and they now demand fairly high qualifications or skills before they employ the services of young volunteers. Calls to fight for King and Country (or the equivalent) are few and far between – and Horatio Algers are few and far between too. It is not, generally speaking, until one has slowly worked one's way up one's career that one can hope for the more obvious rewards of achievement. There are, of course, occupations like teaching, the medical profession, the police and the armed services, and, indeed, several Moonies have had or have been on the way to qualifying for such jobs; but even in such occupations considerable frustration can be experienced by the idealist. Several Moonies who were nurses have told me that they felt that the medical profession was incapable of looking at patients as 'whole' people, or 'we were just expected to treat the disease; no one ever asked about the underlying causes for what was going wrong.'

Jane and Anne are two fairly typical Moonies, both of whom had trained for, and got themselves jobs in, 'service-to-others' professions. Jane had always wanted to be a teacher, but

> I became totally disillusioned with teaching – feeling unable to help children morally. Also, the parents didn't seem to be really concerned about this aspect of education, only in their school grades. When I took the RE lesson, some of the kids said, 'Jesus must die!' I felt I wanted to educate the parents in heart, rather than the children. [This] made me look deeply into what was wrong in education and society at large. I came to realize that there was something wrong with parental values and standards – that there seemed to be no *absolute* standards, that they were unsure of life themselves, so they weren't true guides for their children.

She and her husband decided to give up teaching and took up a job in a Children's Home:

> In the . . . Home I saw how we were only treating the effect of wrongs in society rather than the core of the problem. I felt if we stayed there till we were 90, there would still be children coming in by the thousands. . . .
>
> Teaching had always been my 'dream' career, so when I gave it up it was as if I had lost my direction in life. I was also searching for absolute truth at that time too. When I gave up teaching I felt as if I'd put myself in God's hands completely, so he could lead me directly to this truth. It took five months.

She had then met the Unification Church, and, with her husband, decided to join.

> I felt I had found my 'home' at last, especially that I had found my 'Father' – someone who had suffered so much so I could come to know the truth. I felt *completely* carefree for the first time in my life and a feeling of great hope for the future, not just for myself but for the whole world.

By joining she felt that she could 'help the Messiah to restore the world and take some of our Heavenly Father's burden upon myself'.

Anne is another case of someone who had become upset at the state of the world but could find no way in which she felt she could make any impact:

> I knew that I had to have some kind of direction or just some kind of purpose because I am the kind of person if I can't give everything to what I'm doing, I just don't feel happy. I'm like an all-or-nothing person. . . .
>
> I just took O-Levels. I just couldn't stand it at school. . . . I thought I'll just stick to my nursing. What I'll do, I'll do a specialist course and become really fantastic at that, and then if I do that, maybe I'll really feel happy that I've achieved something – so I was going to do Intensive Care because I have always liked to work under pressure . . . like when I was in Casualty and the theatre. . . . I always felt good when working under pressure. . . .
>
> I was always thinking of the world and what was happening . . . and I was always very concerned about it, and I felt, 'It's all very well me doing this' – and I knew nursing was good work and I knew it was helping people, but somehow I never felt happy, I never felt it was enough. . . . I never felt fulfilled in what I was doing. . . .
>
> . . . my whole feelings about what was happening in the world

began to get so intense. I was just thinking about it the whole time. I remember I saw a programme on Ethiopia, and just seeing the faces of those people - I remember I was sitting in front of the television and I just couldn't stop crying. . . . I thought, 'Well, what am I doing? I can't just stay inside the four walls of a hospital and think that I'm doing something, because I'm not.'. . . there was nobody, there was no politician, there was no person who could do anything about it; things just seemed to go on and on, there was one famine after another, there was one disaster after another. . . I just began to feel very desperate and very kind of afraid – not for myself, but just for the whole situation. I just couldn't think where it was all leading to.

She started reading various philosophies and exploring Eastern religions in an attempt to understand how the world worked, but she found them all very theoretical: 'I mean, it wasn't practical at all; for themselves it was OK, but actually it just couldn't work.'

Of course, it is not only Moonies who are upset at the state of the world. One of the most distressing aspects of my research was discovering the complete hopelessness and helplessness which was expressed by so many of the control group. When they were asked what they thought the world would be like in the year 2000, many of them said that they did not think the world would survive that long. Those who did think that we might still be here, frequently drew pictures of abject misery. One fairly typical answer from a control respondent was:

I don't think the world will last for much later than 2000 as habitable to humans. There will be increasing background radiation and pollution, probably punctuated by accidents (i.e. nuclear, oil tanker) until a nuclear weapon is used in war again – which will automatically result in retaliation in kind. It seems that things will get messier by degrees.

Another member of the control group predicted that the turn of the century would be

Bloody awful, much more unemployment, more inequality in society, much more mechanization, more inequality between rich and poor nations. More old, less young people. No future, or hope. All-powerful state or all-powerful private companies – same thing – lack of individuality, lack of initiative, lack of love. Life focussed on job, marriage, TV. Divided nation as wealth, race, class.

There were, of course, some members of the control group who were optimistic about the future, but most were not. Some were determined to

What Hope For The Year 2000?

—VIOLENCE AND WAR!

—RACISM AND MATERIALISM!

—IMMORALITY AND DELINQUENCY!

—This is our reality—none of which can be completely or even partially solved in an instant. A FUNDAMENTAL AND ETERNAL solution is needed.

The key to truly solving or eliminating any of these problems is knowing and understanding their causes.

THE PRINCIPLE explains these causes and then presents clear and practical solutions.

Knowledge is intellectual and spiritual renewal.

Ignorance is death and destruction.

The revelation that God gave to Sun Myung Moon was given quietly in the East, but it has given men and women throughout the world new happiness and new hope.

(Above and opposite) Leaflet promising hope for the year 2000. The emblems are symbolic representations of the worlds' major religions.

INVITATION

This Sunday, members of the Unification Church would like to extend a welcome to anyone who is willing and open enough to come along to our centre in London and listen to an introduction to the teaching of the Unification Church, the Principle, which we believe has the power to deeply move the human mind and spirit and enables us to experience our own re-creation.

TO-NIGHT we invite you to an evening of dinner and entertainment, as well as a talk outlining one part of the Principle.

Admission . . . £1.00

Programme:

● DINNER ....6.00 p.m.

● TALK ....7.00 p.m.

● MUSIC by the GO WORLD BAND ....8.00 p.m.

---

make the best of a bad job; some were resigned to having a fairly miserable life; many reported being 'bored' and expected to go on being bored; others had adopted an 'Eat, drink and be merry, for tomorrow we die' attitude. Few displayed any faith in politics; politicians were considered either ineffectual idiots or self-seeking hypocrites. As we shall see below, the majority felt that not only had they no control over the world, but they also had precious little control over their own lives. And the Moonies reported having had very similar feelings – until they met the Unification Church.

Seekership

Reading the testimonies of Moonies like Anne and Jane, it seems clear that they were what is sometimes referred to as 'seekers' – that is, they had been actively trying to find something which would satisfy a need or desire which they felt was not being met in their immediate environment. The identification of seekership, like that of 'need' or 'mind-control', can be question-begging when it takes the form 'If Jonathan has found fulfilment in something as "off-beat" as the Unification Church, he must have been looking for something like that – he must have been a seeker.' In fact, Jonathan may have been looking for something which was sort-of-like-that, although it is unlikely that he would have been looking for something precisely-like-that.

Seekership comes in a variety of guises. There are those who are merely playing the social 'role' of a seeker; there are those who seek self-enlightenment and/or self-fulfilment; there are those who seek spiritual enlightenment and/or spiritual fulfilment; there are political seekers who want to change the structure of society by democratic or revolutionary means; there are philosophical seekers who want to understand the meaning of the universe; there are religious seekers who want to find or come closer to God; and there are 'don't know' seekers who are aware of an aching vacuum which they are desperately trying to fill. The Moonie bundle of characteristics tends to contain a mixture of the last two types.

Let me begin by drawing a distinction between, on the one hand, personal, private seekership in which a person is looking, usually by himself, for something for which he is unable to find any fulfilment in his social environment, and, on the other hand, the social *role* of the seeker, which may or may not be available in the culture or subculture in which a person finds himself. Merely playing the social role of a seeker is not likely to result in someone's becoming a Moonie.

I described earlier how many young people have experienced difficulties in finding someone with whom they felt that they could talk about their religious experiences and/or feelings. It might, with some justification, be argued that, while this may be a problem in Stockholm, Brussels, Liverpool or Cincinnati, it could hardly be considered one in San Francisco. In fact, it seems to be just as much of a problem there, but for different reasons. In Scandinavia the role of the seeker is practically nonexistent: while the culture may seem to be unusually permissive in a number of ways, one does not get the impression that one has permission to bring religious or spiritual questions into general conversation. I was, none the less, able to find plenty of evidence that there were young adults who wanted to talk about such things: it was not difficult for a foreign (Scottish) sociologist of religion to unleash a flood of pent-up emotions and questionings about spiritual matters and ultimate meanings.[22] In Britain, many other parts of Europe and, perhaps, most of North America, one has to be fairly careful whom one talks to on these subjects, although one can find groups in which discussion of the 'Beyond' is permitted or even encouraged. In California, however, one's 'spiritual quest' is a favourite topic of conversation for anyone who wants to show that he is 'with it': one can observe the role of the seeker being acted out with enthusiastic verve.[23] But 'proper' seekership has to follow certain stereotypical patterns; the mass individualism which is to be found along the West Coast enjoys a socially institutionalized spontaneity, and anyone who happens not to be following the latest craze, or tossing off the latest expressions of spirituality, can feel just as isolated and frustrated in his search for a religiously 'safe' environment as the personal seekers of Britain or Scandinavia. The trendy Californian 'psychobabble'[24] does not seem to attract Moonies, any more than those playing the role of seeker are likely to be attracted to the Unification Church, although some of them may attend a workshop. Becoming a Moonie is not something one does because it is the 'in thing'.

Turning to the more personal type of individual seekership, it appears that although they will have wanted self-enlightenment and spiritual fulfilment, Moonies are unlikely to have sought it *directly* in the way that Scientologists attempt to become a 'Clear',[25] or those who join the Human Potential movement attempt to explore their inner psyches;[26] nor will many Moonies be the sorts of people who find satisfaction in spending, or suspending, time in the search for spiritual enlightenment in the way that mystic or Premies try to grasp to receive 'inner Knowledge'.[27] Although they will have wanted to see a better world, Moonies are very unlikely to have been involved in any political movement or to have been interested in society as a social structure; at the same time, however, they are likely to have been dissatisfied with the abstractions of philosophy, although several of them (more than the control group) will have tried exploring philosophical writings, including Eastern philosophy. In other words, the potential recruit is likely to have been seeking for self-fulfilment indirectly by seeking a practical way of improving the world while at the same time being less interested in political or revolutionary change than many of his peers.

Considering that the Unification goal is establishing the Kingdom of Heaven on *earth*, that Moonies are dedicated to wiping out communism, and that Moon tells his followers that 'the separation of religion and politics is what Satan likes best' and that they should not abandon politics to non-religious people,[28] it may, at first glance, seem surprising that practically none of the Moonies had been a political seeker. Indeed, table 12 would seem to suggest that Moonies were extraordinarily *un*interested in politics until a political position had been 'poured into' them after they had joined. However, it should be noted, first, that there was, in many cases, already a gap into which something *could* be poured and, secondly, that it would be a mistake to believe that the Moonies have imbibed any very clear political manifesto. The one and only question in my interview schedule which really seemed to stump my interviewees (and it contained

Table 12   What were your political views during the six months before you met the Family, and what are they now?

	Control Group (%)	Moonies 6 months before (%)	Moonies now (%)
Strongly Conservative	4	8	24
Mildly Conservative	25	29	40
Strongly Liberal	6	2	—
Mildly Liberal	10	8	2
Strongly socialist	21	7	2
Mildly socialist	22	12	2
No particular views	10	33	23
Strong rejection of politics[1]			8

Note: [1] Not a pre-coded option.

a lot of very tricky questions) was 'What would you do if you were made Prime Minister tomorrow?' Some people, after embarrassingly long pauses and several 'Well, have a shot' promptings, said that they might try to get rid of pornography or that they would insist that the *Divine Principle* was taught in all schools, but most rank-and-file Moonies just protested that I had asked the wrong question. It was people's hearts, not the structure of society, that needed to be changed, they explained.

Having been a student at LSE during the late 1960s, when it had seemed as if every man and woman at the barricades knew exactly how to transform the whole of society, I was somewhat taken aback by these blank responses. I had not asked the control group for any such practical details in the questionnaire, but I did ask a number of young non-Moonies what they would do if made Prime Minister, and I found myself getting the same non-response. Only a few of my students (who were, after all, at a School of Economics and Political Science) showed any signs of having thought about what someone in power might actually try to accomplish. It seemed as though the Moonies (and possibly quite a number of other young people) were so disillusioned with party politics and/or so convinced that they were in a completely hopeless and helpless situation that they had not bothered to contemplate what they might like to do (or even what they wanted to see done) were they to acquire the power to change things.

Those who joined the Unification Church did, however, feel that they had become part of a group which had a leader – a Messiah – who *did* know what to do, *was* in control and *could* tell them how they too could contribute not just to a higher GNP, better housing conditions or famine relief, but to the even higher goal of restoring God's Kingdom of Heaven on earth. Exactly how this belief is upheld *within* the movement (in so far as it is) cannot be gone into here, but the promise is certainly on offer at the workshops. Table 13 is interesting in that it shows how similar the Moonies' feelings of (lack of) control were to those of the control group before they joined the movement (although it is also of interest that twice as many Moonies claimed that they had had 'complete control' over their own lives). Several of the Moonie respondents made a special note beside their answers to explain that their current feelings of control over others and the world were due not to any individual power but to their being part of a movement which was working according to God's Principle.

I have already described how several Moonies were engaged in religious

Table 13 How much power do/did you feel you actually have/had now/during the six months before meeting the Family:

(i)   to control your own life to do what you want/wanted?
(ii) over other people you know/knew?
(iii) to alter the state of the world?

		Control group (%)	Moonies before (%)	Moonies now (%)
Own life	Complete control	13	26	25
	Quite a lot	57	42	57
	Some but not much	20	22	10
	Very little	7	9	3
	None at all	3	1	2
Over others	Complete control	—	—	1
	Quite a lot	21	19	50
	Some but not much	53	45	27
	Very little	19	22	14
	None at all	7	14	6
To change world	Complete control	1	1	11
	Quite a lot	4	7	75
	Some but not much	21	26	8
	Very little	41	37	3
	None at all	31	28	2

seekership before meeting the Unification Church, but the concept of 'don't know' seekership requires some explanation. Before finalizing my forty-one-page questionnaire, I had asked a score of Moonies to try out a 'pilot' draft. This included several questions in which I tried to gauge the type and strength of seekership to be found among potential Moonies. One member, while discussing his answers to these questions with me, volunteered the information that he had definitely been searching for

Table 14   About the time you went to the 2-day workshop, how important were the following ideals in your life?

		Important and seeking (%)	Important but not seeking (%)	Not often aware of importance (%)	Not at all (%)
High	Joiners	34	36	7	24
standard	Non-joiners	22	44	20	15
of	Leavers	17	11	33	38
living	Control	26	42	22	10
Success	Joiners	44	27	7	22
in	Non-joiners	57	22	8	12
career	Leavers	28	23	11	39
	Control	50	31	8	10
Better	Joiners	66	28	5	2
relationship	Non-joiners	56	29	12	3
with	Leavers	42	58	—	—
others	Control	70	24	4	1
	Joiners	39	48	2	11
Ideal	Non-joiners	26	37	5	32
marriage	Leavers	37	42	11	11
	Control	40	40	8	11
Improving	Joiners	42	51	6	2
the	Non-joiners	29	54	7	10
world	Leavers	53	37	5	5
	Control	24	58	7	10
	Joiners	55	23	18	5
Understanding	Non-joiners	51	15	17	16
God	Leavers	64	24	12	—
	Control	32	24	14	29

Table 14 (continued)

		Important and seeking %	Important but not seeking %	Not often aware of importance %	Not at all %
Spiritual fulfilment	Joiners	55	18	23	5
	Non-joiners	51	20	14	15
	Leavers	66	17	11	6
	Control	45	28	9	17
Control over own life	Joiners	75	18	7	—
	Non-joiners	60	22	9	10
	Leavers	73	17	11	—
	Control	65	19	9	7
'Something' but did not know what	Joiners	56	20	4	21
	Non-joiners	30	12	22	36
	Leavers	40	20	27	13
	Control	16	11	22	50

something but he had had no idea what it was that he was looking for. The questionnaire included a list of values or goals, and the respondents were asked to say how important these were and whether they had been actively trying to achieve them or had just been hoping for their attainment. I decided to add 'Something, but didn't know what' to the list. To my amazement, I found that this was the 'ideal' which, more than any other, discriminated between the Moonies, the non-joiners and the control. Table 14 shows that the Moonies were far more likely than the control or even the non-joiners to have considered this to be important and to have been actively seeking it. Table 14 does not, however, show the number of Moonies who added enthusiastic comments such as 'Yes!!' or the number of confused members of the control group who wrote, 'What??', 'Don't understand', or 'Bloody silly question', in the margin.

10 Conclusions

'What conclusions have you come to?' is a question I have been asked on countless occasions by those (including the Moonies themselves) who have heard that I was studying the Unification Church. I have never quite known how to respond. I have, of course, come to many conclusions, but it is difficult to produce one, or even half a dozen, which could sum up the entire research – or even that part of it which is concerned with the recruitment. Quite often, when it is learned that I have myself been through the 'brainwashing process', the initial question is supplemented with: 'Have you ever felt that you want to join?' The answer to that (to the Moonies' chagrin) is a simple one: 'No, not for an instant; I have always found the movement eminently resistible.' But this is a personal response, and it does not follow that I might not feel that I can understand how others could find themselves wanting to join. Indeed, I suppose that if I were pushed to provide a single conclusion to this part of my study, it would be that I believe it *is* possible to increase our understanding of why certain people become Moonies. Having said that, however, I would also want to insist that no single explanation can be given and, indeed, that any single explanation would be *wrong*. It is necessary to consider a large number of data, not all of which might, by themselves, seem very important, but which, when taken together, can build up a general (possibly an unavoidably *too* general) and rather complicated picture. In this final chapter I try to sketch the outlines of a picture which emerges from the details presented in the earlier chapters.

One cannot, however, order and generalize data without some sort of 'organizing principle', and here, as throughout the rest of the book, I have been guided by an attempt to assess the relative importance and inter-action of the four variables which, it will be remembered, were isolated in chapter 5 as those which would be most significant in deciding the manner and extent to which coercion rather than choice might be responsible for the particular outcome. Put less abstractly, the questions that are being addressed are: to what extent does someone become a Moonie because he decides, in the light of his predispositions and past experiences, that the beliefs and practices of the Unification Church are 'better' than those of the 'outside' society? How far do his experiences of the outside society constitute a 'push' towards the Unification alternative? How far does the Unification alternative present an attractive 'pull' away from other alternatives? and to what extent is the immediate (Unification) environment responsible for *reinterpreting* the person's predispositions and experiences so that he is aware only of what the Unificationists themselves want him to be aware of and thus will recognize only one possible future – being a Moonie?

Starting with what is probably the most contentious of the four variables, it is clear that the Unification environment has played an important role in the recruitment of the majority of the members in the West. Unlike most of the other new religions, the Moonies usually try to persuade their potential recruits to attend residential courses. While this practice may in itself cut down the number of people who are willing to learn about the movement, it does mean that those who attend will be in a carefully controlled situation which can exert a considerable influence on some of the guests.

There is no evidence that any kind of physical coercion is used by the Moonies, or that the diet or workshop activities seriously impair the biological functionings of the guests to the extent that they would be judged incapable of behaving 'normally' were they in another *social* environment at that time. There is, however, plenty of reason to believe that the Moonies will do their best to influence their guests' perception of the situation in which they now find themselves. Some of the guests' memories are more likely to be evoked than others; hopes and fears and, sometimes, feelings of guilt may be played upon; care is taken to find out what 'resonates' with each individual; options are painted in terms most favourable to the Unification Church's alternative; less attractive aspects of the movement are suppressed or, occasionally, denied; in some places, most particularly in California, there has been little opportunity for potential recruits to be exposed to a countervailing influence; and, most significant of all, the experience of a loving, caring community within the Unification environment can foster feelings of personal involvement with individuals, which then developed into feelings of trust and commitment and loyalty to the group – feelings which may encourage the guest to accept, more readily than he would otherwise, the world from a Unification perspective.

But it is also obvious that the Unification environment is not irresistible. Conversion to the movement is the result of a (limited) number of *individual* experiences; it is not the result of a mass-induced hypnosis. The fact that most people who are subjected to the Moonies' attempts to recruit them are perfectly capable of refusing to join the movement rules out those explanations which rely totally on Unification techniques of coercion for an explanation of recruitment to the movement. It also rules out any suggestion that the alternative which the Moonies offer is irresistible – even when it is presented within a Unification context. It points, instead, to the conclusion that the personalities and previous experiences which guests 'bring with them' must play a significant role. This leads us on to the question: in what ways do those who join the movement differ from those who do not?

In chapter 5 I explained how, although we certainly have to examine individual cases if we want to find out what goes into the making of a Moonie, and although we have to recognize that no two cases are ever identical, looking only at the individual Moonie (or ex-Moonie) cannot help us to decide on the type or degree of coercion or choice that may be involved in Unification recruitment. I described how, by means of comparative analysis, it was possible to detect some interesting differences between the bundles of characteristics to be found in five different groups of people: (1) those who became Moonies; (2) those who joined, but then left within a day or two or, at the most, a few weeks; (3) those who went to a workshop, but did not join; (4) a 'non-exposed' control group of a similar age and from a similar background to the Moonies; and (5) the population as whole.

If we look at the population as a whole, it is clear that only a very small proportion has shown any favourable interest in the proselytizing efforts of the Moonies. Those who have responded have tended to be overwhelmingly between the ages of 18 and 28, predominantly male, disproportionately middle-class and usually unmarried. By way of contrast, those who have become Home-Church or Associate members have shared many of the characteristics of that section of the population which is affiliated to the more conventional churches – that is, they have tended to be older, female, of a slightly lower-class (although still disproportionately middle-class) and, frequently, married.

Plenty of reasons have been put forward to explain why young adults will do things which seem to their elders (and some of their peers) to be wrong-headed, irresponsible, incomprehensible, bizarre or insane. Youth is a time for idealism, rebellion and experimentation. If one happens to come from the advantaged middle classes, one can afford the luxury of denying oneself luxuries while following idealistic pursuits. Enjoying the health of youth and unencumbered by immediate responsibilities, one can disclaim material interests – at least until one has 'matured' sufficiently to abandon extravagant fantasies, settle down, accept and probably uphold the pursuits and values of conventional society.

Such observations undoubtedly have a considerable amount of truth in them, and they can help us to understand why those who commit themselves to full-time membership of the Unification Church are liable to be drawn from a particular age range, but by themselves these generalizations are far too sweeping and could apply to many periods throughout history. We might want to ask whether there are more specific features of contemporary society which could be providing a more specific push towards a movement like the Unification Church. Furthermore, such generalizations do not help us to explain why some of these young people should become Moonies while others become Anglicans, Maoists, freedom fighters, punks, glue-sniffers, football hooligans or explorers of the upper reaches of the Amazon. We have seen that not all young people flock to find out what the Unification Church has to offer – in fact, the majority of them express an extreme distaste not merely for the movement as it has been publicized, but also for many of the beliefs and practices which it embodies.[1] How do some of these young people come to see it in a different light?

The assumption that the Unification alternative is universally repugnant to anyone in his right mind has been partly responsible for questions about recruitment to take the form: 'How could *anyone* become a Moonie?' and for the reply to be that no one in his right mind *could* become a Moonie. The fact that there *are* Moonies has then been explained in one of two ways, the simplest explanation being that the person was not in his right mind because he had been subjected to an irresistible technique such as brainwashing or mind-control. I have argued, however, that this leads to another question: how (once he has come into contact with the movement) could anyone *not* become a Moonie? The fact that there are those who do resist the Unification techniques would seem to lead to a second explanation: that those who become Moonies cannot really be said to be in their right minds because they are particularly passive, pathetic or suggestible people. But the evidence suggests that, although a few Moonies might fall into this category, the majority do not; indeed, it seems that, while some such people may be drawn to the workshop, it is precisely those whom one might have expected to be the most vulnerable to persuasion who turn out to be non-joiners, with the few who do agree to join deciding to leave within a very short space of time. It would seem, then, that there is at least a prima-facie case for assuming that although the Unification alternative is not attractive to the majority of young people, it can hold an attraction for some people who appear to be 'in their right minds'.

Before pursuing the distinction between joiners and non-joiners a bit further, it might be helpful to remind ourselves of what it is that the Unification Church would seem to be offering the potential recruit. I present the following summary in terms of the Unification belief system as this is how it is presented to the potential recruit, but I also try to present it in such a way that some of the practical consequences can be recognized in so far as these could persuade certain people (but not others) that the movement is offering them a more important, attractive or compelling alternative than the 'outside' society seems to be offering them. I shall also make a distinction between (1) the movement's vision of an ultimate goal, and (2) the more immediate means which, it is believed, will bring about the goal. I do this because I suspect that a recognition of the peculiar combination of a transcendental goal on the one hand and mundane means on the other hand gives us an important clue about the attraction that the movement can hold for a particular kind of person, while it 'puts off' others. (It also provides several clues as to how the movement can command the kind of obedience that it does from its members).[2] Furthermore, while the belief that there exists (or could exist) a direct relationship between the means and the ultimate goal is possibly the Moonies' greatest act of faith,[3] I suspect (although it is rarely put in such terms) that it is largely the belief that there is *no* such connection which has led many of the movement's opponents to view the Unification Church as fundamentally deceptive and exploitive.

As will be remembered from chapter 3, the Unification goal is conceptualized as restoring the Kingdom of Heaven on earth; the means are conceptualized as following the Messiah, paying indemnity, understanding God's *Divine Principle* and perfecting oneself – the last being a process which has its ritual celebration in the Holy Wine ceremony (held before the marriage 'Blessings') when, it is believed, the participants are purified and cleansed of original sin as the satanic component of their lineage is changed into a heavenly lineage.[4]

The Goal

1 The basic vision is *religious*. Even in California, where it is initially couched in more secular language, the goal is seen primarily as God's goal – it is the restoration of *God's* Kingdom of Heaven on earth.

2 The focus is *'this-worldly' v. 'other-worldly'*.[5] In the special sense that it wishes to change society and to establish a theocracy,[6] the Unification Church is also a political movement. Although restoring the spirit world is important in Unification theology, this can be achieved only through the restoration of the physical world. Jesus was able to bring about spiritual, but not physical salvation.[7] The goal is to build the Kingdom of Heaven *on earth*.

3 An *alter v. ego* orientation: although each Moonie is meant to perfect himself, the Unification goal is primarily for the good of others – for society as a whole and, especially, for God – rather than for the promotion of one's own self-realization. In this the Unification Church differs from movements (such as Scientology, Synanon, *est* or the Human

Potential movement)[8] which strive primarily to promote the individual members' or clients' personal development or self-awareness.

4 *Absolute* Values: when the Kingdom of Heaven is established on earth, the uncertainty of relativism will disappear and absolute, perfect, and eternal truth will be known.

5 The *Ideal Family*: the basic unit of society will be a God-centred family in which men and women complement each other in a harmonious give-and-take relationship and have children who are born without original sin.

6 *An unarticulated end-state*: there is no clear blueprint telling us exactly what the Kingdom of Heaven will be like once established on earth.[9]

The Means

1 The means are *given by God*. It is believed that God knows the best way to restore His Kingdom. His helpers must act in accord with His divine Principle, and follow the Messiah whom He has chosen – or those who, through a chain of sanctioned communication, are in an 'Abel' or 'subject' position.

2 Personal *responsibility*: the goal is achievable only if men and women play their allotted roles. They have to put 100 per cent effort into the 5 per cent of the restoration for which mankind is responsible.[10] If they do not, God's work will be in vain.

3 It must be a *group* effort. Although each individual must perform his role, he must do so as part of the Unification movement. The Kingdom, it is argued, cannot be achieved by each person doing his own, unco-ordinated, thing. The strength of the movement lies in its acting as a whole.

4 *Discipline* is essential. The necessity for obedience to authority follows from points 1 and 3. While the suppression of conscience is at any time wrong, it is essential for the individual to admit that he has not got all the answers. He must put himself in a position in which God can guide him; he must (temporarily) embrace poverty, chastity and obedience in order to purify his motivation and attitude and to bring a 'restored' set of values into a world in which the beneficial use of wealth, the ideal marriage and the honest exchange of opinions are all centred on God rather than on worldly self-interests.

5 *Indemnity* conditions: generally speaking, the harder and more un-pleasant a task is, the greater the indemnity paid for one's own (or others') misdeeds in the past, and the more one is contributing to overcoming the accumulated impediments to the restoration of the Kingdom.[11] The greater the *challenge*, the greater the *sacrifice*, and the more one pushes oneself, the more one can achieve.

6 Both 'internal' and 'external' missions must be accomplished.

(a) *Internally*, each individual must develop his spiritual self. This is done through such 'conditions' as prayer and fasting; through the study and understanding of the *Divine Principle*; through humbling oneself before God and not letting Satan or evil spirits invade one's thoughts. Internal progress is difficult for the individual to assess. Although an individual may himself feel that he is accomplishing the proper attitude, it is always possible that this is arrogance, which is really the work of Satan.

(b) *External* means take a variety of forms, but in the majority of cases these are tasks which consist of achieving very clearly defined goals (such as collecting money or recruiting new members), and each Moonie's success or failure is both visible and quantifiable. At the same time, the pursuit of external means is seen as part of the spiritual (internal) training of the individual.

7 *Urgency*: The *time* element is all-important. If God's side does not win within a certain (not entirely clear, but undoubtedly limited) period,[12] then Satan will be able to claim victory, and the world, if it continues to exist, will be in an even nastier state than it is now.

Put slightly differently, the Unification Church is unlikely to appeal to people who are interested primarily in making money or 'getting on' in a competitive rat race; it offers a 'higher' ideal than the materialism of modern society – it offers a religious ideal. But it is not the sort of religion which offers its followers a method of withdrawing from this world in order to meditate upon the Beyond or to glimpse their own inner godliness through mystical experiences; not is it the sort of religion which enjoins its members to await their rewards in the next world. It is a religion which promises to change this world, for everyone, so that it is a better world – indeed, the best of all possible worlds, the sort of world which God intended there to be when He first created the Garden of Eden. Exactly what the Kingdom will be like in detail may be left to the individual to imagine, but it is known that cruelty, uncertainty and compromise will disappear; everyone will know what is true and good in accordance with God's divine Principle; and everyone will know where he or she stands. It will be a world in which a loving, caring God has a loving, caring relationship with each individual, and in which each individual will also find him or herself as an integral part of a God-centred family into which children, unencumbered by original sin, will be born the inheritors of the New Age.

Whatever the details, the means to achieve the goal are, it is believed, known by God – and by the Messiah who came to reveal God's Principle and to act as the perfect example for the less-than-perfect disciples. And while the goal may in some ways seem abstract, the means most certainly are not. Not only is each individual given spiritual guidance, but he is also set tasks of a highly practical nature. It is possible for Moonies to *see* what they are achieving as they pursue their individual goals, and in so far as these intermediate goals take the form of fund-raising or recruiting new members, it is even possible to calculate the successes and failures of each day's work. The strict organization and the discipline mean that everyone knows exactly what he should be trying to achieve, and that he is part of a larger, unified whole. But the organization is not presented as an impersonal, bureaucratic machine run by interchangeable little cogs; it is seen as a devoted Family of brothers and sisters who are lovingly cared for by 'True Parents'. The concept of indemnity implies that the more arduous his labour, the more the sacrificial Moonie will have accomplished – but the sacrifice is not for ever. The promise is that it need not be long before those who accept the challenge to fulfil their responsibility can enjoy the results of their contribution to the building of the Kingdom.

The Non-Moonie Option

Turning now to the *non*-Unification alternative, one can draw a distinction between specific 'pushes' which affect a particular individual and more general feelings of discontent which can affect a wide range of individuals. Colin provides an example of someone who was experiencing a relatively specific push. He had been taking drugs and was deeply involved with a girl who wanted to marry him. He saw the Unification Church as an undreamed-of haven of peace:

> I could feel the prison doors just closing on me and I could see a really miserable life ahead of me. I used to think, if I've got these things bothering me, why don't other people have these things bothering them? Not knowing everybody has these kind of difficulties in life, nobody exposes them or talks to each other about them, so everybody lives in their own little world, never really getting to know anyone. You find this even with married couples. . . .
>
> I remember after the weekend I just cried – I felt such a happiness inside me like I hadn't felt all my life. And for the first time in my life I saw a real direction and a real hope for mankind, I really did.

Colin's situation was not unique, but the evidence suggests that the typical Moonie is no more likely than his peers to have found himself in a particularly harrowing situation. Far more common are cases in which the society in which the potential recruits found themselves was not posing any immediate threat so much as forming a general backcloth of disillusionment and discontent. It was this backcloth against which the

Unification alternative would be judged and which could result in the sort of direct comparison that could lead a Moonie to declare: 'The bad society around me showed me that the Family life was the right way.'

What, then, are some of these more general experiences of society which the potential recruit takes with him to the Unification workshop? I shall not attempt to represent an account of society 'as it really is'. One would naturally expect Moonies' descriptions to be affected by their current membership of the movement, but what follows is not meant to be a picture of the 'outside' society as it is defined by the Unification Church. What we are concerned with here is an attempt to understand the social environment as it could have impinged upon the consciousness of the potential convert *before* he met the movement, and which other people would also recognize, even if they would not choose the Unification Church as a viable alternative. The description is drawn not only from the Moonies' accounts of their non-Unification lives but also from the direct and indirect responses of the control group and other non-Moonies to whom I have talked. It is a selective description in that it focuses on those aspects of society which could contribute a push towards (rather than a pull from) the alternative offered by the Unification Church for the sorts of people whose more immediate experiences of society were considered in the previous chapter.

In caricature, the potential recruit can see the non-Unification world as a divisive, turbulent, chaotic society, characterized by racial intolerance, injustice, cut-throat competition and lack of direction – a society which seems to be out of control and heading for imminent disaster. He can see an immoral (possibly amoral) society which no longer recognizes absolute values and standards; everything is relative to the utilitarian interests and desires of a pleasure-seeking, money-grubbing, power-hungry population; the pathetic eyes of skeletal children stare accusingly out of Oxfam posters – which are placed, with Kafkaesque humour, beside glossy advertisements for colour television sets, luxurious automobiles and exotic wines. It is a secular society which dismisses religious questions and spiritual quests as irrelevant vestiges of a pre-scientific age, or confines them to the ivory tower of theological colleges; in so far as the traditional Churches still function, they are (sparsely) populated by hypocritical or apathetic congregations and clergy who consider the occasional token ritual to be sufficient energy to offer unto God.

It is a world in which the family is no longer a stable or a happy institution, and in which it is no longer the fundamental building block of a decent society; old people die alone and unloved; babies are battered; relationships are transitory and exploitative; love has been reinterpreted as sexuality. It is a world in which there is no spirit of community; exchanges between people are instrumental, impersonal and fragmented;

A 'Pornography Destroys Love' rally in Trafalgar Square, London.

ticket collectors, shop assistants, colleagues at work are unaware of the dreams, the fears, the longings or loneliness of those with whom they pass the working day; the characters of a soap opera become more real, more relevant, more important than the impersonal persons whose lives are glimpsed only in one or other disparate compartment. It is a world of insecurity in which nations compete for power and for resources, and in which the threats of nuclear war, pollution, ecological disasters, famine, communism, Third World uprisings, terrorist bombings, warfare and street muggings are exacerbated rather than controlled by corrupt politicians and officials and by sensationalist media reports which focus relentlessly upon crime, sex and violence, and cater for the lowest common denominator to be found among the scandal-hungry masses.

What can be done by the youthful idealist who has a heart that is aching to give, bursting to serve, desperate to sacrifice, who wishes to save the world from the awfulness into which it is falling and for the ideals that he has been taught to espouse? His elders smile indulgently and then become irritated. He is now told that he does not understand, that there is nothing to be done, that one must learn to live with the world as it is, that there comes a stage when one must grow up and learn to face reality. But it is a reality that he does not wish to accept.

Of course, not all these visions are conjured up by everyone, and there are plenty of young people who are aware of more pleasant and hopeful aspects of society. The fact remains, however, that a considerable proportion of the population is worried by many of these features. It is not difficult for an awareness of their existence to be brought to the surface. Few people will deny that such things are part of modern society – how important a part, and whether there is a better alternative, is another question.

Disillusionment with society is scarcely a new phenomenon. Glancing briefly at recent history, Western society has observed a series of rejections by vocal sections of its middle-class youth.[13] During the late 1960s it was the 'imperialistic bourgeois structure of capitalism' which was a primary focus of dissent; students in America, in Europe and, for slightly different reasons, in Japan declared that the structure of society must be changed. When the structure seemed remarkably resilient in the face of demos and vindictive rhetoric, the attempt to change it was replaced by an attempt to reject it altogether. Flower children and hippies dropped out of society and into the new counter-culture.[14]

In contrast to the materialistic, dehumanizing, quantifying rat race, the counter-culture was supposed to allow everyone to develop and to fulfil him or herself as a unique individual, in his or her own right, at his or her own level. Everyone could do his or her own thing, unencumbered by the standards of others; everyone could be equal; everyone could achieve everything. But while the counter-culture offered a haven from the rat race for some, for many of those who had been brought up in an achievement-oriented society it offered only a temporary respite during the initial honeymoon of rejection. Lack of direction and a life bereft of goals or purpose still faced those who continued to find themselves seeking a challenge and wanting to *do* something. The individual became bogged down in the vast expanses of anything or nothing which seemed to be his or her sole existential choices. Within the open, unstructured counter-culture, realities and relationships were quickly created, but with no social pressures to reinforce them or hold them together, they crumbled under minor assault. Disillusionment and frustration awaited those who still wanted to know who they were and where they stood in an environment which had chosen to defy definitions and boundaries, and in which sincerity rested upon the rejection of absolute truths. The freedom of spontaneity had become the insecurity of antinomianism. So long as infinity was the only limit for both the means and the goal, nothing was obtainable. There were no benchmarks which allowed one to know whether one had got anywhere. The liberated individual was alone. He was unable to plug into anything with which to pull his lonely, unattached spirit up by its sagging bootstraps.

In theory young people find themselves in a society of opportunity. All have an equal chance to climb the ladder of the achieving society or to enjoy the permissive society in which anything goes. The world is their oyster. But in practice only a few can prise open the oyster and find anything of value inside. In the competitive, claustrophobic rat race, pearls are few and far between; in the agoraphobic counter-culture, all can have as many pearls as they please – but, as a result, pearls have become worthless.[15]

The Moonie Option

By way of contrast, the alternative which the Unification Church offers is one which seems both to recognize and to provide an explanation for the evils of the contemporary world. By making sense of the past, it offers hope for the future; it offers a clear direction, a clear leadership which knows what to do and how to do it. It is, paradoxically, a movement which offers freedom from directionless choices.

It offers a religious community within which God is at the centre of everyday life; God is a living Being with whom each individual can have a personal relationship. It is not only a community in which each individual can feel the comfort of a loving God – it is also one which gives each individual the chance of comforting *Him*. It offers a loving, caring environment which gives its members not only warmth and affection but also a chance to love and sacrifice themselves for others. It is, paradoxically, a community which gives by taking.

The Unification Church offers the potential recruit the chance to be part of a Family of like-minded people who care about the state of the world, who accept and live by high moral standards, who are dedicated to restoring God's Kingdom of Heaven on earth. It offers him the opportunity to *belong*; it offers him the opportunity to *do* something that is of value and thus the opportunity to *be* of value.

This can be pretty heady stuff for some of those who are experiencing an aching vacuum for 'something'. I have already suggested that the potential Moonie is not the sort of person who will accept anything, but it is not difficult to see how the Unification Church might appeal to someone who is idealistic and who has enjoyed the security of a sheltered family life; someone for whom the big decisions may have been taken, but who is, none the less, an achiever – so long as he has a clear idea of what it is that he has to achieve; someone who has a strong sense of service, duty and responsibility but can find no outlet for his desire to contribute; someone whose belief that everything in the world *could* be all right had been held for a longer time than that of his more cynical friends whose illusions had been shattered at an earlier age and with whom he now has some difficulty in finding much in common; someone for whom religious questions are important and who is receptive to religious answers.

At the same time, the Unification Church is *unlikely* to attract those who are bored by or uninterested in religious and/or social issues. It will not appeal (for long) to those who totally reject the idea that there is a God, or who (in Europe) reject the Bible as a source of divine revelation. It is also unlikely to appeal to those who are already firmly committed to a particular faith or secular ideology, or who already have a clear purpose in life, such as achieving success in a chosen career. But those who drift into the movement because they are at a loose end and have nothing better to do are liable to drift out again quite quickly, as are those who are looking for an easy life in which they can accept rather than contribute. People who are interested in achieving material success on the one hand or, on the other hand, in withdrawing from worldly pursuits in order to contemplate higher things or to concentrate on their own inner consciousness are also unlikely to find much of attraction in the Unification Church. And one of the greatest 'protections' against the promise of a loving, caring community is to be happily married or to have a steady and satisfying relationship with a girl/boyfriend.

Once more, it must be stressed that this is a vastly oversimplified picture. There are those who have joined despite the fact that when they met the movement they were happily married, or did not believe in God, or did not give a jot about the state of the world. It is, however, extremely unlikely that someone who was happily married *and* an atheist *and* unconcerned about the world would become a Moonie. Furthermore, as I suggested in chapter 2, different kinds of people join according to the kinds of alternatives which are on offer, and these have differed according to place and time. It appears that those who joined the movement in its earlier days were more likely to have been 'social misfits';[16] and, during the late 1970s, those who joined in California were likely to have been worried more about the social mess the world was in than about its secularity. And, of course, there are those who have joined for reasons other than those which I have enumerated. I have spoken to Moonies who were actively interested in politics before joining, and who claim that they joined because they thought that the movement was the only realistic means of fighting communism; and I have spoken to others, particularly blacks, who say that they were attracted primarily by the multinational flavour and the idea of marriages between people of different cultures bringing the races together; and I have come across one or two people who (like Colin) became Moonies primarily because the movement offered them an escape from an unbearable situation. But these are the exceptions.

It is, of course, the exceptions which make generalizing a risky business, and in the social sciences it is always possible to find exceptions to the rule. But that does not mean that rules (or, rather, discernible regularities) cannot be detected. The qualifications are the inevitable result of the fact that individuals are born different, will grow up in different environments and will react in different ways to the same experiences. But these different reactions do themselves form patterns which allow us to detect the difference that a new variable (such as a new religion) can make to different kinds of people in different societies. By observing and analysing the patterns we may not produce a complete explanation for a specific individual's behaviour, but we can discover that some generalizations are *less* true than others, and we can understand more about the success or failure which the movement enjoys. In doing so we may also find that some features of the wider society are thrown into sharp relief[17] – the analysis may, for example, point to 'gaps' which have been created and left gaping.

There is, furthermore, a paradoxical aspect to greater understanding of how a particular phenomenon 'works' in that this very understanding can itself lead to a change in the situation so that it may subsequently work either more or less effectively.[18] Understanding why a venture of which we approve has failed in the past can result in our making sure that it works more efficiently in the future; conversely, understanding why a venture of which we disapprove has succeeded in the past can lead us to alter the situation which has led to its success. Rather than putting all the blame on the Moonies, those who believe that the Unification Church does not

The first black and white couple to be matched and blessed, February 1975.

provide an ideal way of life for those who join the movement might do better to try to understand the ways in which society has actually *prepared* certain types of perfectly intelligent people to lead the kind of life that they seem unable to find in society but which is, they believe, offered to them by the Unification Church.

The same couple with their first child in 1979.

Those who feel that the Moonies are wasting their lives might, for example, want to recognize the difficulty that young people have in finding an occupation which they feel is worth while and in which they are contributing something of value to others.[19] Most of us do not believe that there are easy answers to the problems of contemporary society, but that does not mean that there are not many ways in which the energy and idealism of youth may not be tapped, with advantages both to the individuals concerned and to the wider society. Of course, some opportunities do exist, and many young people do make a positive contribution to the welfare of others and society in general, but there are many more who are frustrated, feel helpless and hopeless and suffer from a lack of direction and an absence of meaning in their lives. Traditionally, religion has offered direction and meaning in the lives of believers, and indeed it still

'Doing something': Project Volunteer delivering government surplus cheese to local agencies.

International Relief Friendship Foundation (IRFF) in the Upper Volta.

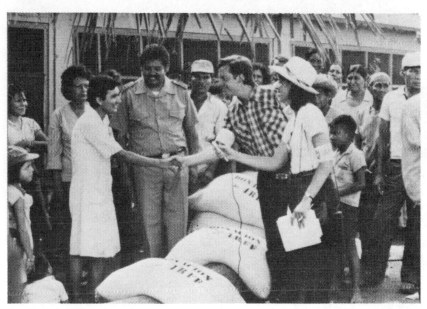

Rice being given to flood victims in Bolivia.

A Unification medical team from Japan in Thailand.

does for large numbers of people. Traditional religion has, however, frequently tended to become bureaucratized and ritualized, and new religions have emerged throughout the course of history to offer their followers a surer, more immediate promise of salvation than the often stagnant institutionalized religions can – especially in times of rapid social change.[20] If they wish to keep their flock, the more orthodox Churches might do worse than try to be slightly more open to discussion about religious questions at a personal level with adolescents. It is not only to those who become Moonies that members of the clergy can appear to be either too remote to approach – or too trendy to be taking either God or religion seriously.[21]

But this is no place to dwell upon the gaps generated by either society in general or the traditional religions in particular. The task I have set myself in this book is confined to addressing the question of why someone will take up the Unification alternative and, as so many people seem to accept that to do so must be the result of brainwashing, my analysis has focused on the evidence and arguments which could support or question such a possibility.

What then are my conclusions? Has my study led me to believe that people join the Unification Church as the result of irresistible brainwashing techniques or as the result of a rational, calculated choice? As will doubtless be clear to anyone who has read thus far, the short reply to such a question is that I do not find either answer satisfactory, but that the evidence would seem to suggest that the answer lies considerably nearer the rational-choice pole of the continuum than it does to the irresistible-brainwashing pole. Such a response frequently elecits a query about why, if this is the case, so many people, including those who knew the Moonie best, insist that he *was* brainwashed. This is a subject which requires a far more detailed response than I can give here, but one or two brief points might be mentioned.[22] At a fairly obvious level, one answer is that 'My child was brainwashed by the Moonies' makes a far better headline than 'Young man decides to adopt Unification faith'. 'Of course,' the questioner will say, 'I don't believe everything I read in the papers but surely, there's no smoke without fire? Anyway, from what I've heard about the movement, that's the only explanation that seems to make any sense.' And, indeed, although (as I argued in chapter 5) brainwashing accounts are usually full of inconsistencies, they can provide a coherent explanation for something which might otherwise seem inexplicable.[23] The idea of someone's washing another person's brain and then inserting alien beliefs and motivations has certainly provided a forceful metaphor for explaining otherwise incomprehensible behaviour, and studies of the 'thought reform' induced in prisoners of war during the last half-century have, as I have already agreed, revealed *some* similarities between the various processes by which people come to change from one set of beliefs to another.

'But why,' I am asked, 'is a direct comparison made with the *Moonies* – why are they picked out?' In fact, the Unification Church is by no means the only movement to have been accused of brainwashing its recruits. Although the actual term 'brainwashing' has been in currency for only a comparatively short time, similar accusations (employing, perhaps, the language of witchcraft or the use of Svengali-like powers) are not new ways of accounting for what have seemed to be undesirable and drastic changes in people's beliefs and practices – changes caused by forces beyond the control of the hapless victim. During the last two decades accusations of brainwashing have been applied (in the 'hard' sense, implying that irresistibly coercive techniques have been used) to groups such as the Symbionese Liberation Army (which kidnapped Patty Hearst) and cases such as that in which a woman in her thirties 'had to be deprogrammed' after declaring that she wanted to marry ('because she was under the power of') an 'unsuitable' partner.[24] At the time of writing ISKCON is appealing against a $9.7 million judgment as the result of a case in which Krishna devotees were accused of brainwashing a 15-year-old girl who had since been deprogrammed (the award to the girl and her mother was originally over $30 million).[25]

The role of the deprogrammers in popularizing the brainwashing account is not without significance. As the First Amendment of the American Constitution, the United Nations Declaration of Human Rights, and the European Convention on Human Rights and Fundamental Freedoms all guarantee individuals the right to believe any religion they choose to believe,[26] it is understandable that legal as well as financial considerations should encourage deprogrammers to insist that their subjects did not *really* choose to believe whatever it is they say they believe. Deprogrammers and councellors are not only likely to claim that Moonies are incapable of escaping without outside intervention,[27] but they are also likely to claim that they always *can* deprogramme a cultist, and that this means that he must have been programmed in the first place. Others have argued that this merely means that it is the deprogrammers who use brainwashing tactics, especially when they employ physical coercion.[28] It would however, be as mistaken to believe that deprogrammers are always successful as it would be to believe that Moonies are always successful. Accurate figures are extremely difficult to come by, but I have interviewed a considerable number of Moonies, and know of many more, who have been through a forcible deprogramming and have subsequently returned to the movement.[29] Usually they express a deep regret that their parents (whom they may now feel they can no longer trust) had been so frightened and exploited by the deprogrammers and the anti-cult publicity. Sometimes they will admit that the experience has left them with some nagging doubts about the movement; more commonly they will declare that their faith in the truth of the *Divine Principle* has been renewed as a result of their having been so sorely 'tested'.[30]

On the other hand, those who are successfully deprogrammed will almost inevitably express profound gratitude to their rescuers[31] and, usually, feelings of guilt for having cost their parents so much suffering and so many thousands of pounds. They are also likely to assert that they would never have left without the intervention of the deprogrammer. It is no doubt true that they would not have left so soon, but it is difficult to be sure that they would not, in their own time, have joined the ever-growing band of voluntary defectors. It would, however, be strange if being presented with another perspective were *not* to make some kind of difference to a person's understanding of the Unification alternative. I am unconvinced that brainwashing (by either the deprogrammers or the Moonies) is necessarily indicated because some people renounce their beliefs after the experience of 'hearing the other side'.[32]

What about the parents and friends who knew the Moonie before he joined the movement? As I have already said, the change in beliefs and life-style can be both sudden and dramatic. At one level the parents will be unable to understand how their offspring could give up a promising future when everything seemed to be going exactly the way they wanted it to go for him. At another level they will be incredulous that he now does many of the things that they had been trying to get him to do for ages – such as cleaning his finger nails and getting his hair cut. One father confided in me: 'He told me he hadn't had sex since he joined, and I believed him. They must have done something to his brain – or something.'

Once the story that brainwashing takes place gains a certain currency, it is easy enough for bewildered and anxious parents to believe that everything seems to fit in with this as the most plausible explanation. Confirmatory evidence is accepted and repeated; other explanations are suppressed or ignored. By now literally hundreds (possibly thousands) of articles have appeared in newspapers, popular magazines and the anti-cult literature which perpetuate the brainwashing hypothesis in more or (usually) less sophisticated forms. Several library shelves could be filled with books (written mainly by ex-members and Evangelical Christians),[33] recounting the various evils of the new movements and, in particular, the sinister control which they have over their members. A number of respectably qualified persons, mostly psychologists or psychiatrists,[34] have published articles of a more scholarly nature and have travelled around the world giving talks to parents and anti-cultist gatherings and testifying in legal proceedings to the effect that the Unification Church and other new religious groups brainwash their members. It has been in an attempt to address the arguments adduced by these fellow academics that I have so peppered this book with methodological considerations.

The Moonies themselves certainly cannot be absolved from blame for fanning the fears that parents may have that their children have been brainwashed. It has often been very difficult for parents to find out what was happening – especially when their offspring have been thousands of miles away from home. Anxious mothers and fathers have flown to California to try to make sure that their sons or daughters were all right, only to be told that their child was not available, or to find that they had the opportunity to talk only in the presence of watchful Moonie companions. This, the Moonies have explained, has been a necessary precaution because of the danger of deprogramming, but it is a practice which has helped to persuade several parents, who would not otherwise have dreamed of illegally kidnapping their own child, that they had to do that very thing. A vicious circle becomes more vicious as each 'side' (as they have now become) provides the other with 'proof' that it indulges in 'dirty tricks' and is not to be trusted. On one occasion in California I asked a British girl why she would not go home to reassure her parents (who I knew were frantic with worry) that she was at least sound in mind and body. Her reply was that she had been about to do so when she had had an hysterical letter from her mother saying that she (the mother) had been so upset that she had taken an overdose of sleeping pills the previous week and that it was all her (the daughter's) fault. 'I knew I couldn't give in to such emotional blackmail,' the Moonie told me. 'They've got to understand that it's my life, and stop trying to run it for me. When they're prepared to accept that, then I'll go home.'[35]

The consideration and understanding that parents have been shown have varied enormously according to the local leadership[36] and, indeed, according to the individual Moonies concerned. But, whatever the circumstances, many parents have undoubtedly had a considerable shock on first encountering their child after he has joined the movement. He may seem to have changed beyond all recognition within a matter of weeks or even days. New converts (to any faith) tend, moreover, to be among the most fanatical of believers. Listening to new Moonies, one can observe that they have not completely 'internalized' their new belief system[37] and therefore tend, when unable to answer a difficult or unfamiliar question, to resort to dogmatic, parrot-like responses, especially when under the emotional stress of trying to explain their new-found faith to their frustrated parents. I have watched Moonies who had been behaving like perfectly sane and rational beings change into jibbering, incoherent idiots when confronted by an angry, uncomprehending parent who (from the Moonie's point of view) has completely failed to listen to what the convert was trying to say and 'just treated me like a kid'. Were I the parent in such circumstances, I am not at all sure that I would not have grave suspicions that my offspring was under some kind of sinister spell. Not being emotionally involved in any particular case, however, and having had the opportunity of observing Moonies when they were not under such pressure (from outside), I have not been persuaded that they are brainwashed zombies.

None the less, I do not wish to argue that the majority of Moonies make a calculated decision to join the movement, consciously taking into account all the relevant details. I do not believe that the majority of joiners expend a great deal of time on weighing up the relative importance of all the pros and cons of membership. Although a few Moonies do claim to have made an entirely rational choice, most will have been swept along by the excitement of having discovered what seemed to be the very answer they had always been looking for, and they will commonly give non-rational (which is not the same as irrational) reasons for their decision to join. Typical explanations are: 'It just made more sense to me than anything else I'd ever heard', 'I felt such relief that someone knew the answers and I didn't have to worry any more', 'I knew I had to give this a chance – it seemed the only hope', 'I could see God was working through these people' or, quite frequently, 'God guided me to the movement.'

While those of us who are not Moonies may accept that a Moonie's reasons for joining may be perfectly valid for him (and that he is not necessarily *wrong*), we may yet remain unsatisfied. We may not accept that his reasons help us to understand sufficiently what has 'really' happened. Of course, no one ever knows precisely what all the factors leading up to a particular outcome have been, and science still has an enormous amount to learn about how the human brain, let alone the human mind, works. We are still grasping for concepts with which to try to express the ways in which we believe that we and others arrive at what we call decisions. Sometimes a distinction is made between 'reasons for' and 'causes of' behaviour; we give reasons for our own behaviour in terms of what makes sense to us (what we believe we took into consideration), and we try to find causes for other people's behaviour, often explaining their actions in terms more of deterministic pushes and pulls than of subjectively understood meanings. This can be a confusing distinction, however, partly because the languages of free will, determinism and causation have so many implicit and ambiguous overtones. Nevertheless, we do question whether people themselves know best what they *really* feel, believe, want, etc. How far are they rationalizing their actions, having been driven by unconscious forces? How far are they aware of the inconsistencies of their arguments? Yet, at the same time, we can ask whether anyone *but* the person concerned can know what he believes or why he acts in the way he does – particularly if we ourselves happen to be the person concerned.[38] If a Moonie insists that the reason why he joined the Unification Church was because God gave him a clear sign, or that God had been guiding him throughout his life, preparing him for membership, what justification has anyone else to suggest that the cause is to be found in his social background, or that he was merely the victim of sophisticated techniques of persuasion?

In this book I have tried to give some justification for the approach that I have taken. I do believe that by comparing the Moonie bundles of characteristics with those of non-joiners and the control group, we have, on the one hand, been able to question whether some of the factors which others have assumed must have been important were in fact all that important, and, on the other hand, we have been able to isolate significant influences which the Moonies might not deny as part of their background but certainly would not use as part of their own explanation. It is, moreover, possible to see how the sorts of explanation which the Moonies give correspond to the kinds of explanation one might expect from people with their sorts of bundles – that is, their own explanations are not all that strange considering the sort of people that they are. For example, the following quotation succinctly epitomizes the kind of response that the Unification Church can elicit from, in this case, a religiously oriented 'doer' with a social conscience: 'I felt that I had been challenged. If you believe it's true, it demands a commitment to action because of what it's saying about the world today and how God's working in the world today.'

Sometimes it may seem as though God is given all the responsibility for the decision ('Once I knew this was God's will, I knew I had no choice'). It should, however, be noted that only certain sorts of people will be prepared to submit to His wish, and although a willingness to submit could be taken to imply that such people are not very strong-willed, it is not difficult to think of plenty of historical examples of men and women who are generally considered to have had extremely strong wills while submitting to what they believed was His will – and I have come across some very strong-willed Moonies. Furthermore, it should not be forgotten that the submitter has to decide that it *is* to the will of God and not an imposter that the submission is being made. I have tried to show that Moonies are frequently people who have had some fairly clear ideas about the sorts of answer and command God might offer, or at least that their preconceived notions have not been incompatible with those proposed by the Unification alternative (while they have been incompatible with some other ideas and ideologies). Despite the fact that non-believers may suspect that the Unification Church is taking advantage of the vacuum that many young people are seeking to fill, the evidence suggests that the movement's revelations are convincing for only a limited number of people, and, of course, for many of these people the vacuum which had been created before they met the movement was not merely a religious one. The religious answer would seem to have required a fair degree of compatibility with more secular hopes and expectations.[39]

Take, for example, the case of William, who came from a respectable lower-middle-class Baptist background and had been a Sunday-school teacher. He gave as his real reason for joining the movement the discovery that the *Divine Principle* cleared up problems that he had been having with his understanding of the Bible. He had, however, also experienced mild difficulties in finding the ideal relationship he had dreamed of having with a girlfriend. He first met the movement when he heard someone lecture at a club that he had visited on several occasions in the hope of meeting people who were more interested in the kinds of questions which he was asking than his fellow university students seemed to be. In the following quotation one can glimpse ways in which all four of the variables which I isolated in chapter 5 could have interacted to play a role in influencing his joining the movement.

> One of the things that really appealed to me was I was looking for something that was based on God's principles because all the groups that I'd been to didn't really bring God into it very much and I thought that was why they didn't last. And then the idea of perfect marriage, where it's God who brings people together: that really struck me because that sort of conclusion I'd reached after a lot of

struggle. I'd reached the stage where I'd say, 'OK, God, it's up to you.' I'd trust Him to lead me to the right person. He knew me better than I knew myself, and He knew the exact, one right person. So the idea of the perfect marriage really excited me. I thought, 'Well, of course, that's the answer,' because all my friends had a lot of unhappiness – their relationships breaking up, not happy marriages. So I was getting a bit disillusioned with things. But that was the real answer, really, when I heard about the Principle. I couldn't question it, it seemed so right. All the things I'd been working on before it brought in, and went so much further, and solved all the things I was a bit uncertain about in the Bible. Reading the Bible, some bits, they don't seem to fit in; it cleared everything up – and the pattern of the whole thing is so wonderful – *pow*! It was really that! I just knew absolutely this had to be right, had to be true.

To point to influences in a person's past life as having an explanatory power in our understanding of why he joined or did not join the Unification Church is not to suggest that no element of choice was involved. Indeed, according to my definition of choice in chapter 5, it would be *necessary* for a person's previous experiences to play at least some role in the process of his coming to a decision. It seems clear that those who become Moonies can be seen as active agents to the extent that their already existing hopes, fears, values and previous experiences of society are 'used'. To some extent, it can be seen that the Moonies also 'use' (play upon) these characteristics, but they are not successful in playing upon *mere* suggestibility. What I have argued is that the data suggest that the potential recruit will have been subjected to not one but many multi-faceted influences and that quite a lot of 'sorting out' will have been done, even if it was at a relatively non-conscious level, with the guests being perfectly capable of 'using' (drawing upon) characteristics which do *not* resonate with Unificationism in order to reject the movement. In other words, it would seem to be possible for the outside observer to recognize a way in which the Moonies' powers of persuasion are effective only when it could 'make sense' to say that there existed a potential affinity between a guest's *pre*dispositions and *pre*suppositions and the Unification beliefs and practices as they have been presented to him – when, in other words, we can understand why 'someone like that' could be attracted to 'something like that'.

Given the enormous diversity to be found between Moonies and between Unification practices according to time and place, it is no doubt foolhardy to attempt too specific a final summary of my conclusions, but it does seem that if one were to gauge the relative influence of the four variables in the recruitment of a large number of Moonies and to plot these configurations at the most appropriate position on (a three-dimenensional version of) table 5, one would find the largest cluster of cases (well over half) around a point at which the four variables were fairly evenly balanced (what I called a situation of 'non-conscious fit'). There would also be a small number of cases in which the Unification environment had had almost no influence (there is, for example, an English Moonie who studied the *Divine Principle* while serving with the army); but I doubt if there would be any cases around the point which represented the Unification environment as the *only* influence. There would be some small clusters of cases in which the Moonie had been particularly open to suggestion because of his immediate or past experience of society, and in a few cases the Moonie would have joined not because of any intrinsic attraction that the Unification alternative held for him but because he just happened to have met the Unification Church and happened to have an unusually suggestible character. But, again very generally speaking, if the 'push' has been much greater than the 'pull', so that there is no obvious 'fit' between the persons character and what the movement is offering, then he is unlikely to remain a Moonie for very long unless he becomes attracted to the people, the beliefs and/or the way of life soon after he has joined.

The influence of the group upon the individual member is, of course, far greater once someone has become a full-time member, spending most of his life within a fairly authoritarian structure and in the company of others of the same persuasion. During the first month or so he will be at his most vulnerable to both the persuasions and the dissuasions of the movement; that is, he will be less sure of himself and therefore more open to suggestion about what to 'put into' the gaps that still exist in his recently acquired vision of reality – for, with his acceptance of an unfamiliar *Weltanschauung*, he will, to some extent, have lost the standards of reference by which he had previously assessed new information. But, at the same time, he will be less committed and thus quite likely to decide that the movement is not really what he thought it was or what he wanted, and he is, therefore, quite liable to leave.

After they have been in the movement for some time Moonies do change in certain ways, but not nearly as much as is sometimes assumed. There is the occasional 'burnt-out case', when someone who has spent a long time on a particular mission (usually fund-raising) breaks down, but Moonies are no more likely to stagnate into mindless robots than are their peers who travel to the city on the 8.23 each morning. They will develop in a number of ways, both emotionally and intellectually, and while they may miss one set of opportunities and experiences, they usually have the opportunity to enjoy many other, often remarkably wide-ranging and challenging experiences. But they will also find that they are presented with a wide range of problems, disillusionments and disappointments, and the majority will, without the need of outside intervention, leave (or at least cease to be full-time members) within a couple of years of joining. The rest may also have problems but will remain convinced that, despite these, the Unification Church is still a better place in which to be than any of the other alternatives open to them. They may continue to hold fast to the ideal of restoring the Kingdom of Heaven on earth, despite the fact that their vision of the Kingdom and their understanding of the means which might achieve its restoration are liable to undergo significant changes as the years pass. But all this is, of course, another story.

Notes and References

Introduction

1 Respectively: *Daily Telegraph*, London, 3 May 1976; *Dallas Morning News*, 2 November 1978; *Sunday Times*, London, 15 June 1980; *Sunday Mirror*, London, 19 September 1976; *New York Times*, 20 February 1979; *Guardian*, London, 27 May 1978; *Sunday Express*, London, 2 March 1980; *Daily Mail*, London, 9 March 1983; *Sunday Telegraph*, Tasmania, 12 August 1979; *Match*, Paris, 1 March 1975; *Bogotá Magazine*, March 1975; *Bunte Österreich*, March 1975; *O Estado de S. Paulo*, 31 March 1983.

2 On 20 March 1984 the Committee on Youth, Culture, Education, Information and Sport passed a subsequent motion for discussion to the Plenary session of the European Parliament ('Report on the Activity of Certain New Religious Movements within the European Community', PE 82.322/fin., 22 March 1984, Rapporteur: Richard Cottrell). On 22 May 1984 an amended version of this motion was passed by the Parliament with 98 votes for the motion, 28 votes against, and 26 abstentions.

3 Mrs Wieczorek-Zeul *et al.*, 'Motion for a Resolution on Distress Caused by Sun Myung Moon's Unification Church', European Parliament Working Document PE 77.807, 9 March 1982.

4 Donald Fraser, Chairman, *Investigation of Korean–American Relations: Report of the Subcommittee on International Relations of the Committee on International Relations, U.S. House of Representatives*, Washington DC, US Government Printing Office, 31 October 1978, pp. 311–92. See also HSA–UWC, *Our Response to the Report of October 31, 1978, on the Investigation of Korean–American Relations regarding Reverend Sun Myung Moon and Members of the Unification Church*, New York, HSA–UWC, 1979.

5 *Daily Mail*, London, 29 May 1978. In fact, the latest estimate is about £300,000, which would mean that the whole case will have cost the Unification Church about £500,000.

6 Rex Weiner and Deanne Stillman, *Woodstock Census: The Nationwide Survey of the Sixties Generation*, New York, Viking Press, 1979, p. 246. In another survey, carried out in the summer of 1978, the Princeton Religion Research Center asked over 1,000 teenagers about their opinion of the Unification

Church. Just over half had not heard of it, but almost all those who had held an unfavourable opinion. Only 1 per cent admitted to a favourable opinion: *Emerging Trends*, vol. 1, no. 2, Princeton, Princeton Religion Research Center, February 1979, p. 4.

7 A further classification of membership is currently being introduced that distinguishes between (a) Associate, (b) Practising and (c) Full members, the latter group being subdivided into Home and Centre members; see chapter 9, n. 9, for the text of a statement signed by Associate members.

8 See, for example, Lee Coleman, 'New Religions and "Deprogramming"': Who's Brainwashing Whom?, mimeo, Berkeley, Ca., undated, and 'Psychiatry the Faithbreaker', mimeo, Berkeley, Ca., 1983 (abridged version published in *Unification News*, March, April, May and June). See also H. Richardson (ed.), *Deprogramming: Documenting the Issue*, prepared fot the American Civil Liberties Union, New York, and the Toronto School of Theology Conference on Religious Deprogramming, 1977; and H. Richardson (ed.), *New Religions and Mental Health*, New York, Edwin Mellen Press, 1980.

9 Albert Somit, 'Brainwashing', in David Sills (ed.), *International Encyclopedia of the Social Sciences*, vol. 3, New York, Macmillan, 1968, p. 138. See also Robert Jay Lifton, *Thought Reform and the Psychology of Totalism: A Study of 'Brainwashing' in China*, New York: Norton, 1961; Edgar H. Schein, *Coercive Persuasion*, New York, Norton, 1961; Denise Winn, *The Manipulated Mind: Brainwashing, Conditioning and Indoctrination*, London, Octagon Press, 1983.

10 Lifton, *Thought Reform and the Psychology of Totalism*; Schein, *Coercive Persuasion*; Somit, 'Brainwashing'; Winn, *The Manipulated Mind*.

11 Even POWER, *Deprogramming: The Constructive Destruction of Belief: A Manual of Technique*, 1975–6, which was a spoof produced by members of the Church of Scientology with the intention of exposing the methods of Ted Patrick (see Ted Patrick with Tom Dulack, *Let Our Children Go*, New York, Dutton, 1976), did not advocate the sorts of atrocity described in, for instance, Lifton, *Thought Reform and the Psychology of Totalism*.

12 Some readers will doubtless feel that I have included too much methodological information. I hope they will bear with me not only for this but also for the constant citing of references to my own work for the benefit of those who may wish to learn further details.

1 Access and Information-Gathering

1 International Cultural Foundation, *Science and Absolute Values*, Proceedings of the Third International Conference on the Unity of the Sciences, 2 vols., New York, ICF, 1975. See also Eileen Barker, 'Sun Myung Moon and the Scientists', *Teilhard Review*, vol. 14, no. 1, 1979, for a further account of the meeting.

2 James A. Beckford, 'British Moonies on the Wane', *Psychology Today*, vol. 2, no. 8, 1976, p. 22, describes the existence of such rumours, although he does not suggest that they are true.

3   See Martin Bulmer (ed.), *Social Research Ethics*, London, Macmillan, 1982, for a discussion of the ethics of 'covert' research or 'disguised' observation.

4   I had hit upon the idea of suggesting to the Moonies that they should give me a list which contained the first name and the first three letters of the surname of the members, their date of birth and date of joining the movement (e.g. Jonathan BRA, 15:4:51; 7:10:74). In this way, if the list were to be stolen, the names would be unrecognizable to those who did not already know them, and I had a means of checking – and, indeed, proving – that I really did have a complete list: if Beckford, or anyone else who knew of a particular member, were to give me a name (e.g. Jonathan Bramwell), I would be able to prove that I really had the member on the list by producing his dates of birth and of joining. This was eventually agreed, and I got the list – with the added bonus that I could calculate information such as the average age of the members on joining and the length of time they had been in the movement.

5   See J. T. Richardson, 'People's Temple and Jonestown: A Corrective Comparison and Critique', *Journal for the Scientific Study of Religion*, vol. 19, no. 3, 1980, for an excellent set of distinctions between Jonestown and other new religions.

6   For methodological points raised in the following sections, see Eileen Barker, 'Confessions of a Methodological Schizophrenic: Problems Encountered in the Study of Rev Sun Myung Moon's Unification Church', *Institute for the Study of Worship and Religious Architecture Research Bulletin*, University of Birmingham, 1978; 'The Professional Stranger: Some Methodological Problems Encountered in a Study of the Reverend Sun Myung Moon's Unification Church', Open University Course Media Notes for D207: *An Introduction to Sociology*, Milton Keynes, Open University, 1980; 'Der Professionelle Fremde: Erklärung des Unerklärlichen beim Studium einer abweichenden religiösen Gruppe', in Günter Kehrer (ed.), *Das Entstehen einer neuen Religion: Das Beispiel der Vereinigungskirche*, Munich, Kösel-Verlag, 1981.

7   For elaborations of different aspects of the contemporary context, see Eileen Barker, 'Apes and Angels: Reductionism, Selection and Emergence in the Study of Man', *Inquiry*, vol. 19, no. 4, 1976; 'Science as Theology: The Theological Functioning of Western Science', in A. R. Peacocke (ed.), *The Sciences and Theology in the Twentieth Century*, London, Oriel Press, and Indiana, University of Notre Dame; 'Who'd Be a Moonie? A Comparative Study of Those who Join the Unification Church in Britain', in Bryan R. Wilson (ed.), *The Social Impact of New Religious Movements*, New York, Rose of Sharon Press, 1981; 'Religion in the UK Today: A Sociologist Looks at the Statistics', in P. Brierley (ed.) *UK Christian Handbook*, London Evangelical Alliance, Bible Society and Marc, 1982; 'New Religious Movements in Britain: Content and Membership', Social Compass, 30–1, 1983.

8   The K, I have been told, stands for Korea.

9   See Max Weber, *The Theory of Social and Economic Organization*, ed./trs. Talcott Parsons, Toronto, Free Press, 1964 (first published by Oxford University Press in New York in 1947), for the classic discussion of *Verstehen*.

10 See n. 4 above.

11 See Alison Lurie, *Imaginary Friends*, London, Heinemann, 1967, for an amusing account of the involvement of a sociologist of religion with a religious sect.

12 A member of the student branch of the Unification Church: see chapter 2.

13 See Kurt H. Wolff (ed./trs.), *The Sociology of Georg Simmel*, New York, Free Press, 1950, Part 5, chapter 3. See also Eileen Barker, 'The Professional Stranger', or 'Der Professionelle Fremde', and 'Supping with the Devil: How Long a Spoon does the Sociologist Need?', *Sociological Analysis*, vol. 44, no. 3, 1983, for further discussion of the ethical and methodological implications of a participant observer's involvement with the movement she is studying (in this latter article my attendance at Unification conferences is discussed).

14 Six cards, each containing eighty spaces for data, were punched for each respondent.

15 The 1,017 application forms gave me information about the applicants' sex, date of birth, nationality, religious background, occupation, and the sex and nationality of their first Moonie contacts. From the centre in which the twenty-one-day workshops were conducted I was able to get similar information concerning just over 600 people who had applied for the twenty-one-day course (some of whom overlapped with the two-day applicants from London, the rest having attended workshops in other parts of the country). I was, furthermore, able to cross-check these names against lists (which were kept in the relevant centres) for the two-day, seven-day and twenty-one-day workshops that had been held throughout 1979; finally, headquarters was able to let me inspect the application forms for actual membership.

16 For a more detailed account of the way in which I obtained data concerning the workshop attenders and the way in which the representativeness of the responses was checked, see my 'The Ones Who Got Away: People who Attend Unification Workshops and do not Become Moonies', in Rodney Stark (ed.), *Religious Movements: Genesis, Exodus and Numbers*, New York, Rose of Sharon Press, forthcoming, and in Eileen Barker (ed.), *Of Gods and Men: New Religious Movements in the West*, Atlanta, Mercer University Press, 1984; Eileen Barker, 'Resistible Coercion: The Significance of Failure Rates in Conversion and Commitment to the Unification Church', in Dick Anthony *et al.*, *Conversion, Coercion and Commitment in New Religious Movements*, forthcoming.

17 See chapter 2, and Anson D. Shupe, Jr, and David G. Bromley, *The New Vigilantes: Deprogrammers, Anti-Cultists, and the New Religions*, Beverley Hills/London, Sage Publications, 1980.

18 Some members do miss their periods for a few months – as do some non-Moonies of a similar age.

19 FAIR newsletter, June 1981, p. 13.

20 The article referred to was my 'Free to Choose? Some Thoughts on the Unification Church and Other New Religious Movements', *Clergy Review*, pt 1, October, pt 2, November 1980; see also my 'Supping with the Devil'.

21 See Max Weber, *The Methodology of the Social Sciences*, ed./trs. Edward A. Shils and Henry A. Finch, New York, Free Press, 1949, for the distinction between value-neutrality and value-relevance.

22   Eileen Barker, 'Facts and Values and Social Science', in *Science and Absolute Values*, Proceedings of the Third International Conference on the Unity of the Sciences, New York, ICF, 1975, elaborates this point.

23   See Karl Popper, *Conjectures and Refutations: The Growth of Scientific Knowledge*, 2nd edn, London, Routledge & Kegan Paul, 1965, chapter 1.

24   See Eileen Barker, 'The Limits of Displacement: Two Disciplines Face Each Other', in D. Martin *et al.* (eds.), *Sociology and Theology: Alliance and Conflict*, Brighton, Harvester Press, 1980, for a fuller discussion of the relationship between social science and religious beliefs.

2   The Unification Church: An Historical Background

1   D.S.C. Kim (ed.), *Day of Hope in Review*, pt 2: *1974–1975*, Tarrytown, NY, HSA–UWC, 1975, p. 2; Unification Church, 'The Unification Church', pamphlet distributed by UC, New York, 1982, p. 5; Young Oon Kim, 'For God's Sake', pamphlet distributed by UC, New York, 1972, p. 23; Chull Paik *et al.*, *Sun Myung Moon: The Man and his Ideal*, Seoul, Future Civilization Press, 1981, p. 67; Unification Church of America, *Sun Myung Moon*, New York, UC, 1976, p. 25.

2   Sebastian A. Matczak, *Unificationism: A New Philosophy and World View*, New York, Learned Publications, 1982, p. 5.

3   Unification Church of America, *Sun Myung Moon*, p. 25; Paik *et al.*, *Sun Myung Moon*, p. 68.

4   Frederick Sontag, *Sun Myung Moon and the Unification Church*, Nashville, Abingdon, 1977, p. 78; Masatoshi Abe (ed.), 'Church Leader's Manual', HSA–UWC, 1980 (originally compiled in Japan, 1977), p. 187; D. S. C. Kim, *Day of Hope*, pt. 2, p. 5; Paik *et al.*, *Sun Myung Moon*, p. 68; Unification Church of America, *Sun Myung Moon*, p. 25.

5   Chung Hwan Kwak, *Outline of the Principle: Level 4*, New York, HSA–UWC, 1980, p. 2.

6   Ibid.; Unification Church of America, *Sun Myung Moon*, p. 25.

7   Kwak, *Outline of the Principle*, p. 2. There was actually an earlier text which Moon finished in 1952 and which is known as 'The Original Text of the Principle'.

8   Hyo Won Eu, *Divine Principle*, Washington DC, HSA–UWC, 1973.

9   For example, Y. O. Kim, *Unification Theology and Christian Thought*, New York, Golden Gate, 1975; Y. O. Kim, *Unification Theology*, New York, HSA–UWC, 1980; Y. W. Kim, *The Divine Principle: Study Guide*, New York, HSA–UWC, 1973 (reprinted London, HSA–UWC, 1977); Kwak, *Outline of the Principle*; S. H. Lee, *Unification Thought: Study Guide*, New York, Unification Thought Institute, 1974.

10   Kwak, *Outline of the Principle*, p. 2.

11   D. S. C. Kim, *Day of Hope*, pt. 2, p. 5; Matczak, *Unificationism*: p. 5.

12   D. S. C. Kim, *Day of Hope*, pt. 2, p. 8.

13   Matczak, *Unificationism*, p. 6; Paik *et al.*, *Sun Myung Moon*, p. 68.

14 W. P. Kim, *Father's Course and Our Life of Faith*, London, HSA–UWC, 1982, pp. 145–6.
15 Paik *et al.*, *Sun Myung Moon*, p. 69.
16 Matczak, *Unificationism*, p. 7.
17 D. S. C. Kim, *Day of Hope*, pt. 2, p. 11.
18 Ibid., p. 12; W. P. Kim, 'Father's Testimony', in *Principle Life*, 2 pts, New York, HSA–UWC, October/November 1979, pt 1, p. 5.
19 W. P. Kim, 'Father's Testimony', pt 1, p. 3.
20 Ibid., p. 4.
21 Ibid., p. 6.
22 W. P. Kim, *Principle Life*, pts 1 and 2; W. P. Kim, *Father's Course and Our Life of Faith*; W. P. Kim, 'Seoul: Chungpa Dong Church and Pioneering', *Today's World*, October 1982; D. S. C. Kim, *Day of Hope*, pt 2, pp. 12, 13; Unification Church, 'The Unification Church', p. 6.
23 D. S. C. Kim, *Day of Hope*, pt 2, p. 16; Neil Salonen, 'History of the Unification Church in America', in R. Quebedeaux (ed.), *Lifestyle: Conversations with Members of the Unification Church*, New York, Rose of Sharon Press, 1982.
24 See, *inter alia*, W. P. Kim, *Father's Course and Our Life of Faith*, ch. 15; W. P. Kim, 'Seoul', pp. 8–21.
25 D. S. C. Kim, *Day of Hope*, pt 2, p. 16.
26 M. L. Mickler, 'A History of the Unification Church in the Bay Area: 1960–74', MA thesis, Graduate Theological Union, University of California, Berkeley, 1980, p. 1.
27 Matczak, *Unificationism*, p. 9; D. S. C. Kim, *Day of Hope*, pt 2, p. 21.
28 Salonen, 'History of the Unification Church in America', pp. 167–8.
29 M. Cozin, 'A Millenarian Movement in Korea and Great Britain', in *A Sociological Year Book of Religion in Britain*, 6, London, SCM, 1973, p. 107, quoting Syn-duk Choi, 'Korea's Tong Il Movement', Transactions *of the Korean Branch, Royal Asiatic Society*, vol. 43, 1967, p. 169.
30 *Northern Daily Leader*, Australia, 3 September 1979, quoted in R. Fraser, *The Jerangle Witch-Hunt: A Study of the Unification Church in Australia and Public Opposition to its Establishment*, Onehunga, New Zealand, distributed privately, 1979, p. 105.
31 In conversations with scores of non-Unificationist Koreans the first information I have been given about the Unification Church has, in almost every instance, been that Moon engages (or has engaged) in immoral sexual practices with his followers.
32 R. Fraser, *The Jerangle Witch-Hunt*, p. 106, shows a reproduction of a Korean record card stating that Moon Yong Myung – alias Sun Myung – was found not guilty of violation of military draft law at Seoul Superior Court, November 1955. See also D. S. C. Kim, *Day of Hope*, pt 2, pp. 26, 31; Bo Hi Pak, *Truth is My Sword*, International Exchange Press, 1978, p. 43.
33 D. S. C. Kim, *Day of Hope*, pt 2, p. 31; W. P. Kim, 'Seoul', pp. 8–13.
34 See, *inter alia*, Abe, 'Church Leader's Manual', pp. 187ff.; W. P. Kim, 'Father's Testimony' and *Father's Course and Our Life of Faith*; D. S. C. Kim,

Day of Hope in Review, Part 1: *1972–1974*, and Part 2: *1974–1975*; Y. O. Kim, 'For God's Sake'; Matczak, *Unificationism*; Paik *et al.*, *Sun Myung Moon*; Unification Church of America, *Sun Myung Moon*; Salonen, 'History of the Unification Church in America'; Sontag, *Sun Myung Moon and the Unification Church*, ch. 4; Ken Sudo, '120-Day Training Manual', unpublished transcript, New York, HSA–UWC, 1975; Master Speaks: 'History of the Unification Church', 29 December 1971.

35 For example, Cozin, 'A Millenarian Movement in Korea and Great Britain'; M. L. Cozin, 'A Religious Sect in Korea and Great Britain', M. Phil. thesis, University of London, 1973.

36 See Sontag, *Sun Myung Moon and the Unification Church*; H. W. McFarland, *The Rush Hour of the Gods*, New York, Macmillan, 1967.

37 Cozin, 'A Millenarian Movement in Korea and Great Britain', ch. 1.

38 For example, F. Clark, 'The Fall of Man in *Divine Principle*', in H. Richardson (ed.), *Ten Theologians Respond to the Unification Church*, New York, Rose of Sharon Press, 1981; M. D. Bryant and S. Hodges (eds.), *Exploring Unification Theology*, 2nd edn, New York, Rose of Sharon Press, 1978; M. D. Bryant (ed.), *Proceedings of the Virgin Islands' Seminar on Unification Theology*, New York, Rose of Sharon Press, 1980; M. D. Bryant and D. Foster (eds.), *Hermeneutics and Unification Theology*, New York, Rose of Sharon Press, 1980; R. Quebedeaux and R. Sawatsky (eds.), *Evangelical-Unification Dialogue*, New York, Rose of Sharon Press, 1979.

39 J. Lofland, *Doomsday Cult: A Study of Conversion, Proselytization, and Maintenance of Faith*, rev. edn, New York, Irvington, 1977.

40 Mickler, 'A History of the Unification Church in the Bay Area'.

41 Ibid., p. 6.

42 Ibid., p. 5; Salonen, 'History of the Unification Church in America', p. 167; Matczak, *Unificationism*, p. 10.

43 Mickler, 'A History of the Unification Church in the Bay Area', p. 3.

44 Lofland, *Doomsday Cult*, p. 35.

45 Ibid.

46 Mickler, 'A History of the Unification Church in the Bay Area', p. 5.

47 Matczak, *Unificationism*, pp. 11, 28.

48 D. Fraser, *Investigation of Korean-American Relations: Report of the Subcommittee on International Relations of the Committee on International Relations, US House of Representatives*, Washington DC, US Government Printing Office, 31 October 1978, p. 446.

49 Matczak, *Unificationism*, p. 26; Mickler, 'A History of the Unification Church in the Bay Area', pp. 93, 97–9; Salonen, 'History of the Unification Church in America', pp. 166–7.

50 Mickler, 'A History of the Unification Church in the Bay Area', pp. 90, 106.

51 Ibid., p. 78; Salonen, 'History of the Unification Church in America', p. 169.

52 B. Hardin and G. Kehrer, 'Some Social Factors Affecting the Rejection of New Belief Systems', in Eileen Barker (ed.), *New Religious Movements: A Perspective for Understanding Society*, New York, Edwin Mellen Press, 1982, p. 272.

53 Ibid.

54   Mickler, 'A History of the Unification Church in the Bay Area', p. 78; Salonen, 'History of the Unification Church in America', p. 169.
55   Mickler, 'A History of the Unification Church in the Bay Area', pp. 78, 85.
56   P. Hartley, 'Early History of the Unification Church in Britain', unpublished typescript, 1983; Mickler, 'A History of the Unification Church in the Bay Area', p. 63.
57   Mickler, 'A History of the Unification Church in the Bay Area', p. 7.
58   Lofland, *Doomsday Cult*, p. 66.
59   For example, Cozin, 'A Religious Sect in Korea and Great Britain', p. 93; Mickler, 'A History of the Unification Church in the Bay Area', pp. 6, 96–7; Salonen, 'History of the Unification Church in America', p. 169.
60   Sontag, *Sun Myung Moon*, pp. 90–1; Mickler, 'A History of the Unification Church in the Bay Area', p. 189.
61   Mickler, 'A History of the Unification Church in the Bay Area', p 189.
62   Ibid., p. 207; Sontag, *Sun Myung Moon*, p. 91.
63   Sontag, *Sun Myung Moon*, p. 9.
64   This is brought out in several places in Mickler, 'A History of the Unification Church in the Bay Area' – for example, pp. 89, 109, 146ff., especially 150, and 180ff., especially 184.
65   Ibid., p. 109.
66   Lofland, *Doomsday Cult*, pp. 32.
67   Ibid., pp. 36–42, 257.
68   Ibid., p. 259.
69   See, *inter alia*, C. Y. Glock and R. Bellah (eds.), *The New Religious Consciousness*, Berkeley, University of California Press, 1976; R. Wuthnow, *The Consciousness Reformation*, Berkeley, University of California, 1976; R. Wuthnow, *Experimentation in American Religion: The New Mysticisms and their Implications for the Churches*, Berkeley, University of California Press, 1978.
70   Mickler, 'A History of the Unification Church in the Bay Area', pp. 91–2.
71   Ibid., p. 97.
72   Matczak, *Unificationism*, p. 26.
73   See Ichiro *et al.* (eds.), *Japanese Religion: A Survey by the Agency for Cultural Affairs*, New York and San Francisco, Kodansha International, 1972, pp. 209–10, 256; Mickler, 'A History of the Unification Church in the Bay Area', p. 99.
74   See McFarland, *The Rush Hour of the Gods*.
75   Mickler, 'A History of the Unification Church in the Bay Area', p. 88.
76   See J. Lofland and R. Stark, 'Becoming a World-Saver: A Theory of Conversion to a Deviant Perspective', *American Sociological Review*, vol. 30, 1965, pp. 862–74; and Lofland, *Doomsday Cult*.
77   Mickler, 'A History of the Unification Church in the Bay Area', p. 101, quoted from 'Report from Japan: Training Programs', *New Age Frontiers*, February 1966.
78   Ibid., p. 102.
79   Ibid., pp. 103, 240 (Matczak, *Unificationism*, p. 26, gives 1962 as the date of the foundation of CARP).

80 Ibid., p. 104.
81 Ibid., quoted from Michiko Matsumoto, 'The Road Rev. Nishikawa Followed', in *Faith and Life*, Tokyo, HSA-UWC, 1976, p. 32, unpublished English translation.
82 Ibid., p. 124.
83 Ibid., p. 123.
84 Ibid., p. 100.
85 Ibid., p. 111.
86 Ibid., p. 112, quoted from Edna Lee, 'The Family', unpublished paper.
87 Ibid., p. 100.
88 Ibid.
89 Ibid., pp. 106–7, 109.
90 Ibid., p. 125.
91 Ibid., p. 126, quoted from Sang Ik Choi, 'Papasan Speaks at Family Meeting', *Epoch Maker*, no. 21, 1970.
92 Ibid., p. 129.
93 Ibid., p. 131.
94 Ibid., p. 132.
95 Ibid., pp. 132–3, 139.
96 Ibid., pp. 136ff.
97 Ibid., p. 142.
98 Ibid., p. 133.
99 Ibid., p. 134.
100 Ibid., p. 175.
101 Ibid., p. 145.
102 Ibid., p. 190.
103 Ibid., p. 155, quoted from Farley Jones, 'Field Work', lecture at Unification Theological Seminary, 23 February 1978.
104 Ibid., p. 156.
105 Matczak, *Unificationism*, p. 27.
106 Mickler, 'A History of the Unification Church in the Bay Area', p. 160.
107 Freedom Leadership Foundation, undated.
108 Mickler, 'A History of the Unification Church in the Bay Area', p. 161.
109 Ibid., pp. 160, 187.
110 D. Fraser, *Investigation of Korean–American Relations*, pp. 319ff; HSA–UWC, *Our Response to the Report of October 31, 1978, on the Investigation of Korean–American Relations Regarding Reverend Sun Myung Moon and Members of the Unification Church*, New York, HSA-UWC, 1979, pp. 48ff.
111 HSA–UWC, *Our Response*, p. 51.
112 A. T. Wood with Jack Vitek, *Moonstruck: A Memoir of My Life in a Cult*, New York, Morrow, 1979, p. 86.
113 A. Ford, *Unknown But Known*, New York, Harper & Row, 1968, ch. 2. See also chapter 3 below.
114 Mickler, 'A History of the Unification Church in the Bay Area', p. 80.
115 'Holy Grounds are small plots of land that are dedicated by a special ritual to God as a condition for restoring the land of the country': Abe, 'Church Leader's Manual', p. 200.

116   Salonen, 'History of the Unification Church in America', p. 170.
117   Mickler, 'A History of the Unification Church in the Bay Area', p. 164.
118   Ibid., p. 196.
119   D. S. C. Kim, *Day of Hope in Review*, pts 1 and 2, give detailed accounts of Moon's public appearances from 1972 to 1975.
120   Mickler, 'A History of the Unification Church in the Bay Area', p. 203.
121   Ibid., p. 196.
122   D. S. C. Kim, *Day of Hope in Review*, pt 1, pp. 2–7.
123   Mickler, 'A History of the Unification Church in the Bay Area', p. 202.
124   Wood, *Moonstruck*, p. 141.
125   Sun Myung Moon, *Divine Principle*, Washington DC, HSA–UWC, 1973; Sun Myung Moon, *Christianity in Crisis: New Hope*, Washington DC, HSA–UWC, 1974; Sun Myung Moon, *The New Future of Christianity*, Thornton Heath, Surrey, HSA–UWC, 1974; Sun Myung Moon, 'America and God's Will', New York, Bicentennial God Bless America Committee, 1976; Sun Myung Moon, 'America in God's Providence', New York, Bicentennial God Bless America Committee pamphlet, 1976; Sun Myung Moon, 'God's Hope for America', New York Bicentennial God Bless America Committee pamphlet, 1976; D. S. C. Kim, *Day of Hope in Review*, pts 1 and 2.
126   Moon, *The New Future of Christianity*, pp. 126–7.
127   Moon, *Christianity in Crisis*, introduction by Col. Bo Hi Pak, pp. vii–viii.
128   D. S. C. Kim, *Day of Hope in Review*, pt 1, pp. 2ff., 24ff., 228ff., 404; Mickler, 'A History of the Unification Church in the Bay Area', pp. 204, 222.
129   Mickler, 'A History of the Unification Church in the Bay Area', p. 235.
130   Lofland, *Doomsday Cult*, p. 116; Mickler, 'A History of the Unification Church in the Bay Area', p. 210.
131   Mickler, 'A History of the Unification Church in the Bay Area', p. 211.
132   Ibid., p. 212.
133   Ibid., p. 214.
134   Ibid., p. 225.
135   Ibid., p. 235.
136   Ibid., p. 236.
137   Unification Theological Seminary, Catalogue 1979–80, p. 5.
138   Mickler, 'A History of the Unification Church in the Bay Area', p. 236.
139   Ibid.; E. Heftmann, *Dark Side of the Moonies*, Harmondsworth, Penguin, 1983, p. 95.
140   Mickler, 'A History of the Unification Church in the Bay Area', p. 236.
141   Master Speaks, MS–447, 10–13–74, p. 7.
142   Matczak, *Unificationism*, p. 25; Mickler, 'A History of the Unification Church in the Bay Area', p. 237.
143   D. S. C. Kim, *Day of Hope in Review*, pt 1, pp. 165–76; Matczak, *Unificationism*, p. 12; Mickler, 'A History of the Unification Church in the Bay Area', P. 239.
144   Ibid., p. 206.
145   Ibid., pp. 219, 218.

146   D. S. C. Kim, *Day of Hope in Review*, pt 1, pp. 33, 161; pt 2, p. 597.

147   Mickler, 'A History of the Unification Church in the Bay Area', p. 240;
       D. S. C. Kim, *Day of Hope in Review*, pt 1, pp. 37ff., pt 2, pp. 137ff. For a
       report by a British student who attended the ILS in 1973 and, like nearly all
       the 'guests', did not become a Moonie, see P. F. Hutton, 'Introduction to the
       Unification Church', diss., mimeo, University of Cambridge, 1974.

148   See D. S. C. Kim, *Day of Hope in Review*, pt 1.

149   F. W. Jones (ed.), *As Others See Us*, Washington DC, HSA–UWC, 1974.

150   Ibid., p. 69.

151   Mickler, 'A History of the Unification Church in the Bay Area', p. 248.

152   D. S. C. Kim, *Day of Hope in Review*, pt 1, pp. 177–225.

153   Ibid., pp. 217–23, 240; Mickler, 'A History of the Unification Church in the
       Bay Area', p. 243.

154   D. S. C. Kim, *Day of Hope in Review*, pt 1, pp. 177–225, 237–59; Mickler,
       'A History of the Unification Church in the Bay Area', p. 244.

155   Mickler, 'A History of the Unification Church in the Bay Area', p. 250.

156   Ibid.

157   Anson D. Shupe Jr and David G. Bromley, *The New Vigilantes: Deprogram-
       mers, Anti-Cultists, and the New Religions*, Beverley Hills/London, Sage
       Publications, 1980.

158   Ted Patrick with Tom Dulack, *Let Our Children Go*, New York, Dutton,
       1976, gives descriptions of some of the more violent deprogrammings which
       Patrick (known by the nickname 'Black Lightning') has carried out.

159   David G. Bromley and James T. Richardson (eds.), *The Brainwashing/
       Deprogramming Debate: Sociological, Psychological, Legal and Historical Per-
       spectives*, New York, Edwin Mellen Press, 1984; M. D. Bryant (ed.),
       *Religious Liberty in Canada: Deprogramming and Media Coverage of New
       Religions*, Documentation Series No. 1, Canadians for the Protection of
       Religious Liberty, Toronto; C. Edwards, *Crazy for God*, Englewood Cliffs,
       NJ, Prentice-Hall, 1979; B. Underwood and B. Underwood, *Hostage to
       Heaven*, New York, Clarkson N. Potter, 1979; H. Richardson (ed.),
       Deprogramming: Documenting the Issue, prepared for the American Civil
       Liberties Union, New York, and the Toronto School of Theology Confer-
       ence on Religious Deprogramming, 1977; H. Richardson (ed.), *New
       Religions and Mental Health*, New York, Edwin Mellen Press, 1980; S.
       Swatland and A. Swatland, *Escape from the Moonies*, London, New English
       Library, 1982.

160   Salonen, reported in *Christianity Today*, 20 July 1979.

161   Nora Spurgin, in R. Quebedeaux and R. Sawatsky (eds.), *Evangelical-
       Unification Dialogue*, New York, Rose of Sharon Press, 1979.

162   Allen Tate Wood, who was a member at the time, reports that there were
       between 100 and 120 members of the Unified Family (Miss Kim's group) in
       1969: Wood, *Moonstruck*, p. 281; Lofland reports that there were at least that
       many in the whole of the United States by June 1974: Lofland, *Doomsday
       Cult*, p. 257.

163   This figure is calculated from Edwin Ang's 'multiplication proposal' made at

the Directors' conference, January 1971, quoted in Mickler, 'A History of the Unification Church in the Bay Area', p. 168. Lofland, *Doomsday Cult*, p. 281, however, estimates that there were 'around 500' members in 1971.

164 Mickler, 'A History of the Unification Church in the Bay Area', p. 254.

165 Salonen, 'History of the Unification Church in America', p. 174.

166 Ibid., p. 241.

167 Mickler, 'A History of the Unification Church in the Bay Area', p. 254.

168 Lofland, *Doomsday Cult*, p. 347.

169 Joseph M. Hopkins, 'Meeting the Moonies on their Territory', *Christianity Today*, vol. 22, no. 20, August 1978.

170 John Maust, 'The Moonies Cross Wits with Cult-Watching Critics', *Christianity Today*, vol. 23, no. 19, July 1979.

171 David Taylor, 'Becoming New People: the Recruitment of Young Americans into the Unification Church', in R. Wallis (ed.), *Millenialism and Charisma*, Belfast, Queen's University, 1982, reports that 'the Church's own internal publication, *The Day of Hope News*, has consistently estimated the total full-time membership at around two thousand.'

172 *Today's World*, July 1982, p. 19; see also p. 23 for some inter-racial and cross-cultural statistics.

173 Fewer than 12,000 couples have taken part in the mass weddings, and several of these are no longer full-time members.

174 Lofland, *Doomsday Cult*, Mickler, 'A History of the Unification Church in the Bay Area', and Wood, *Moonstruck*, are among those reporting on the defection of converts.

175 *Today's World*, July 1982.

176 *Today's World*, November 1982.

177 For example, *Houston Chronicle*, 4 September 1981; *Milwaukee Journal*, 18 January 1979; *New York Times* 28 July 1981.

178 Unification Church of America, *Sun Myung Moon*, p. 18.

179 Moon, 'God's Hope for America'.

180 Ibid., p. 1.

181 *Time Magazine*, 14 June 1976.

182 *Unification News*, January 1984, p. 24. The headline actually says that there were 500,000 people present, though the text gives what I have been told is the more accurate figure of 250,000.

183 *News World* first published 31 December 1976; see Michael Young Warder, *Another Watchdog: A Brief Story of New York's Newest Daily and Sunday Newspaper*, New York, News World Communications Inc., 1977. *New York Tribune* first published 4 April 1983.

184 First published 22 April 1980.

185 First published 17 May 1982.

186 First published 7 March 1983; see *Washington Times, Beating the Odds*, New York/Washington, News World Communications Inc., 1983, for an account of its inception and first year.

187 Mitsuhara Ishii, '*Inchon' Souvenir Book*, One Way Productions Inc., 1982.

188 D. Fraser, *Investigation of Korean–American Relations*.

189   Irving Louis Horowitz, *Science, Sin and Scholarship: The Politics of Reverend Moon and the Unification Church*, Cambridge, Mass./London, MIT Press, 1978, pp. 205–6; Underwood and Underwood, *Hostage to Heaven*, pp. 207ff.

3 Unification Beliefs

1   Both Federal and State courts have, in several cases, held that the Unification Church is religious in nature and thus entitled to the protection of the First Amendment to the Constitution (which guarantees the free exercise of all religions). See, *inter alia*, 'the Unification Church, by any historical analogy, philosophical analysis, or judicial precedent (indeed by INS' own criteria) must be regarded as a *bona fide* "religion".' *Unification Church* v. *Immigration and Naturalization Services*, 547 F. Supp. 623, 628 (1982).

2   'The Master Speaks on the Lord of the Second Advent', MS–1, 1965, p. 3.

3   This has been repeated to me by several Moonies, but see Ken Sudo, '120-Day Training Manual', unpublished transcript, New York, HSA–UWC, p. 399, and Allen Tate Wood with Jack Vitek, *Moonstruck: A Memoir of My Life in a Cult*, New York, Morrow, 1979, p. 120.

4   Hyo Won Eu, *Divine Principle*, Washington DC, HSA–UWC, 1973; Y. W. Kim, *The Divine Principle: Study Guide*, New York, HSA–UWC, 1973 (reprinted London, HSA–UWC, 1977); Chung Hwan Kwak, *Outline of the Principle: Level 4*, New York, HSA–UWC, 1980.

5   W. P. Kim, *Father's Course and Our Life of Faith*, London, HSA–UWC, 1982, pp. 2ff.; J. Lofland, *Doomsday Cult: A Study of Conversion, Proselytization, and Maintenance of Faith*, 2nd ed, New York, Irvington, 1977; chapter 3; Wood, *Moonstruck*, p. 92.

6   See, *inter alia*, *Emerging Trends*, vol. 4, no. 2, Princeton Religion Research Center, February 1982, p. 5; David Hay, *Exploring Inner Space: Is God still Possible in the Twentieth Century?*, Harmondsworth, Penguin, 1982; Alister Hardy, *The Spiritual Nature of Man*, Oxford, Oxford University Press, 1979.

7   Gordon J. Melton, *The Encyclopedia of American Religions*, 2 vols., Wilmington, N. Carolina, McGrath, 1978, vol. 2, pp. 122–5; M. L. Mickler, 'A History of the Unification Church in the Bay Area: 1960–74', unpublished MA thesis, Graduate Theological Union, University of California, Berkeley, 1980, p. 69.

8   Arthur Ford, *Unknown But Known*, New York, Harper & Row, 1968, p. 112.

9   Ibid., p. 123.

10   See P. F. Hutton, 'Introduction to the Unification Church', diss., mimeo, University of Cambridge, 1974, p. 14. See M. B. McGuire, *Control of Charisma: A Sociological Interpretation of the Catholic Pentecostal Movement*, Philadelphia, Temple University Press, 1981, for an excellent analysis of how the leaders of charismatic groups interpret and control the 'speaking in tongues' of those not in positions of authority.

11   Kwak, *Outline of the Principle*, pp. 6–9.

12 For theological criticism see, *inter alia*, Agnes Cunningham, J. R. Nelson, W. L. Hendricks and J. Lara-Brand, 'A Critique of the Theology of the Unification Church as Set Forth in "Divine Principle"', official study document of the Commmission on Faith and Order of the National Council of the Churches of Christ in the USA, 475 Riverside Drive, New York, NY 10027, 1977; H. Richardson (ed.), *Ten Theologians Respond to the Unification Church*, New York, Rose of Sharon Press, 1981; M. D. Bryant (ed.), *Proceedings of the Virgin Islands' Seminar on Unification Theology*, New York, Rose of Sharon Press, 1980.

13 Kwak, *Outline of the Principle*.

14 It has frequently been pointed out to me by less 'fundamentalist' Moonies that these percentages are only notional and not to be taken too literally.

15 Thus representing the three types of love that have to be learned during one's lifetime: first, love for one's (True) parents; second, love for one's spouse; third, love for one's children.

16 'Though Cain and Abel stood on the sides of good and evil, respectively, their positions are relative. Actually, both had Original Sin and Fallen Nature as well as Original Nature – thus both had natures of evil and good': Kwak, *Outline of the Principle*, p. 118. See also Eu, *Divine Principle*, p. 244.

17 Eu, *Divine Principle*, p. 241.

18 Y. O. Kim, *Unification Theology and Christian Thought*, New York, Golden Gate, 1975, p. 116.

19 Sudo, '120-Day Training Manual', p. 400.

20 'Master Speaks'; 'Reverend Sun Myung Moon Speaks on . . .'; Sun Myung Moon, *New Hope*, Washington DC, HSA–UWC, 1973, *The Way of Tradition*, 3 vols, New York, HSA–UWC, 1980 and other HSA–UWC publications. D. S. C. Kim, *Day of Hope in Review*, pt 1: *1972–1974*, pt 2: *1974–1975*, Tarrytown, New York, HSA–UWC, 1974, 1975; and numerous other HSA–UWC publications such as *The Blessing Quarterly*, *Principle Life* and *Today's World*.

21 'The Master Speaks on the Lord of the Second Advent', p. 4.

22 *Today's World*, August 1981, p. 3.

23 Ibid., p. 6.

24 These terms are used, of course, with an application quite different from that used in the Introduction to this book, when I was describing the kinds of knowledge that I was hoping to synthesize in the study.

25 HSA–UWC, *Introduction to the Principle: An Islamic Perspective*, New York, HSA–UWC, 1980.

26 Eu, *Divine Principle*.

27 Y. W. Kim, *The Divine Principle*; Kwak, *Outline of the Principle*.

28 For example, Mose Durst, *The Whole Elephant, The Creation, The Purpose of Mankind, The Cause of Crimes*, Berkeley, Ca., Creative Community Project of New Education Developments Systems, undated.

29 Concluding lines of Durst, 'The Purpose of Mankind'.

30 Moon, *New Hope*, p. ix.

31 For example, Y. O. Kim, *Unification Theology and Christian Thought*; Y. O.

Kim, *Unification Theology*, New York, HSA–UWC, 1980; Sang Hun Lee, *Unification Thought*, New York, Unification Thought Institute, 1973; Freedom Leadership Foundation, *Communism: A Critique and Counter Proposal*, Washington DC, FLF, 1973.

32 For example, M. D. Bryant and H. Richardson (eds.), *A Time for Consideration: A Scholarly Appraisal of the Unification Church*, New York, Edwin Mellen Press, 1978; M. D. Bryant and S. Hodges (eds.), *Exploring Unification Theology*, 2nd edn, New York, Rose of Sharon Press, 1978; Bryant, *Proceedings of the Virgin Islands' Seminar on Unification Theology*; M. D. Bryant and D. Foster (eds.), *Hermeneutics and Unification Theology*, New York, Rose of Sharon Press, 1980; F. K. Flinn (ed.), *Hermeneutics and Horizons: The Shape of the Future*, New York, Rose of Sharon Press, 1982; R. Quebedeaux and R. Sawatsky (eds.), *Evangelical-Unification Dialogue*, New York, Rose of Sharon Press, 1979; Richardson, *Ten Theologians Respond to the Unification Church*; F. Sontag and M. D. Bryant (eds.), *God: The Contemporary Discussion*, New York, Rose of Sharon Press, 1982; C. Tsirpanlis (ed.), *Orthodox-Unification Dialogue*, New York, Rose of Sharon Press, 1981.

4 Meeting the Moonies

1 John Lofland, *Doomsday Cult: A Study of Conversion, Proselytization, and Maintenance of Faith*, 2nd edn, New York, Irvington, 1977.

2 Masatoshi Abe (ed.), 'Church Leader's Manual', HSA–UWC, 1980 (originally compiled in Japan, 1977), and Ken Sudo, '120-Day Training Manual', unpublished transcript, New York, HSA–UWC, 1975, contain instructions on how to go about witnessing to potential recruits.

3 A Moonie's 'spiritual parent' is (usually) the person who first introduced him to the movement.

4 E. B. Rochford. 'Recruitment Strategies, Ideology, and Organization in the Hare Krishna Movement', *Social Problems*, vol. 29, no. 4, 1982; also in E. Barker (ed.), *Of Gods and Men: New Religious Movements in the West*, Atlanta, Ga., Mercer University Press, 1984; David A. Snow *et al.*, 'Social Networks and Social Movements: A Microstructural Approach to Differential Recruitment', *American Sociological Review*, vol. 45, 1980; David A. Snow *et al.*, 'Further Thoughts on Social Networks and Movement Recruitment', *Sociology*, vol. 17, 1983; R. Stark and W. S. Bainbridge, 'Networks of Faith: Recruitment of Cults and Sects', *American Journal of Sociology*, vol. 85, no. 6, 1980.

5 According to responses to my questionnaire. However, about a third of the European Moonies had first made contact through a friend or relative.

6 See, *inter alia*, *Sun*, 4 July 1975; *Sunday Mirror*, 19 September 1976; *Daily Express*, 11 March 1977; *The Times*, 12, 13, 17 December 1977.

7 Eighty-seven per cent British; 96 per cent Europeans; 67 per cent Asians; and 81 per cent Americans.

8 Fifty-two per cent non-joiners; 64 per cent of both those who became members and leavers.

9   Fifty-two per cent non-joiners; 63 per cent joiners; 64 per cent leavers.

10 David Taylor, 'Becoming New People: the Recruitment of Young Americans into the Unification Church', in R. Wallis (ed.), *Millenialism and Charisma*, Belfast, Queen's University, 1982, p. 178, states that the Bay Area Church did not claim affiliation with the Unification Church when he did his research in 1975. See also chapter 5, n. 64.

11 'Holy Salt' is used to purify buildings and food. It is made according to a special ritual – see Abe, 'Church Leader's Manual', p. 203, and the *Blessing Quarterly*, vol. 4, no. 1, 1981, pp. 58–63. Salt is, of course, used for purification purposes in other religious traditions.

12 See chapter 5, n. 64.

13 The 'Pledge' is a short service in which the members dedicate their lives to serving God and Moon. The Pledge is taken on the first day of every week, month and year and on 'Holy Days' all across the world at 5 a.m. (local time).

14 Weekend seminars at Camp K are roughly equivalent to those which have been held at Boonville. Although I draw on my own experiences for this description, similar descriptions are to be found in David Taylor, *Recruitment into the Unification Church as a Socially Organized Accomplishment*, Master's thesis, University of Montana, 1978; Taylor, 'Becoming New People'; D. G. Bromley and A. D. Shupe Jr, *'Moonies' in America: Cults, Church and Crusade*, Beverley Hills/London, Sage Publications, 1979; and several books written by apostates.

15 Highway 128.

16 So called because it consists of the 'sharing' done while eating cereal. When I first heard the term I assumed it was 'serial drama' because the sharing seemed to go on and on from one group gathering to the next.

17 There are various versions of the origin and meaning of this chant. One version is that Onni Durst initiated its use and that it refers to a train either going along the 'straight and narrow' or, as in the children's story, puffing, 'I think I can' as it climbs up a steep hill.

18 In 1979 three-quarters of the British Moonies had attended a twenty-one-day workshop, but less than half the European Moonies had done so, half of them having attended a seven-day workshop. Almost all the British Moonies who have joined during or after 1979 have attended a twenty-one-day workshop.

19 For example, Y. W. Kim, *The Divine Principle: Study Guide*, New York, HSA–UWC, 1973 (reprinted London, HSA–UWC, 1977), was used as a basis for lectures.

20 Abe, 'Church Leader's Manual', p. 121.

21 This is less likely to happen now; the newcomers' courses are more commonly separated from those for members.

22 See Freedom Leadership Foundation, *Communism: A Critique and Counter Proposal*, Washington DC, FLF, 1973.

23 See Sang Hun Lee, *Unification Thought*, New York, Unification Thought Institute, 1973; Sang Hun Lee, *Unification Thought: Study Guide*, New York, Unification Thought Institute, 1974; Sang Hun Lee, *Explaining Unification Thought*, New York, Unification Thought Institute, 1981.

24 There was a period when it was decided that the time for study was so

precious that it should be spent on the more spiritual matters, and new recruits would gain their experience of fund-raising once they had joined a New Hope Team, a special group that new members usually join for about forty days, during which time they will be initiated into the life of the Unification Church in more practical detail than is the case during workshops – they will, for example, be expected to fund-raise and witness, and to say the Pledge (see n. 13). At the time of writing, however, the movement has once more incorporated fund-raising and witnessing into the twenty-one-day course.

25   W. P. Kim, 'Father's Testimony', *Principle Life*, 2 pts, New York, HSA–UWC, 1979; W. P. Kim, *Father's Course and Our Life of Faith*, London, HSA–UWC, 1982; W. P. Kim, 'Seoul: Chungpa Dong Church and Pioneering', *Today's World*, October 1982; W. P. Kim, 'From Pyongyang to Pusan', *Today's World*, April 1983, all provide transcripts of talks given by this early disciple who fled to Pusan with Moon during the Korean War and who gave three lectures at a twenty-one-day course that I attended in 1977. See also *Today's World*, January, September, October 1982, April 1983.

26   *Blessing Quarterly* publishes many such testimonies.

27   See Sudo, '120-Day Training Manual', for the text of a 120-day course.

28   Recently greater use has been made of video recordings of lectures on the *Divine Principle*, which guests can study by themselves in booths. Evidently this has become a particularly popular method of introducing the movement in Japan. See *Vision*, June 1984, p. 47.

5   Choice or Brainwashing?

1   *Daily Mail*, 29 May 1978.

2   Transcript of the official tape recording of evidence given in the High Court of Justice, Queen's Bench Division, before Mr Justice Comyn in the case of *Orme* v. *Associated Newspapers Group Ltd*, Royal Courts of Justice, 9 March 1981, p. 15.

3   Peter Collier, 'Bringing Home the Moonies: the Brain Snatch', *New Times*, 10 July 1977.

4   'I can do no other': Martin Luther at the Diet of Worms, 1521.

5   Such assertions can be found in the anti-cult literature and in most of the books by ex-members and evangelical Christians, but for the most frequently quoted professional assessments, see the following papers by John G. Clark Jr: 'Destructive Cults: Defined and Held Accountable', address to National Guard Reserve Chaplains, Minneapolis, 7 February 1977; 'The Noisy Brain in a Noisy Body', mimeo paper condensed from one delivered at the New Jersey Psychological Association, 5 November 1977, distributed by Free Minds Inc., PO Box 4216, Minneapolis; 'Problems in Referral of Cult Members', *Journal of the National Association of Private Psychiatric Hospitals*, vol. 9, no. 4, 1978; 'The Manipulation of Madness', paper presented in Hanover, W. Germany, 24 February 1978; 'We are all Cultists at Heart', *Newsday*, 30 November 1978; 'Investigating the Effects of Some Religious

Cults on the Health and Welfare of their Converts', paper circulated at FAIR AGM, 1981; 'Testimony to the Special Investigating Committee of the Vermont State Investigating the Effects of Some Religious Cults on the Health and Welfare of their Converts, mimeo circulated by FAIR, London, undated. See also the following papers by M. F. Galper: 'Indoctrination Methods of the Unification Church', presented at the annual meeting of the California State Psychological Association, Los Angeles, 13 March 1977; 'Extremist Religious Cults and Today's Youth', presented at the International Conference on the Effects on Physical and Mental Health of New Totalitarian Religions and Pseudoreligious Movements, Bonn, W. Germany, 20–22 November 1981. See also the following papers by M. T. Singer: 'Therapy with Ex-Cult Members', *Journal of the National Association of Private Psychiatric Hospitals*, vol. 9, no. 4, 1978; 'Coming Out of the Cults', *Psychology Today*, January 1979; 'Where We Were . . . Where We Are . . . Where We're Going', presented at the Citizens' Freedom Foundation Annual Conference, Arlington, Va., 22–24 October 1982. The quotations are from Clark and Galper.

6   L. R. Rambo, 'Current Research on Religious Conversion', *Religious Studies Review*, vol. 8, April 1982, provides an excellent annotated bibliography of different approaches to conversion.

7   Some of the arguments put forward in this chapter are developed more fully in the following papers by Eileen Barker: 'Facts and Values and Social Science', *Science and Absolute Values*, Proceedings of the Third International Conference on the Unity of the Sciences, New York, ICF, 1975; 'Apes and Angels: Reductionism, Selection and Emergence in the Study of Man', *Inquiry*, vol. 19, no. 4, 1976; 'Confessions of a Methodological Schizophrenic: Problems Encountered in the Study of Rev. Sun Myung Moon's Unification Church', *Institute for the Study of Worship and Religious Architecture Research Bulletin*, University of Birmingham, 1978; 'The Professional Stranger: Some Methodological Problems Encountered in a Study of the Reverend Sun Myung Moon's Unification Church', Open University Course Media Notes for D207: *An Introduction to Sociology*, Milton Keynes, OU, 1980; 'Der Professionelle Fremde: Erklärung des Unerklärlichen beim Studium einer abweichenden religiösen Gruppe', in Günter Kehrer (ed.), *Das Entstehen einer neuen Religion: Das Beispiel der Vereinigungskirche*, Munich, Kösel-Verlag, 1981; 'New Religious Movements in Britain: Context and Membership', *Social Compass*, nos. 30–1, 1983; 'Supping with the Devil: How Long a Spoon does the Sociologist Need?', *Sociological Analysis*, vol. 44, no. 3, 1983.

8   Eileen Barker, 'Whose Service is Perfect Freedom: the Concept of Spiritual Well-Being in Relation to the Reverend Sun Myung Moon's Unification Church in Britain', in David O. Moberg (ed.), *Spiritual Well-Being*, Washington DC, University Press of America, 1979.

9   A study of Roman Catholics in England and Wales found that 75 per cent believed, 'At the consecration, the bread and wine are really changed into the Body and Blood of Christ': M. P. Hornsby-Smith and R. N. Lee, *Roman Catholic Opinion: A Study of Roman Catholics in England and Wales in the 1970s*, Final Report, University of Surrey, 1979, pp. 54, 193.

10 Which is not, of course, to suggest that the content of the beliefs cannot be judged by theologians or other individuals – but that is a separate issue.

11 See Karl R. Popper, *The Logic of Scientific Discovery*, rev. edn, London, Hutchinson, 1968, and *Conjectures and Refutations: The Growth of Scientific Knowledge*, 2nd ed, London Routledge & Kegan Paul, 1965, for a discussion of such distinctions.

12 Clark, 'Problems in Referral of Cult Members', p. 27. On the following page he describes one case in which a patient who had been persuaded that 'hallucinations' that she had previously had were manifestations of the God that a particular cult worshipped. When he saw her on a house visit

> she was in a deluded and manic state, highly disorganized, and unable to handle reality. Characteristically she had been told by the cult to act sane if hospitalized.
>
> So effective was her control that the admitting resident could not detect the psychosis, but was persuaded by me and the proper legal cases to effect an admission. Within two weeks, while being evaluated with no medications, she entered into a frank psychotic episode and deprogrammed herself. With further treatment, she made a reasonably satisfactory recovery.

13 See chapters 6 and 8 for further discussion of religious experiences. See also T. Robbins and Dick Anthony, 'The Medicalization of Deviant Religion: Preliminary Observations and Critique', Yale Series of Working Papers in Sociology No. 1, 1980.

14 Acts of the Apostles, ch. 9.

15 See I. L. Horowitz, *Science, Sin and Scholarship: The Politics of Reverend Moon and the Unification Church*, Cambridge, Mass./London, MIT Press, 1978, ch. 12; B. Underwood and B. Underwood, *Hostage to Heaven*, New York, Clarkson N. Potter, 1979, pp. 151ff., for details of such an incident.

16 The 'Lasher Amendment' was successfully passed through all the necessary stages until the final one, when New York Governor Carey vetoed it on the grounds that 'it places in jeopardy constitutionally guaranteed rights and raises false hopes by appearing to create an acceptable procedure . . . but I have asked my Counsel to work with the sponsors of this bill in order to determine whether constitutionally acceptable legislation can be developed in this difficult area': see H. Richardson (ed.), *New Religions and Mental Health: Understanding the Issues*, New York, Rose of Sharon Press, 1980, pp. ix, x.

17 For some of the most widely circulated literature by such psychologists and psychiatrists, see the writings of Clark, Galper and Singer cited in n. 5 above, L. J. West and R. Delgado, 'Psyching out the Cults', *Los Angeles Times*, 26 November 1978.

18 For example, C. Edwards, *Crazy for God*, Englewood Cliffs, NJ, Prentice-Hall, 1979; C. Elkins, *Heavenly Deception*, Wheaton, Ill., Tyndale House, 1980; E. Heftmann, *Dark Side of the Moonies*, Harmondsworth, Penguin, 1983; Susan Swatland and Anne Swatland, *Escape from the Moonies*, London, New English Library, 1982; Underwood and Underwood, *Hostage to Heaven*.

19 J. G. Clark Jr, 'We are all Cultists at Heart'. See also M. R. Rudin, 'Women, Elderly and the Children in Religious Cults', paper presented at the Citizens', Freedom Foundation Annual Conference, Arlington, Va., 23 October 1982, published in *Awareness*, nos. 4 and 5, 1983: see no. 4, p. 5.

20 Comment made by a prominent counsellor at a conference organized by the Graduate Theological Union, Berkeley, Ca., 1981.

21 Official transcript of *Daily Mail* case, 9 March 1981, p. 14 (see n. 2 for details).

22 T. Solomon, 'Integrating the Moonie Experience: a Survey of Ex-Members of the Unification Church', in T. Robbins and Dick Anthony (eds.), *In Gods We Trust: New Patterns of Religious Pluralism in America*, New Brunswick, Transaction Books, 1981, p. 289.

23 Ibid., p. 279.

24 S. A. Wright, 'Post Involvement Attitudes of Voluntary Defectors from Controversial New Religious Movements', paper presented at the Annual Meeting of the Society for the Scientific Study of Religion, Knoxville, 1983, p. 10.

25 M. Galanter, 'Unification Church ("Moonie") Dropouts: Psychological Readjustment after Leaving a Charismatic Religious Group', *American Journal of Psychiatry*, vol. 140, no. 8, 1983, p. 986.

26 The most commonly employed model can be found in R. J. Lifton, *Thought Reform and the Psychology of Totalism: A Study of 'Brainwashing' in China*, New York, Norton, 1961, ch. 22.

27 Lying when the means justify the end of establishing the Kingdom of Heaven on earth: see ch. 7.

28 Galper, 'Indoctrination Methods of the Unification Church', p. 2.

29 Galper, 'Extremist Religious Cults and Today's Youth', p. 1.

30 J. G. Clark Jr, 'We are all Cultists at Heart'.

31 As these data were for private distribution, I shall not cite the source here.

32 T. S. Szasz, *The Myth of Mental Illness*, London, Secker & Warburg, 1962; T. S. Szasz, *Ideology and Insanity*, Harmondsworth, Penguin, 1974 (first published 1970); T. S. Szasz, *The Myth of Psychotherapy: Mental Healing as Religion, Rhetoric and Repression*, Garden City, NY, Anchor Press/Doubleday, 1978.

33 Singer, 'Coming Out of the Cults'.

34 In the *Daily Mail* libel case the following exchange took place:

> MR SHAW (for the Unification Church): To test your hypothesis that Moonies suffer from mind-control – that is your hypothesis, is it not?
>
> PROFESSOR SINGER: Yes.
>
> Q. To test it, would one have to interview, do you think, Moonies as well as ex-Moonies?
>
> A. Not necessarily because it is based upon getting a sufficient history of how the organization works, and from the Moonies while they were in, they described very similar procedures having occurred to them as the ones who come out describe.

Q.   Before one could conclude . . . that [difficulty in concentrating] is a symptom of brainwashing, would not one have to have a group of Moonies whose concentration one can test and a control group who had never been Moonies at all . . . ?

A.   No, because the [methodology] is to study a person in comparison. You use them for their own control case, and that is the way that you take a look at the individual. You get a good history of what they were like, you get records from their school, descriptions from their parents and family, and you use them as their own control.

Q.   . . . is [the symptom of having trouble concentrating] one which one may meet in a variety of contexts and which may present itself whenever someone is suffering from stress or emotions?

A.   It could be but it is very rare in the form that it is in these young adults because they tend to have a lack of the psychiatric symptoms that you often would see that would cause concentration problems.

Q.   Is the trouble they have, concentrating, something that could, given enough time and effort, be measured and assessed?

A.   Yes, in that individual.

Q.   And could be compared, could it not, if one was concerned with sufficient cases, with people outside the Moonies altogether?

A.   Surely.

Q.   Have you made any attempt upon an exercise of that kind?

A.   That is not my personal choice. There are many methods in science and each scientist gets to choose the most appropriate method for testing their hypothesis, that is the best for what they are doing.

Official transcript, 9 March 1981, p. 46.

35   See, *inter alia*, Swatland and Swatland, *Escape from the Moonies*, p. 9; C. Stoner and J. A. Parke, *All God's Children: The Cult Experience – Salvation or Slavery?*, Harmondsworth, Penguin, 1979 (first published 1977).

36   Singer, 'Therapy with Ex-Cult Members', p. 14.

37   Lifton, *Thought Reform and the Psychology of Totalism*; E. H. Schein, 'The Chinese Indoctrination Program for Prisoners of War: a Study of Attempted "Brainwashing"', *Psychiatry*, vol. 19 (reprinted in E. E. Maccoby *et al.* (eds.), *Readings in Social Psychology*, 34d edn, London, Methuen, 1966); E. H. Schein, *Coercive Persuasion*, New York, Norton, 1961.

38   Singer's evidence at the *Daily Mail* trial, pp. 16ff. See also Stoner and Parke, *All God's Children*, p. 240. For a different perspective, see F. Conway and J. Siegelman, 'Information Disease: Have Cults Created a New Mental Illness?', *Science Digest*, January 1982, pp. 86ff.

39   I use the term employed by Lifton in *Thought Reform and the Psychology of Totalism*, as his is the study most frequently cited in this particular argument.

40   For one of the best-known exponents on the behaviourist school, see B. F. Skinner, *Beyond Freedom and Dignity*, Harmondsworth, Penguin, 1973 (first published in the USA 1971); B. F. Skinner, *About Behaviourism*, London, Cape, 1974.

41 For a sophisticated version of this argument, see K. R. Minogue, 'The Myth of Social Conditioning', *Policy Review*, no. 18, 1981, pp. 23ff.

42 See, *inter alia*, Lifton, *Thought Reform and the Psychology of Totalism*; Maccoby *et al.*, *Readings in Social Psychology*, sect. 7; Schein, 'The Chinese Indoctrination Program for Prisoners of War'; Schein, *Coercive Persuasion*; D. Winn, *The Manipulated Mind: Brainwashing, Conditioning and Indoctrination*, London, Octagon Press, 1983.

43 See, *inter alia*, C. T. Tart (ed.), *Altered States of Consciousness*, New York, Wiley, 1969; W. Sargant, *Battle for the Mind*, London, Heinemann, 1957; W. Sargant, *The Mind Possessed*, London, Heinemann, 1973; I. M. Lewis, *Ecstatic Religion: An Anthropological Study of Spirit Possession and Shaminism*, Harmondsworth, Penguin, 1971.

44 See, *inter alia*, J. G. Clark Jr, 'Problems in Referral of Cult Members'; R. Delgado, 'Religious Totalism: Gentle and Ungentle Persuasion under the First Amendment', *Southern California Law Review*, vol. 51, no. 1, 1977; R. W. Dellinger, *Cults and Kids: A Study of Coercion*, Boys Town Center, Boys Town, Neb., undated; R. Enroth, *Youth, Brainwashing and the Extremist Cults*, Grand Rapids, Michigan, Zondervan, 1977; Heftmann, *Dark Side of the Moonies*; Swatland and Swatland, *Escape from the Moonies*.

45 I have yet to discover how a social scientist – or, indeed, anyone – could 'operationalize' the noumenal self, the transcendental ego, the ghost in the machine, the soul or any other such bearer of human free will.

46 See, *inter alia*, P. L. Berger and T. Luckmann, *The Social Construction of Reality: Everything that Passes for Knowledge in Society*, Garden City, NY, Doubleday, 1966.

47 In the language of G. H. Mead, *Mind, Self and Society from the Standpoint of a Social Behaviourist*, ed. C. W. Morris, Chicago/London, University of Chicago Press, 1934, the 'I' can reflect upon the 'Me'.

48 It is not, of course, being suggested that people will always avail themselves of this ability, nor that they will always – or even normally – do whatever sorting they do in a rational manner. It is patently obvious that we can abrogate our active role and that we can be grossly irrational. It is being suggested only that we have a potential for being active and, on occasion, rational beings. See B. R. Wilson (ed.), *Rationality*, Oxford, Blackwell, 1970.

49 Various kinds of multivariate analysis, such as multiple regression, can help us to discover some relative weightings, but although I was able to take advantage of several statistical techniques in my analysis, there was no way in which I (or anyone else) could isolate and quantify the relative effects of the four variables, each of which would have been hopelessly distorted by any such attempt.

50 In other words, the situations are what the sociologist calls ideal types. See Max Weber, *From Max Weber: Essays in Sociology*, eds. H. H. Gerth and C. Wright Mills, New York, Oxford University Press, 1946; Max Weber, *The Theory or Social and Economic Organization*, trs./ed. Talcott Parsons, Toronto, Free Press, 1964 (first published New York, Oxford University Press, 1947).

51 This is a distinction that is similar to that which Popper makes between a first

and a second world. See Karl R. Popper, *Objective Knowledge: An Evolutionary Approach*, Oxford, Clarendon Press, 1972.

52   See, *inter alia*, Ted Patrick with Tom Dulack, *Let Our Children Go*, New York, Dutton, 1976; H. Richardson (ed.), *Deprogramming: Documenting the Issue*, prepared for the American Civil Liberties Union, New York, and the Toronto School of Theology Conference on Religious Deprogramming, 1977; M. D. Bryant (ed.), *Religious Liberty in Canada: Deprogramming and Media Coverage of New Religions*, Documentation Series No. 1, Canadians for the Protection of Religious Liberty, Toronto, 1979.

53   *Unification News*, April 1983, p. 16.

54   See the plaintiffs' deposition testimonies in *David Molko and Tracy Leal* v. *Holy Spirit Association for the Unification of World Christianity*, California Superior Court, City and County of San Francisco, case no, 769–529. A summary judgment was entered in favour of the defendants on 20 October 1983.

55   It is not, perhaps, entirely without relevance that the Northern Ireland MP Bobby Sands was reported in the media as being 'very mentally alert' and capable of engaging in political argument with the Labour Party representatives who visited him in the Maze Prison on the sixty-second day of his hunger strike. See also K. Mellanby, *Human Guinea-Pigs*, London, Merlin Press, 1973 (first published 1945).

56   Which is not to say that the *members* always get sufficient sleep.

57   Again, the Oakland Family *members* might chant, sometimes for two days, in the hope that the guests will accept the Principle. See Ken Sudo, '120-Day Training Manual', unpublished transcript, New York, HSA–UWC, 1975, p. 338.

58   The International Society for Krishna Consciousness is the movement which is popularly known as 'Hare Krishna' because of the chant performed by the devotees.

59   See M. Douglas, *Natural Symbols: Exploration in Cosmology*, London, Barrie & Rockliff, 1970; I. M. Lewis, *Ecstatic Religion*.

60   Definitions of hypnosis are notoriously vague, but see Winn, *The Manipulated Mind*, for a helpful overview of some current theories on the subject.

61   J. G. Clark Jr, 'Problems in Referral of Cult Members', p. 27. See discussions on 'medicalization' in Eileen Barker, 'The Conversion of Conversion', in A. R. Peacocke (ed.), *Reductionism: The Quest for the Unity of Knowledge*, London, NFER–Nelson, forthcoming; B. Kilbourne and J. T. Richardson, 'Psychotherapy and New Religions in a Pluralistic Society', *American Psychologist* (forthcoming); H. Richardson (ed.), *New Religions and Mental Health*, New York, Edwin Mellen Press, 1980; R. A. Kurtz and H. P. Chalfant, *The Sociology of Medicine and Illness*, Boston, Allyn & Bacon, 1983, ch. 2; Robbins and Anthony, 'The Medicalization of Deviant Religion'.

62   This was largely on account of the activities of the International One World Crusade (see ch. 2), which was in Britain at the time.

63   M. Galanter, 'Psychological Induction into the Large Group: Findings from a Modern Religious Sect', *American Journal of Psychiatry*, vol. 137, no. 12, 1980, p. 1575.

64 One of the 'second-level' leaders from Oakland told me that they reckoned that one in ten of those to whom they talked in the street would come to dinner; one in ten of those who came to dinner would agree to attend a workshop; and one in ten of those who attended a workshop would finally become a full-time member. Except for the first figure, which seems much too high, this appears to coincide with the pattern I observed in Britain and would, so far as I am able to estimate, be correct for America. The highest figures from an independent source come from David Taylor, who made six visits to Boonville in 1975 as part of his research for a Master's thesis. D. G. Bromley and A. D. Shupe Jr, *'Moonies' in America: Cults, Church and Crusade,* Beverly Hills/London, Sage Publications, 1979, p. 177, quote D. Taylor, *Recruitment into the Unification Church as a Socially Organized Accomplishment,* Master's thesis, University of Montana, 1978, as saying that about half of those who go on a two-day workshop stay for the week-long seminar. Taylor, 'Becoming New People: the Recruitment of Young Americans into the Unification Church', in R. Wallis (ed.), *Millenialism and Charisma,* Belfast, Queen's University, 1982, p. 202, estimates that slightly more than half those who complete the week-long session stay on and most of these eventually become members. Taylor has told me that the summer of 1975

> was probably the peak of their recruitment success. The Church had no difficulty presenting themselves as Creative Community Project *and* there was very little negative media or other information about them at that time. . . . I believe the 25 per cent figure as a ratio of original weekenders to those who started a second week is fairly accurate. The remaining question is how many of those 25 per cent returned to the Berkeley/Oakland area as committed members? . . . That doesn't mean the [Barker] 10 per cent is that far off. I feel certain at least 15 per cent of those who went to the two-day course at Boonville actually ended up becoming members, at least in the short run – since 25 per cent entered the second week and nearly all stayed for the duration (four weeks), the total could be closer to 20 per cent. *But* this percentage (15–20 per cent) would be reliable only for the summer 1975 recruitment period. Also the disparity in figures may be partly because the Moonies would not count those who did return to the communes from Boonville somewhat committed, but then dropped out almost immediately. There could have been a high attrition rate at this stage since virtually all recruits did *not* have a clue they were committing themselves to the Unification Church. Reverend Moon, of course, was only divulged once recruits were established in the communes. I would have no way of knowing how frequently people dropped out at that stage. (Personal communication)

Further details of the sources and calculations used to reach my figures are given in Eileen Barker, 'The Ones Who Got Away: People who Attend Unification Workshops and do not Become Moonies', in R. Stark (ed.), *Religious Movements; Genesis, Exodus and Numbers,* New York, Rose of

Sharon Press, forthcoming, and in Eileen Barker (ed.), *Of Gods and Men: New Religious Movements in the West*, Atlanta, Ga., Mercer University Press, 1984; see especially n. 11.

Postscript. Since sending this book to the publishers, I have acquired the following evidence concerning the departure rate of guests in Oakland. The first piece of information comes from a former member of the Unification Church who had been a group leader at Boonville before she was deprogrammed. She has herself since been involved in deprogramming and counselling ex-members. She had been a group leader at Boonville. In this sworn testimony she is talking about the dinners and workshops in northern California in the period between 1975 and 1977:

Q.   Of people who came to dinner on Friday night, what percentage would go up to Boonville for a weekend?

A.   Maybe twenty-five people would come for dinner and sometimes we'd get as many as half the people, sometimes as few as a quarter of the people (for the weekend seminar).

Q.   Of that group, how many would stay for the week-long seminar?

A.   There would usually be at least fifteen new people for the week is my recollection. I mean at least that many. Depending on how large, if we'd had, say, sixty people for the weekend, maybe we'd have as many as thirty new people.

Q.   What percentage of those subsequently became members of the group for longer than two or three weeks following the one-week seminar?

A.   Well, say if thirty people came for the weekend, fifteen people stayed for the week, I would guess at the end of that week, ten would probably become members.

Q.   And by members, you mean people that would stay with the group longer than two or three weeks?

A.   Right.

Q.   Of that ten, how many would stay longer than six months?

A.   I would say, five.

Deposition testimony of Barbara Underwood Scharff, 21 June 1983 (pp 71/2) in the case of *David Molko and Tracy Leal* v. *Holy Spirit Association for the Unification of World Christianity, et al.* in the Superior Court of the State of California in and for the City and County of San Francisco, case no. 769–529.

The second piece of information consists of some statistics prepared by Unification Church members who went through their records for the ten-week period from 24 November 1975 to 1 February 1976. These trace the fortunes of 170 persons who had already been to a weekend seminar and had started a seven-day workshop. According to the figures (see next page), there would have been an average of seventeen people going from a two-day to a seven-day workshop around that time. If we assume (as the evidence suggests) that somewhere between two and four times as many would have attended the two-day workshop, it would seem that the Oakland 'rate' was indeed remark-

	No. of guests	Percentage
Left during 1st week	3	1.8
Left after 1st week	54	31.8
Left after 2nd week	20	11.8
Left after 3rd week	7	4.1
Left after 4th week	29	17.1
Joined and left voluntarily	28	16.5
Joined and left through deprogramming	7	4.1
Current members (early 1984)	22	12.8
Total	170	100.0

ably similar to the data collected by Galanter and myself (as depicted in table 5, p. 146).

65 See, for example, Citizens' Freedom Foundation, *Information News*, October 1981, p. 3: 'No one is free from their psychological coercion.'

66 A national poll of college campuses in America showed 93 per cent of students saying that there was 'No chance' and a further 5 per cent saying 'Very little chance' that they would join a religious cult such as the Reverend Sun Myung Moon's Unification Church; 1 per cent answered, 'Some chance'; fewer than 1 per cent answered, 'Good chance': the *Newsweek* on Campus Poll, 1983, see *Emerging Trends*, Princeton Religion Research Center, vol. 5, no. 5, 1983, p. 2.

6   Reactions to the Workshop

1 Much of this chapter is a shortened version of Eileen Barker, 'The Ones Who Got Away: People who Attend Unification Workshops and do not Become Moonies', in R. Stark (ed.), *Religious Movements: Genesis, Exodus and Numbers*, New York, Rose of Sharon Press, forthcoming, and in Eileen Barker (ed.), *Of Gods and Men: New Religious Movements in the West*, Atlanta, Ga., Mercer University Press, 1984.

2 'Leavers' differ from the 'apostates' (who do not concern us here), the latter having been in the movement for several months or years before leaving.

3 Responses from people who joined as either Home-Church or CARP (student) members are not included. This is because the numbers were too small (eleven and thirteen respectively) to make a significant comparison, but, broadly speaking, they appeared to be even more appreciative of the workshop than the full-time joiners. A section in chapter 9 deals with some characteristics of Home-Church members.

4 See, for example, the judge's summing up in the *Daily Mail* court case (see ch. 5, n. 2 for details of the case).

5 This process of 'growth charisma' and the beliefs which I call 'Moonology' are described in Eileen Barker, *Moonies in Action*, Oxford, Blackwell, forthcoming.

6   I am indebted to the Religious Experience Research Unit, Manchester College, Oxford, and to David Hay for permission to use in my research the wording of some of the questions that they used. See T. Beardsworth, *A Sense of Presence*, Religious Experience Research Unit, Manchester College, Oxford, 1977; A. Hardy, *The Spiritual Nature of Man*, Oxford, Oxford University Press, 1979; D. Hay, *Exploring Inner Space: Is God still Possible in the Twentieth Century?*, Harmondsworth, Penguin, 1982; E. Robinson, *The Original Vision* (1977) and *Living the Question* (1978), both published by the Religious Experience Research Unit, Manchester College, Oxford.

7   Although I cannot accept their argument in its entirety, it does seem to me that F. Conway and J. Siegelman, *Snapping: America's Epidemic of Sudden Personality Change*, Philadelphia/New York, Lippincott, 1978, provides one of the more useful models for conceptualizing sudden conversion, which they see as a holographic crisis in the brain that occurs when a very small change in information produces a massive 'catastrophic' change in the structure of a person's hologram (his or her picture of reality). See also E. C. Zeeman, *Catastrophe Theory: Selected Papers, 1972–1977*, London, Addison-Wesley, 1978, especially chs. 8, 12; and R. Ofshe, 'Obedience to Authority: Re-analysis and Alternative Explanation', mimeo, University of California, Berkeley, 1982, for further suggestions of relevance in conceptualizing and evaluating the time element in sudden conversion. See also L. R. Rambo, 'Current Research on Religious Conversion', *Religious Studies Review*, vol. 8, 1982.

8   See Citizens' Freedom Foundation, *Information News*, October 1981, p. 3, and quotation at the beginning of ch. 5.

7   Environmental Control, Deception and 'Love-Bombing'

1   Ken Sudo, '120-Day Training Manual', unpublished transcript, New York, HSA–UWC, 1975, p. 338.

2   See S. E. Asch, 'Effects of Group Pressure upon the Modification and Distortion of Judgments', in E. E. Maccoby *et al.*, *Readings in Social Psychology*, 3rd edn, London, Methuen, 1966.

3   D. Taylor, 'Becoming New People: the Recruitment of Young Americans into the Unification Church', in R. Wallis (ed.), *Millenarianism and Charisma*, Belfast, Queen's University, 1982, p. 183. M. Galanter, 'Psychological Introduction into the Large Group: Findings from a Modern Religious Sect', *American Journal of Psychiatry*, vol. 137, no. 12, 1980, has drawn an interesting parallel between this practice and the sponsorship system in AA. He also points out that it has antecedents in other Christian sects, such as the Moravian Protestants and the Anabaptists, which employed group-oriented explorations of belief and feelings. 'Indeed,' he continues 'the technique of mixing "successful" veterans and initiates in conjoint group experience for modelling and identification is regularly seen in contemporary self-help programs.' See also T. Oden, 'The New Pietism', in E. Barker (ed.), *New*

Religious Movements: A Perspective for Understanding Society, New York, Edwin Mellen Press, 1982.

4   Here I use the term 'objectified' in the sense that the 'truth' is reified or 'made into' a 'real thing'. See P. L. Berger and T. Luckmann, *The Social Construction of Reality: Everything that Passes for Knowledge in Society*, Garden City, NY, Doubleday, 1966.

5   My data showed that less than one in five British and European Moonies (but a third of the American seminarians) joined within two weeks of their first contact with the movement; on the other hand, only just over one in five of the British (and a third of the Europeans and American seminarians) took more than three months to join after first contact. Stilson Judah, who very kindly has allowed me to analyse his unpublished data, found 60 per cent of his San Francisco sample joined within three weeks of first meeting the movement. See also D. G. Bromley and A. D. Shupe Jr, *'Moonies' in America: Cults, Church and Crusade*, Beverly Hills/London, Sage Publications, 1979, p. 174.

6   Around three-quarters of the Moonies did not break contact for more than a week between meeting and joining the movement (a third kept up daily contact). Well over three-quarters suggested that they had either wanted to join (18 per cent) or had had some interest in joining from the time of first contact (63 per cent). A further 13 per cent said that they had not been particularly interested, 5 per cent claiming that they definitely had *not* wanted to join; 1 per cent reported that, having managed to break contact, they had then been recontacted by the Moonies – others who broke contact intimated either that they had been open to renewal of contact or that they themselves had been responsible for returning to the movement.

7   Moonies have frequently told me that it was the media which first introduced the term 'love-bombing'. It is not a concept normally used by British or European members, although I have heard them, and Americans from the East Coast, accuse the Oakland Family of the practice, and, as can be seen from the quotation at the beginning of this chapter, the Oakland Family has used the term with approval. See also D. Taylor, 'Becoming New People', pp. 188ff.

8   Genesis 27: 1–36. See Chung Hwan Kwak, *Outline of the Principle: Level 4*, New York, HSA–UWC, 1980, pp. 135–9. In the first 120-day training session Jacob's deception is explained with the words: 'Jacob deceived Satan not God. Satan deceived God, therefore, in order to indemnify this failure, Satan must be deceived from God's side. This is the reason why Jacob deceived his elder brother Esau, also Isaac, and his Uncle Laban': Sudo, '120-Day Training Manual', p. 265. Sudo does, however, end this lecture with the admonition: 'One thing is that Jacob deceived others, but we must not deceive others. Okay? This dispensation is different. . . . Don't misunderstand me, we must buy, don't steal. Don't deceive others' (p. 268). See also p. 272.

9   Including, according to J. E. Milligan, 'The Persistence of the Salvation Army: a Challenge to the Sociology of Sectarianism', unpublished Ph.D. thesis, University of Glasgow, 1982, the Salvation Army, which is nowadays usually looked upon with respect for its charitable work.

10   I have offered a critical analysis of the Unification Church on some of these
       questions in Eileen Barker, 'Doing Love: Tensions in the Ideal Family', in
       G. James (ed.), *The Family and Unification Thought: A Comparative Study*,
       New York, Rose of Sharon Press, 1983; Eileen Barker, 'Quo Vadis?', in
       P. Hammond and D. E. Bromley (eds.), *Towards the Twenty-First Century*,
       Belton, Ca., Wadsworth, forthcoming; E. Barker, *Moonies in Action*, Oxford,
       Blackwell, forthcoming.

11   W. Sargant, *The Mind Possessed*, London, Heinemann, 1973; E. H. Schein,
       Coercive Persuasion, New York, Norton, 1961; A. Somit, 'Brainwashing', in
       David Sills (ed.), *International Encyclopedia of the Social Sciences*, vol. 3, New
       York, Macmillan, 1968; D. Winn, *The Manipulated Mind: Brainwashing,
       Conditioning and Indoctrination*, London, Octagon Press, 1983. See also
       B. Bettleheim, 'Behaviour in Extreme Situations', in Maccoby *et al.*, *Readings
       in Social Psychology* (first published in *Journal of Abnormal and Social Psy-
       chology*, vol. 38, 1943, pp. 417–52), for a description of how prisoners in
       Dachau and Buchenwald 'adjusted' to Gestapo values.

12   W. Sargant, *Battle for the Mind*, London, Heinemann, 1957, quoted in Winn,
       The Manipulated Mind, p. 28.

13   Winn, *The Manipulated Mind*, p. 28.

14   J. Lofland and R. Stark, 'Becoming a World-Saver: a Theory of Conversion to
       a Deviant Perspective', *American Sociological Review*, vol. 30, 1965, p. 871.
       For further developments of Lofland's thinking about conversion, see
       J. Lofland, '"Becoming a World-Saver" Revisited', in J. T. Richardson (ed.),
       Conversion and Commitment in Contemporary Religion, special issue of *American
       Behavioral Scientist*, vol. 20, no.s 6, 1977; J. Lofland, 'Social Movement
       Culture', in Hammond and Bromley, *Towards the Twenty-First Century*;
       J. Lofland and N. Skonovd, 'Conversion Motifs', *Journal for the Scientific
       Study of Religion*, vol. 20, no. 4, 1981 (of which a longer version appears in
       Eileen Barker (ed.), *Of Gods and Men: New Religious Movements in the West*,
       Atlanta, Ga., Mercer University Press, 1984).

15   R. Traviso, 'Alteration and Conversion as Qualitatively Different Trans-
       formations', in G. P. Stone and H. Farberman (eds.), *Social Psychology
       through Symbolic Interaction*, Waltham, Mass., Ginn-Blaisdell, 1970, quoted in
       Lofland and Skovnod, 'Conversion Motifs', p. 375.

16   For an analysis of the Unification Church from the perspective of a 'resource
       mobilization model', see Bromley and Shupe, *'Moonies' in America*.

17   It is an interesting feature of movements like the Unification Church that,
       despite the fact that they advocate the existence of absolute values, they
       frequently find that their actions are guided more by pragmatic, Utilitarian
       principles than by Kantian ethics in so far as they accept that the means can
       justify the end. See Karl R. Popper, *The Open Society and its Enemies*, 2 vols.,
       London, Routledge & Kegan Paul, 1945, for a discussion of some of the
       political/philosophical issues arising from such a position.

18   Some Moonies do put pressure on people with threats of how Satan or the
       spirit world can attack those who, having had the opportunity to hear the
       Divine Principle, do not follow the Messiah. This, however, plays only a

minor role in recruitment practices; it has a far more important role as a means of controlling those who are actually in the movement.

19   Barker, 'Doing Love'.
20   See E. Goffman, *Asylums: Essays on the Social Situation of Mental Patients and Other Inmates*, Garden City, NY, Anchor Press/Doubleday, 1961, and R. J. Lifton, *Thought Reform and the Psychology of Totalism: A Study of 'Brainwashing' in China*, New York, Norton, 1961, for accounts of, respectively, the 'total institution' and 'totalism'. It should, however, be stressed that throughout history people have joined *voluntary* associations (s' .ch as monasteries and convents) which share some characteristics with compulsory organizations (such as prisons and asylums). See M. Hill, *The Religious Order: A Study of Virtuoso Religion and its Legitimation in the Nineteenth-Century Church of England*, London, Heinemann, 1973, pp. 72–82, for a helpful discussion of the limited applicability of the concept of the total institution to the religious order. See also A. Etzioni, *A Comparative Analysis of Complex Organizations*, Glencoe, Ill., Free Press, 1961.
21   In many respects the Unification Church is an organization which can be defined as one of 'high group' and 'low grid' control – see M. Douglas, *Natural Symbols: Explorations in Cosmology*, London, Barrie & Rockliff, 1970.

8   Suggestibility

1   See H. J. Eysenck, *Uses and Abuses of Psychology*, Harmondsworth, Penguin, 1953; Karl R. Popper, *Conjectures and Refutations: The Growth of Scientific Knowledge*, 2nd edn, London, Routledge & Kegan Paul, 1965, ch. 1; T. S. Szasz, *The Myth of Mental Illness*, London, Secker & Warburg, 1962; T. S. Szasz, *Ideology and Insanity*, Harmondsworth, Penguin, 1974 (first published 1970); T. S. Szasz, *The Myth of Psychotherapy: Mental Healing as Religion, Rhetoric, and Repression*, Garden City, NY, Anchor Press/Doubleday, 1978, for swingeing criticisms of psychoanalytic methodology for such questions.
2   I use the word 'reliability' in the technical sense in which it means that the results are reproducible (as opposed to the 'validity' of a measurement which refers to whether or not it is measuring what we want to measure).
3   W. Kuner, 'New Religious Movements and Mental Health', in Eilcen Barker (ed.), *Of Gods and Men: New Religious Movements in the West*, Atlanta, Ga., Mercer University Press, 1984.
4   M. Galanter *et al.*, 'The Moonies: a Psychological Study of Conversion and Membership in a Contemporary Religious Cult', *American Journal of Psychology*, vol. 136, no. 2, 1979.
5   'The comparison group was drawn from a residentially and socially more stable population than that usually associated with persons entering this sect. . . . The difference in scores might therefore be partly attributed to the considerable amount of social disruption experienced by many people who elect to come to the workshops': M. Galanter, 'Psychological Induction into the Large Group: Findings from a Modern Religious Sect', *American Journal of Psychiatry*, vol. 137, no. 12, 1980, p. 1579.

6   Ibid.

7   It might also be mentioned that in my role as a university teacher and as Dean of Undergraduate Studies, I have come across many young people whose backgrounds would seem to have prepared them equally 'well' for membership of a Unification-type movement – if, that is, we were to accept merely the trauma/inadequacy/seeking-for-security sorts of explanation that have been given for people's becoming Moonies.

8   Galanter *et al.*, 'The Moonies', p. 166, reports that 30 per cent of his sample of Moonies had sought professional help for emotional problems and 6 per cent had been hospitalized. Americans are, however, much more prone to consult psychiatrists or psychotherapists than the British or Europeans, so, without a control group, it is difficult to evaluate this information. It is interesting, however, that he also found that 9 per cent from the Divine Light Mission had been hospitalized for emotional problems (Galanter, 'Psychological Induction into the Large Group', p. 1579). Galanter does not, unfortunately, tell us how many of his workshop subjects had a history of mental health problems, but he does report that the workshop staff, apparently respecting the vulnerability of some guests, asked for six of the thirty guests who stayed beyond the two-day workshop to leave because of 'psychological instability'. The staff accepted the fact that not all those interested in joining were suitable for membership (ibid.).

9   Or, to be more technical, the standard deviation tended to be greatest for the leavers, then the non-joiners, and lowest for the joiners. If one were to plot graphs in which *actual* susceptibility to the Unification Church was on the Y axis, along which the leavers (who had had more exposure to the movement's persuasive techniques) were deemed to be lower than the non-joiners (the joiners scoring highest), and in which the X axis represented the variables on the checklist of *presumed* suggestibility, the data would reveal a number of (albeit somewhat lopsided) inverted U curves.

10   That is, student members. See chapter 2, p. 50.

11   See J. A. Beckford, 'Accounting for Conversion', *British Journal of Sociology*, vol. 29, 1978, pp. 246–62.

12   The periods were for the Moonies:
         (1) 'from birth to the age of 10 years'
         (2) 'between the ages of 11 and 16 years'
         (3) 'from 17 years until six months before first meeting the Unification Church'
         (4) 'during the six months before meeting Unification Church'
         (5) 'now' (i.e. time of filling in the questionnaire)
      and for the control group:
         (1)–(2) as for the Moonies
         (3) 'from 17 years to the last six months'
         (4) 'during the last six months' (before filling in the questionnaire).

13   For a fuller discussion of the concept of spiritual well-being in relation to the Unification Church, see Eileen Barker, 'Whose Service is Perfect Freedom: the Concept of Spiritual Well-Being in Relation to the Reverend Sun Myung

Moon's Unification Church in Britain', in D. O. Moberg (ed.), *Spiritual Well-Being*, Washington DC, University Press of America, 1979.

14 The questionnaires, which contained forty-one pages for the Moonies and thirty-six pages for the control group, had a large number of open (i.e. not pre-coded) answers.

15 One of whom was a Roman Catholic monk, the other a non-believer from a strict Nonconformist background.

9 Susceptibility

1 For example, Eileen Barker, 'Who'd Be a Moonie? A Comparative Study of Those who Join the Unification Church in Britain', in B. R. Wilson (ed.), *The Social Impact of New Religious Movements*, New York, Rose of Sharon Press, 1981; Eileen Barker, 'The Ones Who Got Away: People who Attend Unification Church Workshops and do not Become Moonies', in R. Stark (ed.), *Religious Movements: Genesis Exodus and Numbers*, New York, Rose of Sharon Press, forthcoming, and in Eileen Barker (ed.), *Of Gods and Men: New Religious Movements in the West*, Atlanta, Ga., Mercer University Press, 1984.

2 It is possible to increase the statistical density of British Moonies fortyfold by referring merely to the variables of age, sex and class. Taking the situation as it was in 1980, roughly 1 person in every 100,000 (or 0.001 per cent) of the total British population would have been a Moonie. However, in the category of middle-middle- and upper-middle-class males who were aged between 21 and 26, roughly 1 in every 2,500 (or 0.04 per cent) would have been a Moonie. This is because half the Moonies but only about 7 per cent of the general population were between 21 and 26 years old; half the Moonies but only about 13 per cent of the general population came from the middle-middle or upper-middle classes; two-thirds of the Moonies but roughly half the general population (at that age) were male. But while such a statistic gives us some general idea of the Unification membership, we still have a lot to find out: 80 per cent of Moonies were not male *and* 21–6 *and* middle-middle- or upper-middle-class; and, of course, 2,499 persons out of every 2,500 in that category were not Moonies.

At that time (1980) there were 588 members of the 'British Family', a number which has never been greatly exceeded. Curiously enough, the proportion of the American population which comprises full-time members of the Unification Church is in almost exactly the same area of magnitude (i.e. roughly 0.001 per cent).

3 Less than 1 per cent of the British membership.

4 This is definitely the case in Britain, but it seems to be a pattern also found in America, judging from the data which Stilson Judah kindly allowed me to analyse after he had collected it from fifty members of the Oakland Family, and also according to a survey carried out in June 1976 by a Unification Church member with a sample of more than a thousand full-time members: Nora Spurgin, 'Unification Church Membership Profile', privately distributed paper, New York, HSA–UWC, 1977.

5   See Spurgin, 'Unification Church Membership Profile', p. 1, for American data.

6   The majority of British members leave within two years of joining, and several will do so after this period – sometimes after eight, nine or ten years in the movement. Quite a few have left after a 'matching' (when their marriage partners have been suggested for them by Moon). Although I cannot be so certain about the drop-out rate in other countries, all the evidence I have suggests that it is similar to that in Britain.

7   Spurgin, 'Unification Church Membership Profile', p. 6.

8   See P. Brierley (ed.), *Prospects for the Eighties*, London, Bible Society, 1980, p. 23, for English data, and G. Gallup Jr, *Religion in America, 1981*, Princeton Religion Research Center, 1981, for American Data.

9   Associate members will have signed a form stating that they support the aims of the Unification Church, which are defined thus:

> The Unification Church, being a Christian church with Rev. Sun Myung Moon as its founder and spiritual leader, has the following aims:
> 1. To build a society of goodness centred on God's love, fulfilling the prayer of Jesus, 'Thy will be done on earth, as it is in heaven', by helping people in all fields of endeavour to take up their responsibility in building such a society.
> 2. To promote the moral and spiritual education of people of all ages, teaching them to love God, love one another and love the creation unselfishly, and how to bring God into all human affairs – social, cultural and scientific.
> 3. To create God-centred families as a foundation for a moral and healthy society, and to create one human family transcending race and nationality, centred on God.
> 4. To solve the ideological and moral confusion which has resulted from the spread of atheistic materialism, by convincing people that a solution with a religious core – and not purely secular one – is the most practical and most moral way to right the wrongs of the world.
> 5. To strengthen Christianity and other religions and to encourage all religious people to cooperate and take the lead in solving world problems, not just spiritually but also socially and materially.

10   See Introduction, n. 7.

11   Despite the fact that there now exists an Islamic version of the *Divine Principle* (*Introduction to the Principle: An Islamic Perspective*, New York, HSA–UWC, 1980), it appears to be difficult for Muslims to reconcile its teachings with the Koran. Although about sixty Muslims started a two-day workshop in the London area during 1979, at least a third of these left before the end of the two days. Smaller numbers of Buddhists and Hindus attended, but they stayed the course (and, in a couple of cases, even joined), their assessment tending towards the view that the *Divine Principle*, rather than being either right or wrong, was just one of the many ways which can be 'acceptable'. In Britain Jews very rarely attend the workshops and practically never join. This

is in marked contrast to the situation in the USA, where they are over-represented in the movement: Spurgin, 'Unification Church Membership Profile', p. 3, reports that 5.3 per cent of full-time members were from a Jewish background; Gallup, *Religion in America, 1981*, pp. 8, 11, found that Jews comprised 2 per cent of the total US population.

12 P. Brierley (ed.), *UK Christian Handbook*, London, Evangelical Alliance, Bible Society and Marc, 1982, p. 14.

13 'There was significantly more religious belief in those who joined the Unification Church than in the general population. Also members came from significantly more religious homes. Unification Church members were generally religious people before joining the Church. Many were independently religious, implying dissatisfaction with traditional religion and established churches': Spurgin, 'Unification Church Membership Profile', p. 2.

14 I had for example, included a Catholic priest, a Presbyterian minister and a Methodist youth worker among my 'distributors' as, by the time I came to distribute the control group questionnaires, I knew that a significant proportion of Moonies had a religious background and I did not want that difference to affect the discovery of other differences which I did *not* know about.

15 About a quarter of the Moonies had attended a denominational school.

16 Seventy-eight per cent Moonies, 63 per cent non-joiners, 52 per cent leavers and 57 per cent of the control group attended church weekly up to the age of 10. The national average for weekly attendance in the UK is about one in seven of the child population (up to age 14), and one in ten of the adult population (Brierley, *Prospects for the Eighties*).

17 Given the propensity of most commentators to lump together members of all the new religions, it is interesting that a small group of Premies (members of Guru Maharaj Ji's Divine Light Mission) to whom I gave the questionnaire tended not to define themselves as achievers in the educational system at *any* time.

18 My data for the Americans suggest that an even higher proportion of them than of British Moonies believed in God at the time of meeting the Unification Church, but as the American population tends to confess to belief in God more than European populations (Gallup, *Religion in America, 1982*, Princeton Religion Research Center, 1982), and as we have no information about those who go to American workshops and do not join, this information cannot, in itself, tell us very much. In the *Newsweek* on Campus Poll, 1983 (*Emerging Trends*, Princeton Religious Research Center, vol. 5, no. 5, p. 2) 91 per cent of American students said that they believed in God or a universal spirit, 5 per cent that they did not, and 4 per cent that they were not sure. At the same time, only two-thirds of the students were *members* of a church or synagogue.

19 I asked both (1) the question used by Andrew Greeley in *The Sociology of the Paranormal: A Reconnaissance*, Beverly Hills/London, Sage Publications, 1975: 'How often have you felt as though you were very close to a powerful spiritual force that seemed to lift you out of yourself?', to which 23 per cent of the Moonies replied, 'Never' for the period before meeting the movement and

14 per cent for the period since meeting the Unification Church, and 43 per cent of the control group replied, 'Never' (69 per cent of the British population answered, 'Never' when asked by a National Opinion Poll – see D. Hay, *Exploring Inner Space: Is God still Possible in the Twentieth Century?*, Harmondsworth, Penguin, 1982, p. 118 – and 65 per cent gave a negative answer to Greeley in the USA); and (2) the question devised by Sir Alister Hardy: 'How often have you been aware of, or influenced by, a presence or power, whether you call it God or not, which is different from your everyday self?', to which 13 per cent of the Moonies said, 'Never' for the period before meeting the Unification Church and 4 per cent replied, 'Never' for their time in the Unification Church, and 39 per cent of the control group replied, 'Never' (64 per cent answered, 'Never' to the British National Opinion Poll – Hay, *Exploring Inner Space*, p. 118). See also T. Beardsworth, *A Sense of Presence*, Religious Experience Research Unit, Manchester College, Oxford, 1977; E. Robinson, *The Original Vision* (1977) and *Living the Questions* (1978), both published by the Religious Experience Research Unit, Manchester College, Oxford.

20 Hay, *Exploring Inner Space*, p. 122.
21 Ibid., p. 158.
22 Cf. N. G. Holm (ed.), *Religious Ecstasy*, Stockholm, Almquist & Wiksell, 1982.
23 See C. McFadden, *The Serial: A Year in the Life of Marin County*, New York, Knopf, 1976, for an amusing account of seekership in Marin County.
24 R. D. Rosen, *Psychobabble*, London, Wildwood House, 1978.
25 R. Wallis, *The Road to Total Freedom: A Sociological Analysis of Scientology*, London, Heinemann, 1976.
26 D. Stone, 'The Human Potential Movement', in C. Y. Glock and R. Bellah (eds.), *The New Religious Consciousness*, Berkeley, University of California Press, 1976.
27 See J. V. Downton Jr, *Sacred Journeys: The Conversion of Young Americans to Divine Light Mission*, New York, Columbia University Press, 1979.
28 HSA–UWC, *Our Response to the Report of October 31, 1978 on the Investigation of Korean–American Relations regarding Reverend Sun Myung Moon and Members of the Unification Church*, New York, HSA–UWC, 1979, p. 40.

10 Conclusions

1 I was, however, surprised to find that although the majority of the control group expressed a strong dislike of the idea of their marriage partner being chosen for them, a significant minority said that it could be a great relief, and that the two people involved might not (as they themselves had found to their cost) be the best judges of who was the right person for them.
2 At the same time, an understanding of the sorts of people who join, and their reasons for having done so, provides clues as to why the movement *cannot* command complete obedience, but either has to temper its demands or risk

losing some of its members. See E. Barker, 'Doing Love: Tensions in the Ideal Family', in G. James (ed.), *The Family and Unification Thought: A Comparative Study*, New York, Rose of Sharon Press, 1983; E. Barker, 'Quo Vadis?', in P. Hammond and D. E. Bromley (eds.), *Towards the Twenty-First Century*, Belton, Ca., Wadsworth, forthcoming; E. Barker, *Moonies in Action*, Oxford, Blackwell, forthcoming.

3   The Moonies will point to the various Unification ventures mentioned in chapter 2 (ICUS, the God conferences, CAUSA, VOC, the newspapers, the Little Angels, the machine-tool industry, the rallies, etc.) as proof that the means are being employed to achieve the overall goal of establishing the Kingdom of Heaven on earth. As such ventures progress, the Moonies argue, the gap of faith narrows.

4   See Moon's speech 'The Engagement and Holy Wine Ceremonies', 13 May 1979, printed in the *Blessing Quarterly*, vol. 3, no. 1, 1980.

5   See M. Weber, *The Sociology of Religion*, trs. Ephraim Fischoff, London, Methuen, 1963, ch. 40.

6   Sun Myung Moon, *The Way of Tradition*, 3 vols., New York, HSA–UWC, 1980, vol. 1, pp. 31ff.; Master Speaks: 'The Significance of the Training Session' (3rd Directors' Conference), p. 12; HSA–UWC, *Our Response to the Report of October 31, 1978 on the Investigation of Korean–American Relations regarding Reverend Sun Myung Moon and Members of the Unification Church*, New York, HSA–UWC, 1979, pp. 39–42.

7   Chung Hwan Kwak, *Outline of the Principle: Level 4*, New York, HSA–UWC, 1980, p. 169.

8   See R. Wallis, *The Road to Total Freedom: A Sociological Analysis of Scientology*, London, Heinemann, 1976; R. Ofshe, 'Synanon: The People's Business', in C. Y. Glock and R. Bellah (eds.), *The New Religious Consciousness*, Berkeley, University of California Press, 1976; S. Tipton, *Getting Saved from the Sixties: Moral Meaning in Conversion and Cultural Change*, Berkeley, Los Angeles, London, University of California Press, 1982; D. Stone, 'The Human Potential Movement', in Glock and Bellah, *The New Religious Consciousness*.

9   Try looking at Moon, *The Way of Tradition*, vol. 1, section on Kingdom of Heaven (pp. 311ff.), and various speeches in Master Speaks and Reverend Sun Myung Moon Speaks On. . . , such as 1 January 1975, 1 January 1977, 17 April 1977, 1 January 1978, 26 March 1978, 1 January 1979, 1 January 1980, 1 January 1981, 20 December 1981.

10   Kwak, *Outline of the Principle*, pp. 89–90.

11   Ibid., p. 106.

12   see ibid., chs 8, 14; see also numerous speeches by Moon.

13   For an elaboration of the points made in this section, see E. Barker, 'Whose Service is Perfect Freedom: The Concept of Spiritual Well-Being in Relation to the Reverend Sun Myung Moon's Unification Church in Britain', in D. O. Moberg (ed.), *Spiritual Well-Being*, Washington DC, University Press of America, 1979; E. Barker, 'New Religious Movements in Britain: Content and Membership', *Social Compass*, vol. 30, no. 1, 1983.

14   See N. J. Demerath III, G. Marwell and T. Aitken, *Dynamics of Idealism*, San Francisco, Jossey-Bass, 1971, for a valuable account of the rise and fall of a particular kind of student activism. An excellent analysis of some of the consequences of the counter-culture is to be found in B. Martin, *A Sociology of Contemporary Cultural Change*, Oxford, Blackwell, 1981.

15   The situations that I am contrasting draw on Weber's vision of the 'iron cage' of increasing rationalization, and a version of Durkheim's concept of anomie: see M. Weber, *From Max Weber: Essays in Sociology*, ed. H. H. Gerth and C. Wright Mills, New York, Oxford University Press, 1946; M. Weber, *The Theory of Social and Economic Organization*, trs./ed. Talcott Parsons, Toronto, Free Press, 1964; E. Durkheim, *The Division of Labour in Society*, trs. G. Simpson, New York, Macmillan, 1933; E. Durkheim, *Suicide: A Study in Sociology*, ed. G. Simpson, London, Routledge & Kegan Paul, 1953.

16   J. Lofland, *Doomsday Cult: A Study of Conversion, Proselytization, and Maintenance of Faith*, 2nd edn, New York, Irvington, 1977.

17   See E. Barker (ed.), *New Religious Movements: A Perspective for Understanding Society*, New York, Edwin Mellen Press, 1982, especially the essays by B. Wilson, Z. Werblowsky, R. Wuthnow, N. Smart, W. Lewis, R. Wallis, C. Campbell, D. Anthony and T. Robbins, B. Hardin and G. Kehrer, J. Beckford, and D. Bromley, B. Busching and A. Shupe.

18   This is related to one of the most fundamental differences between the subject matter of the natural and social sciences. Regularities can occur within the social world because people share certain 'knowledge' or visions of reality. Knowledge of that knowledge can lead to the regularity no longer obtaining. Generally speaking, this is not a problem (or advantage) when investigating the 'behaviour' of, say, metals.

19   The Moonies would probably denounce L. Tiger and R. Fox, *The Imperial Animal*, London, Secker & Warburg, 1971, as being written from an atheistic, reductionist and Marxist perspective, but the argument in chapter 5 (which is entitled 'Give and Take') is about how necessary it is for the Imperial Animal (mankind) to have the opportunity to give as well as to take, and there is a discussion about the difficulties that modern society has in enabling its members to feel that they are contributing to a worthwhile goal.

20   B. R. Wilson, *Religion in Sociological Perspective*, Oxford, Oxford University Press, 1982. See also D. Martin, *The Breaking of the Image: A Sociology of Christian Theory and Practice*, Oxford, Blackwell, 1980, ch. 9.

21   After attending the confirmation ceremony of a 15-year-old godchild, I listened to the vicar's account of the interesting discussions that had taken place in the classes leading up to the confirmation. 'What do the young people do *after* confirmation?' I asked. The vicar looked blank. 'I mean, do you have any meetings for them now?' 'Oh yes,' he replied, 'there's ping-pong every Tuesday evening.' For some interesting and relevant statistics, see L. Francis, *Teenagers and the Church*, London, Collins Liturgical Publications, 1984.

22   For a detailed analysis of reactions to the new religions, see A. D. Shupe, Jr, and D. G. Bromley, *The New Vigilantes: Deprogrammers, Anti-Cultists, and the New Religions*, Beverley Hills/London, Sage, 1980. See also D. G. Hill, *Study*

of Mind Development Groups, Sects and Cults in Ontario: A Report to the Ontario Government, Toronto, 1980, esp. ch. 6.

23 I am grateful to James Beckford for drawing this distinction between consistency and coherence in relation to brainwashing accounts (personal communication); see also Beckford, 'Accounting for Conversion', *British Journal of Sociology*, vol. 29, pp. 246–62.

24 Since the practice began, adults (in their twenties and thirties) have been subjected to forcible deprogramming because they have changed from a Protestant to a Catholic faith, shown signs of homosexuality or wanted to marry someone of whom their parents disapproved. See D. Bromley and J. Richardson (eds.), *The Brainwashing/Deprogramming Debate: Sociological Psychological, Legal and Historical Perspectives*, New York, Edwin Mellen Press, 1984; M. D. Bryant (ed.), *Religious Liberty in Canada: Deprogramming and Media Coverage of New Religions*, Documentation Series No. 1, Toronto, Canadians for the Protection of Religious Liberty, 1979; H. Richardson (ed.), *Deprogramming: Documenting the Issue*, prepared for the American Civil Liberties Union, New York, and the Toronto School of Theology Conference on Religious Deprogramming, 1977; H. Richardson (ed.), *New Religions and Mental Health*, New York, Edwin Mellen Press, 1980.

25 *George* v. *ISKCON*, Santa Ana, California, 1983.

26 See R. Delgado, 'Religious Totalism: Gentle and Ungentle Persuasion under the First Amendment', *Southern California Law Review*, vol. 51, no. 1, 1977; W. C. Shepherd, 'The Prosecutor's Reach: Legal Issues Stemming from the New Religious Movements', unpublished paper presented to GTU meeting, 'Conversion, Coercion and Commitment in the Religious Movements', Berkeley, June 1981; St J. A. Robilliard, *Religion and the Law: Religious Liberty in Modern English Law*, Manchester, Manchester University Press, 1984; T. Robbins, W. Shepherd and J. McBride (eds.), *The Law and the New Religions*, Chico, Ca., Scholars Press, forthcoming; E. Barker, 'By Law Established: the British right to Discriminate', *Society*, May/June 1984, for discussions on the subject of new religious movements and the law.

27 See *inter alia* the remarks attributed to Jean Merritt in *News*, Citizen's Freedom Foundation Information Services, vol. 6, no. 5, 1981, p. 3, and those made by Galen Kelly in 'Whose Mind is it Anyway', *Jaywalking*, ATV, April 1981.

28 See Introduction, n. 8.

29 One deprogrammer told me that out of over a hundred cases he had had only two 'failures'. I met six of them at the Unification Theological Seminary the next day.

30 For one of the less sensational accounts, given by a 28-year-old Moonie who returned to the Unification Church after being detained by deprogrammers for two and a half months, see N. Raine, 'The Faith Breakers', *New Tomorrow*. no. 46, 1983. E. Barker, 'With Enemies Like That . . . : Some Functions of Deprogramming as an Aid to Sectarian Membership', in Bromley and Richardson, *The Brainwashing/Deprogramming Debate*, discusses some of the effects of deprogrammees returning to the movement.

31   See, for example, the dedication in S. Swatland and A. Swatland, *Escape from the Moonies*, London, New English Library, 1982:

> This book is dedicated to Joe Alexander, Chris, Dennis, Mark, Matthew, Michael and Virginia, a band described in different ways by different people.
>   The Moonies called them Agents of Satan.
>   The police called them Kidnappers.
>   We prefer to call them Rescuers, modern Knights on White Horses.
>   Without their courage, without their compasssion, there could have been no happy ending.

32   This book is not the place to go into this question further, but it ought to be mentioned that *how* someone leaves (voluntarily or through force) affects the way in which they subsequently face up to life outside the movement.

33   Not all Evangelical Christians have been entirely unsympathetic to the Unification movement. See R. Quebedeaux and R. Sawatsky (eds.), *Evangelical-Unification Dialogue*, New York, Rose of Sharon Press, 1979; I. Hexham and M. Langley, 'Cracking the Moonie Code', *Crux*, vol. 15, no. 3, 1979.

34   A small number of social scientists have come down on the brainwashing 'side', but nearly all the sociologists who have studied the new religions tend to be sceptical about the concept's having any useful explanatory power for the movements which they have studied. Some of this disagreement between the disciplines may be due to the fact that sociologists tend to get their data by observing the membership *in situ*, while the psychologists and psychiatrists are more likely to get their information from clients and patients, either after the latter have left the movement or while they were being deprogrammed, or interviewed, possibly against their will, for evidence of 'impaired capacity to form "realistic" appraisals of reality' for a conservatorship order. See T. Robbins and D. Anthony, 'The Medicalization of Deviant Religion: Preliminary Observations and Critique', *Yale Series of Working Papers in Sociology*, no. 1, 1980, and J. T. Richardson, 'Psychotherapy and New Religious Movements in a Pluralist Society', *American Psychologist*, forthcoming, for further suggestions about why some psychiatrists and psychologists may favour brainwashing accounts.

35   See Wallis, *The Road to Total Freedom*, for an application of the 'deviancy amplification' model to Scientology.

36   The British movement has, on occasion, asked members of the Parents' Asssociation to address potential recruits at the 21-day workshops and to advise them to inform their parents about what they are doing, and to discuss their plans with them. (The Parents' Association is an organization run by parents who, while not themselves Moonies, try to liaise directly with the movement in sorting out problems that arise. Similar groups exist in other countries.)

37   This is a consequence of conversion being a rather longer process than is usually assumed, which continues (or discontinues) for some time after commitment.

38 See B. Wilson (ed.), *Rationality*, Oxford, Blackwell, 1970, esp. Introduction.
39 Some of the questions raised by social scientists looking for 'fits' between religious beliefs and secular characteristics are discussed in E. Barker, 'The Limits of Displacement: Two Disciplines Face Each Other', in D. Martin, J. Orme-Mills and W. S. F. Pickering (eds.), *Sociology and Theology: Alliance and Conflict*, Brighton, Harvester Press, 1980.

Index